FOR B...
OUR
ON
Any...

Sydney, July 1990

THE *Sea Horse* AND THE *Wanderer*

THE *Sea Horse* AND THE *Wanderer*

Ben Boyd in Australia

Marion Diamond

MELBOURNE UNIVERSITY PRESS
1988

First published 1988
Typeset by Allset Graphics Pty Ltd
Printed in Australia by Globe Press Pty Ltd,
50 Weston Street, Brunswick for
Melbourne University Press, Carlton, Victoria 3053
U.S.A. and Canada: International Specialized Book Services, Inc.,
5602 N.E. Hassalo Street, Portland, Oregon 97213-3640
United Kingdom, Europe, Middle East, Africa:
HB Sales
Littleton House, Littleton Road, Ashford, Middlesex
England TW15 1UQ

This book is copyright.
Apart from any fair dealing for the purposes of private study,
research, criticism or review, as permitted under the Copyright Act,
no part may be reproduced by any process without written permission.
Enquiries should be made to the publisher.

© Marion Elizabeth Diamond 1988

National Library of Australia Cataloguing-in-Publication entry

Diamond, Marion, 1948-
    The Sea Horse and the Wanderer: Ben Boyd
in Australia.
    Bibliography.
    Includes Index.
    ISBN 0 522 84355 7.

    1. Boyd, Benjamin, 1803?-1851. 2. Businessmen
    —New South Wales—Biography. 3. Pioneers—
    New South Wales—Biography. I. Title.
338.7'6'0924

With ample fortune, and no common mind,
    A heart by nature generous and free,
    B[oy]d, is not most pitiful in thee
To herd with Things as pithless as the wind
Even in their noise? To spit thyself abroad
    With men who spout for patriotic gold
    Their innate brass—nay, even with such to hold
Factious community for Public Fraud!
Contemn—abandon them! Be timely wise;
    Nor sow for honour thus with moral chaff!
Stern, watchful Clio has thee in her eyes!
And if yon Clique, with logic of their lies,
    Mislead you to the end (howe'er you laugh
    Now at the threat), behold your Epitaph!

                        Sonnets Dedicated to Senators, no. IV
                        Weekly Register, 22 February 1845

Contents

	Acknowledgements	xi
	A Note on Spelling	xiii
	Conversions	xiv
	Introduction	1
1	Early Life of a Merchant Adventurer	5
2	Establishment of the Royal Bank of Australia	17
3	First Speculations	30
4	A Lust for Land	50
5	The Squatting Interest	68
6	Boydtown	93
7	Labour Problems	111
8	The British Lobby	141
9	Retrenchment	166
10	The Wanderer	187
	Appendix	212
	Abbreviations	214
	Notes	215
	Select Bibliography	240
	Index	247

Illustrations

Plates

Benjamin Boyd as a young man   between 82 and 83
Family collection, London
The *Wanderer*, RYS
Mitchell Library, Sydney
The *Sea Horse*
Mitchell Library, Sydney
Boyd's six imported stallions
Family collection, London
Mafra Homestead, Maneroo
Mitchell Library, Sydney
The lighthouse at Boydtown   between 114 and 115
Family collection, London
Map of Twofold Bay, with whaleboat
Mitchell Library, Sydney
Portrait of Benjamin Boyd
From *Heads of the People*, 1 May 1847
Whaling at Twofold Bay
Mitchell Library, Sydney
Benjamin Boyd's house, Sydney
La Trobe collection, State Library of Victoria

Figures

Cartoon of Ben Boyd and 'Quaker' Robinson	99
Three islanders recruited by Boyd	127

Map

An indication of Boyd's land holdings Prepared by Gordon Sonnenberg	59

Acknowledgements

ALL BOOKS ARE co-operative efforts: they rely on the contributions of many generous people. All acknowledgements are invidious: there are many people whose names I never knew to whom I am grateful, for help in libraries, for encouragement during the down periods, and stimulation during the highs. I wish to thank the following friends who helped me in many ways. They are not, however, responsible for its deficiencies. Frank Broeze, Patricia, Lady Boyd, Georgina Brady, Barrie Dyster, Noeline Hall, Terry Irving, John and Kitty Millbank, Hugh Stewart-Killick, Helen Taylor and Sandy Yarwood all helped to make this book possible—as did the anonymous reader for Melbourne University Press, whose suggestions were helpful and wise.

Margaret O'Hagan and Spencer Routh were anything but anonymous librarians at the University of Queensland Library, but I can only refer in more general terms to those at other libraries and archives who also helped me. My thanks to the staff of the Mitchell Library and New South Wales Archives in Sydney, the Archives of Business and Labour (Australian National University) and the manuscripts room of the National Library of Australia in Canberra, the Alexander Turnbull Library and the New Zealand Archives in Wellington, the Hawaiian Archives in Honolulu, the manuscripts room of Cambridge University Library, the public library at Dumfries, the Mitchell Library in Glasgow, the Scottish Record Office in Edinburgh, and the British Library, the Goldsmiths Library (University of London), the Guildhall Library and the Public Record Office in London.

I am grateful to the Department of History, University of Queensland, which helped fund my trip to Britain in mid-1985, after I discovered the existence of further papers at a critical point in the project.

I am also grateful to two men whose historical research paved my way, but who, to my regret, died before I had a chance to meet them: Lord Boyd of Merton, historian of his family, and local historian H. P. Wellings of Eden, Twofold Bay.

I also owe quite a lot to Phil.

A Note on Spelling

SPELLING WAS less rigid in the nineteenth century. In dealing with personal names, I have used the form of spelling used by the person himself, even if this causes slight inconsistencies. William Sprott Boyd signed himself so; Alexander Sprot chose the spelling which the family now prefers. Geographical names are more difficult. The names of squatting runs vary enormously; where there is a current version of the name, such as Deniliquin, I have used that.

The name of the southern squatting district reaching inland from Twofold Bay is a particular problem. During the 1840s it was known as Maneroo, spelt in several ways, and accented on the final syllable. The region currently known as Monaro covers a smaller area, and does not extend to the coast. I have used 'Maneroo' to denote the area of coast plus hinterland which formed the squatting district, and 'Monaro' as the name of the present Monaro district, described by W. K. Hancock in *Discovering Monaro*.

Boyd and his contemporaries spoke of the island in the Solomons called 'Guadalcanar'; I have called it by its present name, 'Guadalcanal'. With the coming of independence, many Pacific island groups have taken new indigenous names. To avoid confusion, I have included these in brackets where appropriate.

Conversions

1 foot	0.30 metre
1 yard	0.91 metre
1 mile	1.61 kilometres
1 acre	0.40 hectare
1 pound	0.45 kilogram
1 ton	1.02 tonnes
1 gallon	4.55 litres
1s (12d)	10 cents
£1	$2

To avoid anachronisms, imperial measures have been retained throughout.

Introduction

ON 18 JULY 1842 an aristocrat sailed into Sydney Harbour after a long and leisurely voyage from England. That aristocrat was *Wanderer*, a racing yacht of the Royal Yacht Squadron. The shoreline was crowded with onlookers as she entered the harbour, and her arrival was publicized by a salute, fired in her honour by her companion ship, *Velocity*.

Her credentials were impeccable. As a member of the Royal Yacht Squadron, *Wanderer* had all the rights and privileges of a British man-o'-war while sailing in colonial waters, and the ensign of the squadron was the sign of her acceptance as a member of a select flotilla whose crew included those enthusiastic sailors, Victoria and Albert. The Australian colonies had never before played host to one of the Cowes squadron. Little wonder, then, that *Wanderer*, RYS, with her ambience of royalty and high society, captured the imagination of the inhabitants of Sydney. Small wonder, too, that in this colonial outpost the aristocratic nimbus of the ship was transferred to its owner, Benjamin Boyd.

Ben Boyd was no aristocrat, but his veneer was as shiny as the polish in his yacht's walnut stateroom. From his arrival in New South Wales in 1842, Boyd made a mark on the economic and political life of the colony that demands explanation. Within two years he headed the main opposition party in the colony; within three he had entered, and left, the colonial legislature. He claimed land amounting to more than a million acres, and built a town with four hundred inhabitants as his own personal property. He helped to destroy one governor, was creditor to

1

another, and threatened the New Zealand government with bankruptcy. Yet within eight years his personal credit and financial empire were destroyed, and he left the colony ignominiously, to disappear in mysterious circumstances, a subject of fascinated horror.

Boyd was an enigma, even to his contemporaries: half successful businessman and half scoundrel. On the one hand, he was a visionary, a romantic speculator whose extravagant ideas are exemplified by *Wanderer*; for the squadron represented more than pleasure, it stood for privilege and the power of patronage. In Australia the yacht became a part of his stock-in-trade, an effective reminder of his aristocratic background with which to overawe the local colonists. But *Wanderer* was dangerous as well as beautiful, armed with eight guns on her deck and along the rails, and a brass twelve-pounder known as 'Long Tom' and reputed to have seen service at Waterloo.[1]

In the same way, Boyd concealed a ruthless and completely amoral personality behind his splendidly extravagant facade. The romantic colonial adventurer was counterbalanced by the legitimate entrepreneur.

The Australian colonies had already been introduced to this other, sober side of Boyd. On 1 June 1841 another remarkable ship, *Sea Horse*, had arrived in Sydney. Built at Dundee in 1839, she was, at 600 tons burthen 150 feet in length, and driven by two steam engines of 220 horsepower each, the largest steamship yet to operate in Australian waters.[2] She was a product of the most advanced technology of her day, but a technology as yet only imperfectly developed.

If *Wanderer* reflected Boyd's craving for aristocratic splendour, *Sea Horse* was the workhorse of his fleet. His objective was to establish a profitable steam shipping service between the colonial ports, but she failed to achieve this. She was too large for the colonies' limited traffic, and too greedy for coal, and her gargantuan appetite, like that of her owner, proved her undoing. She had already demonstrated her unprofitability when in 1843 she was wrecked in the Tamar River.

Boyd's legitimate schemes were likewise wrecked on the shoals of economic depression, unfavourable public opinion and management failure. In 1848 he lost control of his bank and his businesses, but retained ownership of his pleasure craft. The more pragmatic values represented by *Sea Horse* henceforth ebbed away. Instead, Boyd and *Wanderer* embarked on a fantastic voyage of discovery and ultimate ruin. At four o'clock one Sunday morning in 1849, using a special privilege of the Royal Yacht Squadron exempting members from normal port regulations, Boyd sailed out of Sydney Harbour, escaping the charges of fraud that were probably his due. He visited the Californian goldfields and Hawaii before vanishing in the Solomon Islands, a known haunt of cannibals. Her crew sailed *Wanderer* back to New South Wales but she, too, was wrecked—scuttled?—on the bar at Port Macquarie.

The privileged and anachronistic *Wanderer* and the technically advanced but unprofitable *Sea Horse* together serve as images for Boyd's enterprises in Australia. A charismatic and enigmatic figure, Boyd had considerable influence on political and economic developments in New South Wales during the 1840s. Unlike most participants in colonial affairs, he was neither native born nor a settler, but a transient. His attitude towards the colony was coloured by this impermanence. To interpret his role, he needs to be seen against an imperial, as well as a colonial, background, for the source of his influence lay in the network of his associations in Scotland and England.

Boyd was both an individual capitalist and the chairman of the Royal Bank of Australia, a British company which he founded and from which he derived his wealth. Through the London office of the bank, Boyd's contacts with the City of London gave him access to the colonial bureaucracy far greater than mere colonials could muster, and a status with the British government that wealth alone could not give him. Boyd operated on the assumption that the source of colonial patronage and power lay not in the colonies, but in Britain. Until the end, that assumption served him well.

Boyd's significance in the history of New South Wales therefore has two aspects. As squatter, politician and financier, Boyd helped to determine the outcome of the great conflict between Gipps and the squatters over the control of Crown Lands. As employer and capitalist, Boyd articulated a position on the problems of labour in the squatting industry which intensified dissatisfaction in the colony with various types of bonded labour. His final solution, the importation of Melanesians, tainted labour relations in the colony as nothing else could.

On the other hand, Boyd was also the British expatriate chairman of the Royal Bank of Australia. For his own purposes he developed a network of contacts in London, which he made available, also for his own purposes, to the squatting party in New South Wales. The campaign for control of Crown Lands was fought in London more than in Sydney; Boyd's family, friends and cronies directed the battle.

An understanding of Boyd's Australian experience begins with the history of his early life. In this background lies the origin of the network of connections which gave him his later power.

1
Early Life of
a Merchant Adventurer

BENJAMIN BOYD was born, probably in 1797, the second son of a Scottish landowning family which traced its descent from the Earls of Kilmarnock in the sixteenth century. Ben was born in London, his next brother, Mark, in Scotland, and the family divided its time between their London home at Waterloo Place, just off Pall Mall, and Merton Hall, a large pebble-dash house built at the turn of the century on the Boyd estates, which had been carved out of the much larger holdings of the Earls of Galloway near the town of Newton Stewart in Wigtonshire.

In all the south-west of Scotland the population in 1801 was only 106 700, and Wigtonshire itself was an isolated, under-populated area of landowners, their tenants and their sheep. Within that small world, the Boyds were important figures. Dr William Boyd, Benjamin's grandfather, was both landowner and minister of the Church of Scotland, and when, in 1787, he drew up his will, he established an entail, giving his eldest son, John, a life interest in his major property at Culbratton, while the younger sons, Edward, William and James, together with his widow, Joanna Maitland, were to share the income from his other estate, Merton Hall.[1]

Dr Boyd's testament illustrated the stability of the society in which he lived, and expected to die. His estates represented considerable wealth in an underdeveloped countryside where agriculture, and the rents of tenant farmers, were the most important and socially acceptable form of income. He willed this property with due respect for the unchanging virtues of landed wealth and primogeniture, a part of the continuing generations of Boyds who had kept their heads, their names, and their lands, through the centuries. By the end of the eighteenth century, however, the old certainties of landed property, its privileges, and its unquestioned transfer from one generation to the next, were under challenge.

His will was never implemented. In 1798, because of 'sundry debts' and dissatisfaction with his eldest son, Dr Boyd overturned his careful adherence to the right of primogeniture and allocated the bulk of his property to his second son instead. Edward Boyd, in his turn, incurred further debts on the security of the estate, so that by the time Benjamin and his brothers reached their majority, there was little to inherit except the entail itself.[2] The property remained important only for the status that land gave, even in a society where upward mobility was increasing, and increasingly associated with more liquid forms of wealth.

Edward Boyd himself characterized this change, investing his wealth in various speculative activities, including the Glaswegian West India trade, maritime insurance, and cotton milling. He and his wife, Janet, a daughter of Benjamin Yule, had six sons and three daughters. The children grew up, in Scotland and at Waterloo Place, during a time of rapid economic change. By the end of the eighteenth century the industrial revolution had reached Wigtonshire, and new technologies, imported from the south but fed by local resources and local initiative, brought new problems and challenges to the lowland Scottish landowners. Some took up that challenge, and Newton Stewart became an early centre of textile manufacturing.

Close ties existed between the south-west of Scotland and northern Ireland. In earlier years, Scottish Presbyterians had migrated from the region to become members of the Protestant Ascendancy; amongst them was a collateral branch of the Boyd family. With the growth of industrialization in Scotland, the flow reversed, and Catholic Irish labourers arrived to work in the cotton mills. They brought new social problems: Mark Boyd described how his father, as magistrate, called out the local militia to deal with riots between Catholic and Presbyterian workers, and sectarianism promoted the growth of a local freemasonry.[3]

Despite occasional such incidents, however, Benjamin's early years appear to have been uncomplicatedly happy ones. The family had numerous kin in Scotland. His most successful relative was his maternal uncle, Mark Sprott of Garnkirk, who was married to Janet Yule's sister Mary, and was a trustee of Edward Boyd's marriage settlement. At the turn of the century, Garnkirk, a village some five miles east of Glasgow, had become a centre of heavy industry. Sprott's estate of nearly 1500 acres contained iron, limestone and clay, and he established clayworks to produce 'vases and flower-pots, and cans, and pots, and crucibles...which for elegance and durability are perhaps rarely equalled'.[4] By the time Ben Boyd reached manhood, his uncle was both wealthy and powerful in Glasgow business circles, with interests that extended far beyond his original Garnkirk estate. In 1823 Sprott bought Riddell, a country estate in Roxburghshire, signifying his new-found position in society. Riddell was a famous country house, mentioned by Sir Walter Scott in *The Lay of the Last Minstrel*, and in Sprott's day it had one thousand acres turned over to lawns—an indication of great wealth in land-hungry Scotland.

Riddell was only about ten miles from Broadmeadows, in Selkirkshire, where Boyd's cousins Archibald and Wilson Maitland Boyd grew up. Ben and his brothers appear to have been frequent visitors both at Riddell and Broadmeadows. These family connections with his cousins, Alexander and Thomas Sprott of Garnkirk and Riddell, and the Boyds at Broadmeadows, were an important formative influence in Ben Boyd's life. In his fashion, he remained exceptionally loyal to his kin, using his companies to find them positions or to lend them money, with a generosity which was often not in the interests of his shareholders. He also expected this family patronage to be reciprocated; the bitterness of his later conflict with his other cousins, William Sprott Boyd and his brother Archibald, of Hillhousefield and Leith, can best be explained in terms of their willingness to put sound business principles ahead of family loyalty, exemplifying the conflict implicit in the shift from pre-industrial loyalties based on vertical patronage to nineteenth-century capitalist Scotland.[5]

Riddell was only about eight miles from Abbotsfield, the home of Sir Walter Scott, who was for many years Sheriff of Roxburghshire. It is likely that Ben Boyd and his brothers met Scott at Riddell, where he was a regular visitor, and were influenced by his Scottish romanticism, and his vision of a pre-industrial Scotland based on feudal ties of loyalty and patronage. In 1833 Mark Boyd became secretary of the Abbotsford appeal to rescue Scott from bankruptcy.[6]

Boyd's vision of an ideal ancestral Scotland remained important throughout his life. He made much of his Scottish origins. Based in London, both he and Mark were members of the Dumfriesshire and Galloway Club, a social club where expatriate Scots in London met to drink, and which offered companionship, and a sense of separateness from London society. Through such social arrangements the Boyds formed a part of an interlocking network of relationships. William Jardine and James Matheson, who established a trading empire in the Far East, were both lowland Scots and members of the same network, and Benjamin's cousin, William Sprott Boyd, went to Canton to work for their firm. The Hon. Francis Scott, the member of parliament for Roxburghshire, was another member of the network. But the nostalgic yearning for Scotland which led successful businessmen like Jardine or Andrew Carnegie—or Mark Sprott—to retire to the highlands at the end of their careers had little to do with the real world.

Boyd extended the Scottish patriotism to Australia. He commonly appeared in the garb of a highland chieftain at the numerous costume balls held in Sydney throughout the 1840s,[7] and his friendship with the Presbyterian radical, John Dunmore Lang, can best be explained in terms of Scottish sentiment. However, such gestures owed more to Sir Walter Scott than to Scotland. Rather than an hereditary chief of the highlands, he was the son of a bankrupt lowland landowner, and behind the romantic imagery his association with Scotland was based not on the currency of traditional folk imagery but on that other traditional Scottish asset—money.

Edward Boyd's large family was born into the privileged security of the upper middle-classes, but it was a world less secure than outward appearances suggested. Despite their land, they lived on the brink of disaster, threatened poverty, and the fragility of an income based not on land, the traditional and appropriate means, but on speculation and the clever manipulation of finance.

Edward Boyd was associated, in part through Mark Sprott, with the eighteenth-century Glasgow traders. Like other merchants from the west of Scotland, he was a shipowner, trading with America, the West Indies and the East. Glasgow was a major port for the Atlantic trade. Edward's younger brother died in Guadalupe in 1794.[8] Mark Boyd, writing of his father's shipping interests, declared:

> For ten years of the last century and down to the period of Mr. Pitt's death [1806] my father was extensively connected as a merchant with America and the West Indies, and in this capacity was frequently sent for and consulted by Mr. Pitt.

Mark may have exaggerated his father's influence; he was also capable, according to his son, of exerting pressure on the East India Company, and on the Duke of Clarence, whom he managed to persuade to give support to 'those who conscientiously and disinterestedly advocated the cause of the West India planter and proprietor' against moves, in 1804, to abolish the slave trade.[9]

The Glasgow merchants were deeply involved in the slave trade. Edward Boyd kept a black boy, who was brought back to Scotland after the ship's surgeon decided he was too ill to be landed in South Carolina. 'Dick' subsequently became a family retainer within the Boyd household, totally loyal to their interests and something of a family 'pet'.[10] The presence of this coloured 'boy', an anomalous figure within the family circle, seems to have influenced Benjamin Boyd's attitude towards race: his later employment of coloured labour in Australia, while thoroughly exploitative, also owed something to the image of the trustworthy family retainer.

Edward Boyd's mercantile activities declined as the nineteenth century continued, but alternative opportunities for investment were opening up. The industrial revolution brought a great increase in the size, variety and resourcefulness of institutions providing credit to support industrial development. One such financial institution was the insurance company. Insurance, from its origins in the maritime insurance industry well known to the Glasgow traders, was well placed to tap the new demand for credit for other purposes. Mark Boyd called his father 'an extensive underwriter'.[11]

By the early 1820s Boyd senior was in financial trouble. The advertisements in the local newspapers chart his decline, as he gradually alienated part of the estate to meet his rising debts. On 9 August 1826 Edward Boyd was declared bankrupt. His failure probably followed his investment in a local cotton mill at Newton Stewart, which collapsed that year, but he had dabbled in many speculative ventures—shipping, trade and insurance.[12] Because the estate was entailed, the land itself could not be sold to meet his debts. Instead, the estate was placed in the hands of trustees, and its income sequestered, but the land itself remained intact for the next generation. Everything moveable, however, was sold up. The advertisements give the flavour of the Boyd family's catastrophe, as everything associated with their childhood home—stock, carriages, furniture, farm implements, crops and even the 'cut ryegrass and meadow hay'—went under the auctioneer's hammer. Even the Boyds' private right to shooting was leased. A way of life, it seemed, had come to an end.[13]

The eldest son, William Sprott Boyd, had left for India in 1819 as an official of the East India Company. In his absence it was Benjamin, with help from the third brother, Mark, who was called upon to restore the family's fortunes. In March 1825 he became a member of the London Stock Exchange, where two years later Mark joined him as his clerk.[14]

From its distant beginnings in the coffee houses of Restoration London, the Stock Exchange had expanded, in the years since the end of the Napoleonic Wars, beyond its traditional business in government bonds, to deal with the investment needs of increasing numbers of private companies. In the early years of the cotton and iron masters, most capital was generated by individuals or families, or within partnerships where the number of contributors was sufficiently small to allow personal control to be exerted. The partnership remained the norm for many forms of business throughout the nineteenth century, but for some projects, capital formation on a larger scale became necessary. The railway boom in particular increased the demand for investment capital, and tapped the resources of the small investor, tempted away from the safety, and the lower yield, of government paper. Such operations offered opportunities for small investors to place their money at call, or to purchase shares, in these ventures. Colonial companies, too, had a small but well-publicized share of the market. Railway companies were notorious for their instability, and colonial companies involved unforeseen risks. This new and unsophisticated class of investor was vulnerable in an age when government regulation of the money market lagged far behind current sharp practice. Until joint-stock legislation in the 1840s, however, such enterprises entailed risks, for only chartered corporations had limited liability, and such companies were rare.

In the 1830s Benjamin and Mark Boyd followed their father into the insurance business, as resident directors of the Edinburgh-based North British Insurance Company, which established a London branch in 1832. The London board of the company had a decidedly Scottish flavour. Besides the Boyd brothers, the other local directors included Sir Peter Laurie (Chairman), A. Cockburn, John Connell, W. P. Craufurd, George Webster, Isaac Sewell and W. A. Urquhart. From the first, the London branch seems to have caused problems for the company; throughout the 1830s concern was expressed in Edinburgh that the expenses of the branch were heavy in proportion to the business contracted, and that no proper records were kept. Nevertheless, the Boyds were well rewarded for their involvement: as resident managers, they received £400 each per annum, with a commission of 5 per cent on all premiums. The lease of their premises, No. 4 New Bank Buildings, was paid by North British, but the Boyds were at liberty to carry on their own business there, and may have lived there as well from time to time.[15]

Seven years after the Merton Hall shooting rights had been lost, and a year after his appointment to the board of North British, Benjamin Boyd was able to advertise in the local papers that 'no Person will Shoot or Course upon the Lands of Mertonhall, all permissions having been withdrawn'.[16]

Their association with Sir Peter Laurie was particularly profitable to the Boyd brothers. Laurie, born into an unassuming family in Stitchell, Roxburghshire, came to London as a saddler's apprentice. He made a fortune from military contracts during the Napoleonic War, and by 1832 had become Lord Mayor of

London. He joined the North British Insurance Company, he said, 'for my good opinion of the Talents [and] Integrity of the Resident Directors B & M Boyd', and was elected chairman. In 1835 the same directors established the London Reversionary Interest Society, at the same address, and with Ben and Mark Boyd once again as resident directors.[17]

Soon the same group of speculators was interested in establishing a bank. On 23 April 1838 *The Times* devoted its regular column on city intelligence to rumours that the 'Commercial Bank of London' was about to be floated with a capital of two million pounds. Behind the rumour lay an attempt by Boyd, in company with the brewer Thomas Meux and James Matheson of the Hong Kong based firm of Jardine, Matheson and Co., to form a new bank. This attempt failed, or rather was merged in a less ambitious project, the Union Bank of London. Peter Laurie became chairman, and Ben and Mark Boyd were directors of the board, which met for the first time on 9 January 1839.[18]

As well as financial enterprises, Boyd also followed his father into shipping. Of particular significance for his colonial ambitions was his connection with the St George Steam Packet Company which operated passenger steamships from Liverpool across the St George Strait to Ireland. Through it Boyd developed contacts with the Liverpool shipping establishment, and became friendly with another director, the Quaker Joseph Phelps Robinson, whose family had further business interests in London and New York. The two also became partners in a brewing business.[19]

By 1840 the significant features of Ben Boyd's life were firmly established. He was a member of the London Stock Exchange. Most of his work involved the raising of investment money, the lifeblood of the industrial revolution, through the banks and insurance companies with which he was associated. He had links with the merchants of the British Empire through family associations in India, the Far East, and the West Indies. His directorship in St George Steam Packets gave him a contact with Liverpool, and indirectly with America as well. He had a widespread, if tangled, network of kin and connections in Scotland and, through the North British Insurance Company, he was in a position to milk this network for investment funds. His other interests, ranging from banking to brewing, were substantial. As the eldest son of the family remaining in Britain, he was effectively head of his large family for Edward, 'the old gentleman', was in poor health by 1840 and died in 1846. Even in a legal sense, Ben and Mark were joint heads of the family, for in 1832 they had become their father's creditors, and trustees of their parents' marriage settlement.[20]

From all these details, a picture emerges of Benjamin Boyd as an established figure, a man of stature in the business community, a man approaching forty in the bosom of his family, unmarried, but otherwise fitting the stereotype of the early Victorian capitalist. But Boyd also emerges from the records as a personality. His brother Mark portrayed him, with admiring affection, as a larger-than-life character, and though the portrait he paints may be blurred by affection and nostalgia, his anecdotes are still telling. Ben Boyd, it seems, knew everybody. 'I like your brother', Rothschild told Mark, 'but [he] is a tight hand at a bargain, for when I deal with him in French Rentes I always lose money by him; he is such a screw'. He knew Louis Napoleon during his exile in England, and from the Elysée Palace the Emperor of the French wrote, urging the Minister of Marine to search for Boyd after his disappearance in the Pacific. Mark Boyd tells how his brother managed, by sheer gall, to persuade the Duke of Sussex to give him a ticket to Queen Victoria's Coronation. And his hobby was ballooning, a risky and expensive sport which attracted only the most *outré* of young bloods.[21]

Such anecdotes may be of little relevance to the wider issues of Boyd's involvement with the Australian colonies, but they serve to illustrate his personality, and to explain the fascination with which he was regarded by his contemporaries. He challenged conventions and risked physical dangers, but he never challenged the class structure. On the contrary, his many outrageous actions were undertaken in the knowledge that his position in society gave him a certain immunity. Only someone supremely confident of that position would attempt to wheedle an invitation to the coronation from the Duke of Sussex. Boyd was not quite respectable, perhaps; he was too closely associated with his father's rather dubious bankruptcy, and with somewhat shady interest in speculative dealings, but he was accepted by society for his birth, his wealth and, above all, for his style. Moreover, he was a man with a permanent stake in the London financial world and any number of useful associates.

Why, then, did Boyd decide, some time between 1838 and the beginning of 1840, to focus his speculations on the far-away world of New South Wales? There are two aspects to this question: why the colonies? and why Australia? On the one hand, investment in the colonies was not, in itself, a remarkable shift of direction. Boyd's west-of-Scotland inheritance had brought him into contact with the trans-Atlantic trade out of Glasgow, through his father, Mark Sprott, and other associates. Boyd's connections with Liverpool introduced him to the shippers involved in bounty emigration to New South Wales. Colonial investment was a legitimate and important feature of the London and Scottish money markets, and investment, particularly in colonial land, had been stimulated by private colonial enterprises in South Australia, Canada and Texas. Plans were already under way in England to repeat Wakefield's South Australian experiment in New Zealand. Several specifically Scottish companies, too, had set their sights on Australia. The Clyde Company, for instance, also based on money drawn from the west of Scotland as the name suggests, became an important pastoral company in the Port Phillip District from 1836.

Boyd's colonial speculation therefore fits within a general pattern of British, and particularly Scottish, investment. This was a time of rising interest in Britain's colonial empire, not politically, but amongst private investors. It would be a misreading of Boyd's personality, however, to assume that his reasons were entirely rational. Boyd loved travel, adventure and risk-taking. While the systematic colonizers introduced respectability into private colonization, more idiosyncratic colonial adventures were also under way. James Brooke, for instance, the future 'White Rajah' of Borneo, sailed in 1839 for the East Indies in *Royalist*, another vessel of the Royal Yacht Squadron. Boyd and Brooke probably knew each other from Cowes, and it is possible that Boyd was inspired to emulate his more famous compatriot.

Boyd's attention was drawn to New South Wales by a combination of family circumstances. In the late 1830s, Ben's cousins, Archibald Boyd of Broadmeadows and William Mitchell

1 *Early Life of a Merchant Adventurer* 15

Boyd, went out to New South Wales and took up squatting licences in the New England District. Another cousin, Alexander Sprott, was in the Port Phillip District by the early 1840s and possibly arrived during the late 1830s. And on 22 May 1841, at the British Embassy in Florence, Boyd's younger brother, John Curwen Christian Boyd, married Margaret, the daughter of one of Sydney's leading merchants, Robert Campbell Senior.[22]

The lady married 'very much to the annoyance of her mother and family',[23] but willingly or not the Campbell clan, with its Scottish, Indian and Australian mercantile tradition was now wedded to another Scottish clan. They shared much in common: each family was Scottish and Presbyterian; each was involved in shipping and commerce. Though the Campbells had no embarrassing bankruptcy in their background, this was balanced, in contemporary estimation, against their undoubted inferiority as a colonial family, which compared poorly with the Boyds' metropolitan status and landed, albeit sequestered, estates. Curwen, though, was a younger son, and the estate was entailed. In 1841 Curwen and Margaret Boyd sailed for Sydney.

Perhaps the most interesting point of convergence between the Boyd and Campbell clans is that both had collateral branches in India, and were involved in trade with the East. William Sprott Boyd, Benjamin's eldest brother, had done well in the East India Company. Steadily promoted through the service, he reached the position of Political Commissioner in Guzerat [Gujarat] and Resident at Baroda, and was sufficiently important to be mentioned by the London newspapers as a possible President of Bombay. A cousin, also called William Sprott Boyd (known as 'the elder'), worked for Jardine, Matheson in Macao, and later in Hong Kong. Ben Boyd was associated with James Matheson, and by the time he reached Australia he was keenly interested in establishing trade with the Far East. The Campbells, likewise, were linked to Indian trade through the firm of Campbell and Co. of Calcutta. The first Australian Campbell had arrived in Sydney in 1798 as an agent of the company, and the connection was maintained during the next fifty years.[24]

Across the generations and the links of kinship, the Boyd family had spread in many directions from its original Scottish base. To India and the Far East, to the West Indies and America, and now to New South Wales, Boyd sons had gone out for two generations to tap the resources of the Empire, to trade and to exploit the opportunities of new lands—and to return home to invest their colonial fortunes in good Scottish land. Benjamin Boyd's decision to invest in New South Wales was part of this continuum, part of a tradition of exploitation rather than colonization which reached back to the eighteenth century, and was approached in a largely eighteenth-century manner.

Ben Boyd's plan was both grandiose and rapacious, based on the tradition of the merchant adventurers of an earlier age. His successes, such as they were, derived from his supreme confidence in his ability to succeed, a confidence based on his family's history of daring the odds. His ultimate failure, however, lay in his reliance on the eighteenth-century coin of influence—patronage and privilege. His family background taught him to put his faith in such currency, though they had already failed his father. These eighteenth-century characteristics of the mercantile system, though still potent forces, ultimately proved inadequate to cope with the reality of nineteenth-century capitalism, and the greater efficiency its competitive system demanded.

2

Establishment of the Royal Bank of Australia

ON 19 FEBRUARY 1840 Benjamin Boyd brought together a group of investors to establish the Royal Bank of Australia. During the mid-1830s, the expansion of the wool industry in New South Wales drew attention to Australia in London. The foundation of South Australia in 1836 provided further publicity for the Australian colonies. Expanding trade with the colonies extended the importance of banks to tap this trade and the wealth of the expanding squatting movement. Boyd, through his directorships in the Union Bank of London and the North British Insurance Company, was well placed to recognize and develop the potential of colonial banking. Wool growers depended on the export of their produce, but this involved them in long supply lines, a long time lag between export and sale, and hence a need for credit. In the speculative climate of New South Wales in the 1830s the greatest part of squatting business was done on credit. An effective interest rate of 10 to 15 per cent indicated the intensity of the demand. The dividend paid—or promised—by the colonial banks was a reflection of these high expectations: during the two half-years of 1835, for instance, the Bank of New South Wales paid its shareholders 24 and 20 per cent.[1]

In response, a number of banks were formed in Britain to tap this remarkable source of profit, of which the Bank of Australasia (1835) and the Union Bank of Australia (1837) were the most important. The Royal Bank of Australia followed this general trend. The indenture of 3 August 1840, under which it was formed, stated that its object was to carry on 'the trade or business... of Bankers or of Banking', including issuing banknotes and bills payable on demand, and making loans to customers on the basis of such security as real estate, merchandise, livestock, wool or other property.

Just as its potential financial scope was wide, the Royal Bank of Australia had, despite its name, been designed to allow virtually unlimited geographic expansion. From its principal office in London the company could extend throughout Great Britain, and to the colonies of Australia, New Zealand, the Cape of Good Hope, the territories of the East India Company, or 'within any other islands, countries, or territories to which Her Majesty's subjects may lawfully trade beyond the Cape of Good Hope to the Straits of Magellan'. On the other hand, not one of its 128 clauses gave any indication that the bank should expand beyond legitimate banking business into the many fields of enterprise that Boyd was to pursue in New South Wales.[2]

Boyd's intention in setting up the bank is not easy to identify. One possibility is that the bank was, from the time of its inception, merely a cover for his own schemes, a conduit by which money could be raised from unsuspecting investors and transferred into his own companies. This was the suspicion of the bank's official receiver, W. C. Wryghte, who was appointed to wind up the company after it failed. His *Report*, published in 1854, revealed that great confusion existed between the personal affairs of Boyd and the affairs of the bank. Boyd appears to have treated the capital and credit of his bank as a personal source of funds, and had inextricably, and perhaps deliberately, entangled the connection between his own enterprises and those of the bank.

Certainly, he paid little heed to his responsibilities to his shareholders. On the eve of his embarkation for New South Wales, in November 1841, Boyd sent a private letter to John W. Sutherland, the Deputy Chairman of the bank, in which he outlined the precautions he wanted the directors to take in their dealings with shareholders. No more shares should be sold, he recommended; on the contrary, 'I should prefer continuing to buy any Shares, offered on the market at par, more especially the London proprietors, who add no weight to the undertaking and are calculated to give trouble at General Meetings', and he continued, outlining a policy of secrecy for the directors to pursue:

If any proprietors apply for a statement of the affairs of the Bank you must reply to them in very general terms, it is quite sufficient to tell them that the concern is going on steadily but that the Directors thought it prudent in the unsettled state of affairs in Australia to do very little until these commercial difficulties had blown over. If this is not enough to satisfy them it will be well if their shares can be bought up as they will prove troublesome proprietors.

With regard to a general Meeting upon *no account have one* a day sooner than the last authorised by the Deed, which I believe is in July 1845 when I am sanguine of showing a [?profit] that has never been equalled.

[B]y no means either print or give copies or extracts of the Deed of Settlement it only affords parties facilities for getting up similar establishments or opportunities for cavil to troublesome parties.

If any such applications are made the usual & proper answer is that the deed of Settlement lies at the office of the Co, for the inspection of the share holders, but that there is no copy of it printed.[3]

Whatever Boyd's intentions may have been, the potential for fraud certainly existed within the system he had established. For this reason it is important to establish the measures that were taken to protect investors, and the cause of their failure. Clause 25 of the indenture attempted to provide the company with the advantages of limited liability: 'In any Contracts or Engagements entered into in behalf of the Company, it may be stipulated that the properties of the Company shall be the only security for the performance of such Contracts or Engagements'. The reality, however, was that no such agreement carried the force of law. Banking in 1840 was an unregulated business, for major reforms came only in 1844 with the Joint Stock Banking Acts (7 & 8 Vic., c.113).

The bank's capital, in 20 000 shares of £50 each, was to be one million pounds. This nice round figure reverberates through the literature on the Royal Bank, but the truth was that nothing like this amount of money was raised from shareholders. Apart from the twenty shares which each of the ten directors was required to purchase, by 31 March 1841 only 4501 shares had been sold to about 150 proprietors. Boyd himself purchased 6000 shares in the bank, but gave only promissory notes in exchange.[4]

The bulk of the bank's capital, about £300 000, was raised not from shares but by the sale of debentures. An agent, Robert Allan, was appointed in Edinburgh, and 'there was quite a rage'[5] for the debentures in Scotland generally, and more particularly in the south-west where Boyd's associations were greatest. To encourage investors, the Royal Bank of Australia guaranteed a dividend on these debentures of 5 per cent for the first five years and 6 per cent thereafter. Both the Perth Banking Company and the Edinburgh and Glasgow Bank took large parcels as investments and to sell on commission.

The face value of the shares was £50, and shareholders paid an initial deposit of £10 per share. As proprietors in the company, they were liable to the extent of the remaining 80 per cent of their shares on call for the debts of the bank, and might be liable for more if the bank's claim of limited liability was called into question. But it is clear from the later correspondence of disillusioned shareholders that they were encouraged to believe that they would have to pay no more than the initial deposit. Later calls on the shares met a poor response. By 1842 sales virtually ceased, the shares were unlisted, and to shore up their face value the bank itself bought any such shares as were offered for sale on the open market.

The debenture holders, on the other hand, many of them large institutional investors, were the bank's creditors. Herein lay the seed of serious conflict between the two groups involved in floating the bank, and set the scene for the legal battles which ensued when the bank finally crashed at the end of the decade.

The indenture allowed five years for the bank's initial establishment before the first meeting of shareholders fell due. For those five years, the ten directors were responsible to no other authority. In return for participating in a weekly directors' meeting, each received an annual director's fee of £100, with twice that amount for Benjamin Boyd as chairman. These fees, payable from 3 March 1840, were an initial annual expense of £1100 on the bank.

Boyd's choice of director reflected the variety of his associations with the business communities of Scotland and London. Thomas Meux came from a family of brewers in London, and had been involved in the earlier 'Commercial Bank of London' proposal. On his death he was replaced by a Scots businessman, Adam Duff. Alexander Cockburn, a wine importer, was connected with Robert Cockburn, the Chairman of the Edinburgh Board of the North British Insurance Company. William Petre Craufurd was Deputy Paymaster of Her Majesty's Forces. He was involved in other colonial enterprises, such as the British American Land Company. George Webster was a close associate of Sir Peter Laurie. He had interests in Australia through his sons, John, a squatter and trader who later moved to New Zealand, and Alexander, a merchant in Sydney.

John Mitchell, from Glasgow, also had Australian connections. His brother, Sir Thomas Mitchell, was Surveyor-General of New South Wales, and he was a director of the Van Diemen's Land Company. John Connell was a businessman and a director of the North British Insurance Company. John Sutherland, the Deputy Chairman of the bank, became particularly important in the bank's London office after Boyd left for Australia in 1841. Sutherland lived near Croydon, where he was Deputy Lord Lieutenant of the County of Surrey, and an important figure in the local Tory party.[6]

The two directors of most significance to Boyd's wider Australian activities were Benjamin's brother and business partner, Mark Boyd, and Joseph Phelps Robinson, the only director, other than Boyd himself, who actually went out to Australia.

Mark Boyd was his brother's closest business associate. They had worked together since 1827 on the Stock Exchange and later, from their address at New Bank Buildings, they were involved in a variety of other business activities. Mark Boyd became a lobbyist, both for the interests of the Royal Bank of Australia, and for the wider interests of the squatting party in the Australian colonies, pursuing such concerns as immigration, land policy and steam communication.

It was possibly through his brother that Ben Boyd first met Joseph Phelps Robinson.[7] Robinson, born about 1815, was considerably younger than the Boyds. He was a member of an American Quaker family with interests in shipping and coal in

New York, and further interest in land in South America.[8] Through a cousin, Joseph Pim, he was connected to the Liverpool shipping interest, and his elder brother, Anthony Robinson, was a merchant in London. Despite his youth, Joseph Robinson was the Managing Director of the St George Steam Packet Company and on matters of shipping he was more knowledgeable than Boyd. He may have been responsible for drawing Boyd's attention to the opportunities offered by steam communication with Australia; this was certainly a theme that Robinson pursued during his time in New South Wales.

Through its directors, the Royal Bank was associated with banking, shipping, importing, and some of the manufacturing activities of the industrial revolution. No general profile of the directors is possible, for they came from a variety of backgrounds, but they seem to have shared some financial interests. Connell, Craufurd, Cockburn, Webster and, of course, the two Boyds, were all on the London board of the North British Insurance Company and of the London Reversionary Interest Society.[9] Several, including Duff, Mitchell, Cockburn and Craufurd, had Scottish connections. Some, such as Sutherland and Connell, had landed property, and several were magistrates. Sutherland, as Deputy Lord Lieutenant of Surrey, held an office traditionally associated with the aristocracy, but at best the directors were members of the *haute bourgeoisie*. At a time when titled office holders were often specifically sought by a new company to add tone to its lists of directors, none of the Royal Bank's directors had so much as a knighthood.

It is hard to tell how seriously they took their obligations to the bank. Only Sutherland, Connell, Duff and Mark Boyd attended board meetings regularly. After Craufurd's death, his heir complained that his director's fee had not been paid—though he acknowledged that Craufurd had not attended a meeting in more than two years. When the board of directors later attempted to assert its will over Boyd, to disentangle the financial difficulties into which he had led them, only some directors were knowledgeable about the bank's business.

In the absence of firm control from above, the bank's employees had considerable power in daily affairs, but lacked responsibility or authority to act, particularly to act to control their Chairman, Benjamin Boyd. The Secretaries of the bank,

Thomas Huggins and then George Henry Wray, were in fact Boyd's employees, and the bank operated out of New Bank Buildings, along with other business activities of the Boyd brothers.

At the same time that he established the Royal Bank of Australia, Ben Boyd set up several partnerships through which he intended to organize his activities in Australia. He and Mark Boyd already operated in partnership under the title 'Boyd Brothers' or 'B. and M. Boyd', from their business address in London. Much of Benjamin's business in the colonies was directed through Boyd Brothers, including many activities that were legitimately the concern of the Royal Bank of Australia.

The same was true of the Australian Wool Company, floated in November 1840, in which he and Mark were joined by William Smith, a Liverpool shipowner. Smith's ships were engaged in the bounty immigration traffic to Australia, and he had an agent in New South Wales, A. B. Smith. In November 1840 the board of the Royal Bank of Australia agreed to Boyd's proposal that the bank should exchange £20 000 of bank debentures for £10 000 worth of debentures of the Australian Wool Company. The difference was to be made available to Boyd as cash.[10]

This exchange of paper was typical of a number of deals done between the Royal Bank and other companies with which Boyd was associated. The North British Insurance Company lent the Royal Bank £27 000, accepting bank debentures in return. The Union Bank of London agreed to give the Royal Bank credit of £30 000, at 5 per cent interest, in return for maintaining a sum of £5000, interest free, in the Union Bank. The St George Steam Packet Company accepted bank debentures worth £20 000 as mortgage on the *Juno*, one of the steamers sent to Australia.[11]

In this way Boyd obtained finance and ships. However, his deals rendered both the bank and the other companies highly vulnerable in the event of a failure anywhere within the interlocking network. The companies eventually found themselves obliged to shore up the Royal Bank long after any reasonable expectation of profitability had vanished, for on its solvency rested the security of some much larger companies as well.

Wryghte, the Official Receiver of the bank, came to believe that Boyd's financial manipulations had been deliberately conceived for fraudulent purposes. Certainly the potential for double dealing existed within the system that Boyd had devised. The fact that the Australian Wool Company was formed so soon after the Royal Bank of Australia, and was so rapidly involved in a transfer of debentures and cash, tends to confirm this point of view.

However, it is at least worth considering the possibility that the formation of the bank was a response to the unsophisticated nature of capital formation in the colonies. The Royal Bank of Australia failed to fulfil the promises of its indenture to act as an orthodox banking institution. Instead, it may perhaps be seen as a forerunner of the late nineteenth-century pastoral companies which provided much of the funding for Australian rural development, by providing an outlet for small British investors.

The Royal Bank of Australia was floated in March 1840, but Boyd did not leave for Australia until November 1841. He used these intervening months to establish the basis of much of his future political influence in New South Wales. Patronage played an important part in determining the success or failure of colonial enterprises, and Boyd spent time cultivating the sources, public and private, of influence.

The most obvious place for any aspiring colonial entrepreneur to establish contacts was the Colonial Office. Boyd, it seemed, represented exactly the type of imaginative, wealthy investor that the British government hoped to attract to the Australian colonies, for officials of Downing Street treated him sympathetically. In October 1840 he wrote to request special permission to purchase coastal land, on his own terms, for coaling stations and repair harbours. The Colonial Office agreed

> to direct the Australian Colonies . . . to appropriate as the Sites of Public Wharfs and Landing Places any points on the Coasts of those Settlements which you may point out to them as particularly adapted to promote the success of Steam navigation in the adjacent Seas.[12]

Such a recommendation gave Boyd considerable advantage over less favoured settlers. Land in New South Wales was sold only after survey, and in the past the pace of surveying had frequently fallen behind that of land sales. Boyd was being given the

2 *The Royal Bank of Australia* 25

opportunity to choose land, in the knowledge that the governor would give priority to clear it for sale.

Boyd's second request was more eccentric and the Colonial Office responded more cautiously. What, he asked the secretary of state, would be the attitude of Her Majesty's government to a proposal to found a 'republic' in the South Seas? At that moment Lord John Russell was dealing with a ticklish dispute respecting the colonist William Charles Wentworth's private land claims to the South Island of New Zealand. He was therefore understandably wary, but he did not totally oppose Boyd's ambition, merely stating that he '[did] not feel, that he [could] enter into any engagement on behalf of H.M. Government at present'.[13]

The Colonial Office did not take this request very seriously. Neither, in all probability, did Boyd, with more immediate plans to pursue; his vision of a South Seas republic, unknown to his financial backers, remained stored away for the future.

Outlandish though it may appear, Boyd's vision of a private state had numerous predecessors in the nineteenth century. Wentworth's scheme for New Zealand had been a purely commercial proposition. More extravagant visions of independent empires were nurtured by a particular type of colonial adventurer, of which James Brooke was the most recent exemplar, but Sir Stamford Raffles in Singapore and Clunies Ross in the Cocos Islands were earlier models. Ben Boyd's emulation of such personalities shows another dimension of his character. The comparison with Brooke is emphasized by Boyd's association with the private and privileged world of the Royal Yacht Squadron.

Benjamin Boyd had become a member of the Royal Thames Yacht Club in 1839. The following year, he purchased *Wanderer*, a topsail schooner yacht of 141 tons, and through her virtually purchased his membership of the Royal Yacht Squadron.[14] The squadron represented more than pleasure; it stood for privilege and the power of patronage. Begun in the early years of the nineteenth century, its membership was drawn largely from the old Corinthian group which had formed the Prince Regent's set. By the 1830s that set was being challenged by a new, equally wealthy group of whom Boyd was a typical example, socially adequate to mix with true aristocrats, and accepted in the exclusive world of yachting for their wealth—always a necessity for this particular sport—and for their sporting prowess. Risk-taking was, after all, a manly trait, and if a few speculators such as Boyd weighed anchor off Cowes, they were accepted on their individual merits. In Boyd's case, those merits consisted of charm, good humour, and lavish hospitality aboard *Wanderer*.

Membership at Cowes gave Boyd the entrée to a most select circle. The Earl of Yarborough was commodore of the squadron, and its membership included some of the more powerful figures in the social and political world. The young Queen Victoria and Prince Albert were enthusiastic participants, and a persistent legend records that Boyd 'entertained royalty' aboard *Wanderer*.[15]

Boyd met the beau monde on the Isle of Wight. He also met two of his most loyal subordinates, Oswald Brierly and Henry Sewell. Brierly was a young artist with a passion for ships and the sea, whom Boyd met at Cowes where he was developing his talent for painting maritime subjects. Boyd invited him to join his expedition to Australia, and Brierly's illustrated diaries of their travels, and of his years in New South Wales in Boyd's employment, give one of the fullest accounts of Boyd's colonial experiences.

Henry Sewell was a solicitor on the Isle of Wight. In 1841 he came to London to work on Boyd's concerns. His father Isaac was already a member of the North British Insurance Company board, and Henry became known as Ben and Mark Boyd's 'private and confidential agent ... and also the advisor of some of the other Directors of the Royal Bank of Australia'.[16]

Both men did well, with no thanks due to Boyd. When the affairs of the bank began to collapse, Sewell used his experience of colonial affairs to join the Canterbury Association for the colonization of New Zealand. He went out to New Zealand to wind up the company's affairs in 1852, and by 1856, when New Zealand became a self-governing colony, he was elected as the first premier. Brierly returned to England in time to record the naval battles of the Crimean War. He became marine painter to the Queen, and was eventually knighted in 1885.

The image of a yacht has changed since 1840, when the private vessels of wealthy men were, despite their luxurious fittings, large, heavily armed ships with a fighting capacity. Brooke's private yacht, *Royalist*, proved herself against pirates in the East Indies. Consequently, the squadron was recognized as an arm, albeit private and privileged, of the British navy and its vessels were exempt from normal port duties and allowed the rights and privileges of men-o'-war.

Such prerogatives might seem no more than an amusing aristocratic conceit, but for Boyd they were to have unexpected consequences. In 1839 Brooke sailed to the East on a voyage of exploration and adventure. At the Cape of Good Hope the authorities subjected him to port charges from which he would have been exempt in home waters. He wrote back to the squadron to complain, and Yarborough took up the matter with the British government.

The Colonial Office responded by agreeing to treat such yachts as 'subject to the same treatment as men-o'-war', and sent out a circular to all colonial governors to this effect. In due course Sir George Gipps replied from New South Wales:

> this Government will be happy to receive vessels belonging to the Royal Yacht Club, in the way that they are received in England, and that the Colonists of New South Wales hope to see the Commodore and his entire Squadron in Port Jackson before the end of the ensuing year.

'This should be communicated to the Club', James Stephen minuted, 'although I fear, it will be received as a sachasm, and was not improbably so intended'.[17] Despite Gipps's 'sachasm', the privilege of avoiding all port charges was a useful one for Boyd. Irrespective of the money he saved by sailing in *Wanderer*, he also avoided all official control over or knowledge of his movements in the colonies.

Where Brooke led, others followed. Boyd sailed from Plymouth in *Wanderer* in November 1841. The *Plymouth Herald*, reporting his departure, drew clear comparisons between the two:

> gentlemen of large private fortunes, who voluntarily quit all the ease and enjoyment which the most ample means command at home, and go out to encounter the perils and privations which are the lot of every adventurous traveller in long and distant voyage and travel.[18]

A question mark hangs over the timing of Boyd's departure. The Royal Bank of Australia was founded in early 1840; it was not until twenty months later that the chairman of the bank left to establish the bank in New South Wales. Employees of the bank, together with Ben's youngest brother Curwen, were despatched in *Sea Horse* on 2 September 1840, taking £1000 in sovereigns and £10 500 in notes.[19] They were followed during 1841 by the steamships *Juno*, carrying Curwen Boyd and his bride, and *Cornubia*, which sailed in January 1842 with J. P. Robinson.

The employees were given instructions to assess the financial situation, to establish a shipping service, and to open agencies in the different ports, but they were ordered not to begin banking operations until Benjamin Boyd, the Chairman of the bank, arrived in New South Wales. The original prospectus gave the directors five years in which to establish the bank in New South Wales. Boyd's procrastination was therefore a serious matter. By 31 March 1841, one year after the formation of the bank, only £45 010 had been raised from shares, but by the end of that year preliminary expenses had already reached £12 177, and would rise higher before any return on investment could be expected.[20] Moreover the financial situation in the Australian colonies was steadily worsening throughout this long delay. Meanwhile the bank did a little desultory business in London.

Boyd seemed in no hurry to leave. His departure was constantly expected, and constantly postponed. 'I notice that Ben starts in a fortnight', wrote a Liverpool friend on 15 September 1840, but another fourteen months passed before he sailed. There is a rumour that he fell in love at this time, and did not want to leave with the affair unresolved. The lady's name was Emma Green, and she was probably the sister of Charles Green, the 'aeronaut' who had shared Boyd's ballooning exploits. Little more is known about this romance, but Boyd never married, and Emma later married another shipowner.[21] After Boyd's death, a portrait of a woman, said to be Emma Green, was discovered in a locked cabinet aboard *Wanderer*.

Meanwhile, the delay to Boyd's departure was of more than personal consequence, for the affairs of the bank were left in limbo. Boyd's irresolution was an early symptom of the procrastination and managerial inefficiency that were to dog the company in the following years. In naming the last Wednesday in

July 1845 as the date for the first shareholders' meeting of the Royal Bank of Australia, the prospectus had set a time bomb ticking. After an initial five years, the chairman and directors would have to account for their stewardship to the bank's investors.

All appeared optimistic, however, as Ben Boyd sailed west from Plymouth Sound in his luxury yacht, accompanied by congenial companions, in November 1841. Untroubled by the economic disasters that had befallen New South Wales, he expected to make an easy fortune. Meanwhile, in the village of Avonholm by Strathaven, shareholder James Struthers sat down to protest at 'the very meagre account of the business of the company afforded to the shareholders in the present circular', and added, dourly, 'I for one will not remain satisfied with the bare assurance that Mr Boyd has gone yachting to Australia, and has got a large amount of other peoples money with him, but thinks it unnecessary to state how he is applying it'.[22]

3 First Speculations

IN AUSTRALIA the population waited with some bemusement for Ben Boyd. His arrival was first anticipated by the *Sydney Herald* which reported in December 1840 that 'he may be expected in about a month in one of nine steamers which have been purchased for these Colonies by a number of men of capital in Britain.... Mr Boyd brings with him a large amount of specie.' More than a year later, the *Herald* was still plaintively noting:

> For the last eighteen months the Sydney Newspapers have been announcing the approach of Mr Boyd ... At one time we have been told that he had left England, another time that he was seen at Rio, and a third announcement left him at the Cape; every one of them however ending with a declaration that he might be 'daily expected'.[1]

Publicity about Boyd and the Royal Bank of Australia was carefully nurtured to arouse interest amongst the colonists. The arrival of Boyd's steamships, though their number had fallen from nine to three, maintained interest and promoted curiosity in such a small and isolated community. Even one of Boyd's sailing ships, the brigantine *Velocity*, managed to gain publicity for her owners when her captain, Samuel Browning, brought her into Fremantle in the record time of ninety days.[2]

These ships—the steamships *Sea Horse*, *Juno* and *Cornubia*, and the sailing ships *Velocity* and *Terror*—brought the bank's employees, together with a considerable amount of banknotes

3 First Speculations 31

and cash with which to establish operations. Although ordered by the bank in London not as yet to seek banking business, Edward Rennie and David M. Laurie opened an agency in Sydney; they rented a large property at Church Hill, so-called because St Phillip's, St Patrick's and Scots Church all stood within a short distance of each other at the end of York Street. The agency was well placed, within two blocks of the wharves of Darling Harbour, and its location and size were reflected in the high annual rental of £500. A regular steamship service to the southern ports was advertized in the press, and *Sea Horse* left on her first voyage to Port Phillip on 27 July,[3] carrying amongst her passengers Robert Fennell, who was to start an agency in Melbourne, Thomas Crawford (or Craufurd), who became the bank's agent in Adelaide, and George Robinson, the younger brother of Joseph Phelps Robinson. Later agencies were established at Launceston, under Richard Webb, and in Hobart under Laurie. These young men were given considerable independence by the Royal Bank. They were paid handsomely, and were allowed to establish their own businesses in addition to their work for the bank. Given the system of patronage which operated in Britain during the 1840s, it is no surprise to find from their surnames that several directors' relatives seem to have been employed by the bank.[4]

Although he left England after Boyd, in January 1842, Robinson was the first of the partners to arrive in Sydney with the smallest steamer, *Cornubia*, in April after a brisk voyage via the Cape of Good Hope. Boyd, on the other hand, took his time. He left Plymouth in *Wanderer* on 14 December 1841 and reached Madeira on Christmas eve. After five days at Porto Santo, the yacht sailed on to Teneriffe, where Boyd and his companions visited the British consul and spent several days sightseeing and shooting game. They finally sailed on 14 January, not for the Cape of Good Hope, as might be anticipated, but for South America. A fortnight later, on 31 January, they arrived in Rio where for nearly three weeks the party again spent time on social visits, sightseeing, and further shooting expeditions. Captain Tom Bushby, one of Boyd's companions, left *Wanderer* at Rio following an apoplexy which forced him to return to England. They left Rio on 19 February, this time travelling south because, as Brierly recorded, 'it was decided to visit Tristan da Cunha'[5]—where they arrived on 19 March.

The island fascinated the travellers, who spent another two weeks sightseeing there. Brierly devoted one full book of his journal to this fortnight, and Boyd's description of its apparently idyllic social system was published in the *Athenaeum*. The community was patriarchal, twenty-seven of the seventy-odd inhabitants being direct descendants of Governor Glass. Boyd called it 'a perfect model of a republic—the laws very simple, as you may suppose. Thus each person on the Island in turn supplies ships with provisions, the profits of which sale are his own; and this rule being never deviated from, all are contented and happy.' Tristan da Cunha was probably at the back of Boyd's mind when, much later, he envisaged a 'Republic in the South Seas' on a comparably patriarchal model. Glass's latest granddaughter was christened during *Wanderer's* visit, and Boyd made his first purchase of sheep—five sheep to give to the baby as a marriage portion.[6]

On 28 March *Wanderer* sailed for the Cape of Good Hope, which they reached on 6 April. There they took time for yet another shooting excursion, with their quarry this time being springbok. They sailed for Australia on 22 April, with a final pause at the Indian Ocean islands of Amsterdam and St Pauls, where they spent a day sailing around the islands so that Brierly could make sketches. On 1 June they had their first glimpse of Australia, and on 10 June they entered Port Phillip. 'Here the little vessel & her adventurous cruise excited the greatest interest, crowds coming down daily from Melbourne in the Steamer to look at her, and we experienced on every hand the warmest hospitality and attention.'[7] In all, the journey had taken 179 days, of which 66 days had been spent ashore. Some shore leave, certainly, was necessary to provision the ship, but the unnecessary South American leg added three months to the length of the voyage.

Boyd showed no sense of urgency. With agreeable companions and a luxurious ship, he treated the journey as a pleasure cruise, rather than as part of the serious business of capital accumulation with which he had been entrusted by his associates in the Royal Bank of Australia. His companions on board, his younger brother James and Oswald Brierly, seemed equally unconcerned. Boyd appeared to be drifting, as effectively cut off from the affairs of the real world as if he were still floating in one of his balloons. The same sense of exhilaration and remoteness from the pressures of the City shaped his attitude. As long as there remained another wild animal to shoot, an exotic place to visit, Boyd seemed as free as if blown by whim. But his irresponsibility involved others besides himself. His casual attitude, his willingness to procrastinate and to ignore the object of his voyage, were a source of increasing irritation to the bank's shareholders and co-directors.

Boyd 'descended upon quiet plodding Melbourne like a Dives of unfathonable wealth'. The settlement was small, isolated and economically depressed. Small wonder, then, that the arrival of *Wanderer*, and the social prestige of her passengers, caused a flutter amongst the local citizenry. Boyd came ashore to be 'made much of, and feasted and feted by the Melbourne Club'. Georgiana McCrae, a fellow Scot, was a natural daughter of the Duke of Gordon. She recorded Boyd's social visit in her diary with gentle irony—noting, one suspects, the poseur behind the larger than life image:

> Mr Benjamin had rubbed his shoes, and was still smoothing his hair when I received him. He is Rubens over again. Tells me he went to a *bal masque* as Rubens with his broad leafed hat, and was considered *comme il faut*.[8]

Charisma and charm are elusive qualities for a later generation to identify. They lie in the eye and the heart of the beholder, who may be only partly aware of the impact the stronger personality is exerting. Later he may resist that influence when he comes to record his impressions. There seems little doubt, however, that Boyd had both; they made him the focus of attention at any social gathering. No doubt his money, and the lavish hospitality he bought with that wealth, played some part in Boyd's social influence. But he had an impact on his peers in Britain as well. Above all, his dominance over his own brothers suggests the impact of his personality. Mark Boyd had five brothers, but when, in his *Reminiscences*, he speaks of 'my brother', it is invariably Benjamin who is his subject. Even when, towards the end of the decade, Boyd's empire and reputation were crumbling, his followers found it a painful and disillusioning experience to be forced to confront his limitations. In mid-1842, enthusiastic, ebullient and optimistic, and with access, so he said, to one million pounds in credit, Benjamin Boyd's personal presence was overwhelming.

One of his first actions on landing at Port Phillip was to buy sheep. William Westgarth shared accommodation with Robert Fennell, the bank's Melbourne agent, and later worked for Boyd himself. He graphically described Boyd's method of purchase: 'He... made a hasty run up to Colac, [saw the owner], bought him out, and left him in charge of this first of many purchases'. On this occasion, Boyd's impetuosity was rewarded with good fortune. The former owner of Colac Station, who now became Boyd's manager, was Augustus Morris, a young man who knew both land and sheep. Subsequently Morris explored the saltbush country of the Riverina district on Boyd's behalf, and took sheep north from the Port Phillip District to the area around Deniliquin where Boyd established further stations. Like Brierly and Sewell, Morris also achieved success in subsequent years, as a pastoralist, politician, and co-author with George Ranken of the 1883 report of the New South Wales government into free selection.[9]

Boyd could not expect that all the appointments he made would be so fortuitous. However many of the young men he employed achieved later success in their chosen careers, suggesting that Boyd's eye for talent was remarkably keen. Yet despite his skill as a talent spotter, he had been in Australia less than a fortnight when he purchased Colac, and he could have had little knowledge of the economic situation he had entered. Nor had he any directive to extend the activities of the Royal Bank. His purchase implied a major change of direction, but the board of directors was left in ignorance of the changes he was foreshadowing. In fact Boyd did not write home at all until several weeks later, and the first news of his arrival reached his anxious friends and relatives from a different source. On 16 November, a letter from George Webb reported that *Wanderer* had put in to Hobart because of bad weather. Six weeks later the bank still had not heard from Boyd but relied on rumours: 'A Gentleman has just called who has a letter from his Brother at Port Phillip stating that you had been buying Sheep there', Wray wrote to

Boyd on 21 December. It was an inadequate way in which to run a serious commercial enterprise.[10]

Boyd reached Sydney on 18 July 1842. Publicity had been intense, especially since *Wanderer* had arrived in Port Phillip. The arrival was well prepared; *Velocity* fired a salute, and crowds of onlookers lined the heights of Sydney Harbour to see the first yacht of the Royal Yacht Squadron to pass through the Heads.[11]

In establishing himself in New South Wales, Boyd's first priority had to be the development of a relationship with the governor. Sir George Gipps tended to treat with justifiable cynicism the many British capitalists and adventurers foisted on him by the casual sponsorship of the metropolitan government.[12] He was therefore likely to treat with some suspicion the patronage Boyd had received from the British government. In other respects, however, Boyd's birth, wealth and prospects assured him of the governor's hospitality.

In personality the two men were opposites. Gipps was a worrier, conscientious to a fault in his administration, but rigid and lacking in imagination. Imagination was Boyd's dominant characteristic. He was ebullient and flamboyant, with the pervasive self-confidence of inherited position. The governor, on the other hand, was a self-made man, a soldier and bureaucrat who had reached his high position through diligence and a meticulous attention to detail. Loyal to his office, Gipps attempted to implement the policies of the British government in the interests of all colonists. His balancing act was often difficult, sometimes impossible, especially since the British government was often uncertain of the details of its policy and sometimes changed it under pressure from outside interests.

Two years had elapsed since Boyd's initial decision to invest in New South Wales, and there had been a sharp reversal in the fortunes of the colony. By July 1842 New South Wales was suffering from an economic depression which affected both public and private sectors. The slump not only affected the prospect of profits for the Royal Bank of Australia, it also affected the bank's reception in the colony, for public opinion was increasingly hostile towards the ambitions of newly arrived capitalists like Boyd.

The colony depended on the pastoral industry, but the price of wool had never recovered from its 1836 peak. Instead, as the frontier expanded into marginal land squatters were faced with rising transport costs. With the end of convict transportation in 1840, labour became more expensive and less servile. To add to the troubles of the pastoralists, a drought began in 1839. During the 1830s many sheepmen had relied on the sale of the year's increase of lambs to new squatters to meet their expenses during the following season, before they could expect any return from the London wool sales. Now, with contraction rather than expansion on the frontier, this supplementary income was no longer available, and the squatters found themselves unable to service their substantial debts.

The problems of the pastoral industry rebounded on their creditors, the banks and the merchant community, and from them to the colonists in general. These difficulties were compounded by changing British government policy, for with the end of the convict system Britain reduced her contribution towards the cost of the police and the gaols, the infrastructure of the system. Nevertheless, the mother country continued to expect that New South Wales would, and could, absorb large numbers of assisted immigrants, and pay for the privilege from the sale of Crown Lands.

For a variety of reasons, then, the easy fortunes of the 1830s were over, money was flowing out of the colony, and public opinion, seeking an explanation for the downturn, blamed the banks. The squatting boom had been based on easy credit. The banks had profited from this system of easy borrowing, for interest rates and consequent banking profits were high. Westgarth reported rates of 10 per cent for discounting three-monthly bills, with 2 per cent additional for longer periods or overdrawn accounts.[13] Pressure to reduce interest rates was growing, yet high rates were only symptomatic of the high risks involved in colonial finance. Such risks culminated, in March 1843, in the collapse of the Bank of Australia, a failure which revealed the inherent weakness of colonial banking.

When Boyd arrived, however, the hazards of colonial banking were less evident than its profitability. On the very day of his arrival the Bank of Australia and the Sydney Bank announced half-yearly dividends of 6 per cent and 5½ per cent respectively. Such profits caused discontent amongst colonists facing troubled times. As depression increased, the role of the banks, particularly the Anglo-Australian banks and finance companies, was questioned not only by colonists but even by officials of the British colonial system itself. On 11 August the Legislative Council debated the issue. Governor Gipps emphasized the danger to the colony if overseas interests gained control of the financial system, which 'would ... convert the whole property of the colony into rent rolls for absentee proprietors, and, by the bye the wool of Australia would be sent to England to pay the interest of money owing in England in the shape of mortgages, or bank shares, or loans of some sort'.[14]

Gipps's strong stand against the economic imperialism of private entrepreneurs from the City of London was also expressed officially in his despatches to the Colonial Office. He told the Secretary of State that he opposed the establishment of further British banks:

> this Colony has never derived, nor is it ever likely to derive any advantage from companies formed in England—neither from the Australian Agricultural Company, the Bank of Australasia, nor any other; and ... I cannot but apprehend, that the high pretensions of the recent Companies which have started into existence elsewhere...will end in disappointment if not in disaster.[15]

Gipps's antagonism to foreign moneylenders was reiterated in the local press. The *Herald* reserved its harshest criticism for the 'Anglo-Colonial' banks, which they distinguished from local banks as more greedy, because 'over-grasping British capitalists' withdrew their profits from the colony, thus adding to the financial crisis.[16]

Thus by the time of Boyd's arrival, both government and public opinion was opposed to any new British-based bank. Moreover the days of easy credit, and easy profits, were drawing to a close. An early indication of this trend came in September, when the local banks reduced their rate on three-monthly bills from 10 to 8 per cent.[17]

Boyd lacked the local connections to break into an already overcrowded financial market and, with public opinion raised against any such attempt, he made the sensible business decision not to develop the banking functions of the Royal Bank of

Australia in an atmosphere of such active hostility. The Royal Bank therefore never became a bank of note issue, and its banking business remained limited, being mostly concerned with the transfer of bills of exchange between England and Australia. The bank's opening hours, from twelve until two every day, suggest the desultory nature of its public business.[18]

Boyd reported to Sutherland that the economy was in a parlous condition:

> there is scarcely a leading House in the Colony solvent. The system of accommodation has been and is carried on to such a frightful extent and the ramifications of one House is so mixed up with another that hitherto the great Crash has been staved off as each Bank has been obliged to support its customers being well aware that if one House is allowed to go all must follow.

Such was the state of the economy, he had decided not to issue banknotes as originally intended but to 'discount settlers bills, holding a lien over the property, for there is little probability of stock falling much lower, but if it did, it would be of little consequence, as the following year's increase would much more than make up any deficiency'.[19]

With this sanguine expectation, he directed his activity towards the accumulation of mortgages on stock. The economic climate was certainly unfavourable for the establishment of a new bank, but Boyd's early purchases of land, the bank's early association with shipping, and above all the way in which the bank's money was transferred into Boyd's other enterprises, demonstrate how far beyond normal banking activities the Royal Bank had gone, even before Boyd's arrival.

In 1854 the bank's official receiver argued that, from its inception, the bank was a fraud, the Australian Wool Company a 'fiction', and Boyd's operations were based on 'the *mere pretense* of carrying on a Bank'. His claim will be dealt with later, but it must be noted that the bank's employees began buying stations before Boyd arrived, and that Rennie, the agent in Sydney, operated two sets of books, one for the Royal Bank, the other for the Australian Wool Company.[20]

With Boyd's arrival the pace of non-banking activities increased. He purchased squatting runs, he enlarged his fleet of whalers, and he bought land at Twofold Bay for a projected township and port. In all these purchases, the Royal Bank provided the funds, but Boyd paid little heed to its interests. It had cost the bank approximately £1200 to send out its employees. They were now sent inland 'to herd sheep, until the business of the Bank required their services'. In vindication of his activities six years later, Boyd argued that on his arrival the colony was 'on the eve of a great & general convulsion ... Paper ... was totally valueless—& had I employed the funds at my disposal in discounts, the result would have been that every penny must have been lost'. Instead, 'exceedingly desirous to render the money immediately productive', he looked to 'the only real wealth' of the colony—its pastoral resources.[21]

Unfortunately for Boyd's companies, the system of squatting licences under which he made his purchases required that the holder of a licence should be 'a fit and proper person'—in other words, an individual, not a company. During July, Westgarth noted Boyd's purchase of Colac Station for 'the great "Australian Wool Company," or whatever other title was to suit the great schemes of this busy head which had turned up amongst us'.[22] Ultimately the creditors of the Royal Bank found it equally difficult to identify, and to disentangle, the various purchases Boyd made through his different companies and partnerships.

Boyd made few gestures towards the ostensible purpose for which he had come to Australia. Instead he used the Royal Bank as a source of funds for other purposes. On 22 August 1843, on behalf of the Australian Wool Company, Boyd borrowed £100 000 from the Royal Bank, at 10 per cent per annum interest, giving debentures of the Australian Wool Company in exchange. He thus became the largest customer of his own bank.[23] Apart from such dubious internal transfers, few significant banking ventures were initiated during this period. Those loans that were arranged were not based on normal economic grounds, but on political or personal factors, or as a way of gaining leverage over debtors for other purposes.

Such a case was Boyd's decision to lend money to a fellow member of the Royal Yacht Squadron, the Honorable James Erskine Murray, who was languishing in Melbourne at the time of Boyd's arrival. There could be no clearer example of the faulty priorities on which Boyd chose his bank's clients. Murray was deeply in debt, with no property in Australia, but the Royal Bank lent him money, rumoured to be £10 000. This allowed him to escape his Port Phillip creditors and sail his yacht to Borneo in yet another attempt to emulate James Brooke. The expedition ended in abject failure. Murray was killed by pirates, and Brooke commented: 'Thus ended a rash and ill-advised adventure, which was consulted without reference to the character or temper of the natives, and might, had it been pursued here, have led to worse events than have now occurred'. The events were serious enough for the Royal Bank of Australia.[24]

Sir Eardley Wilmot, the newly appointed Governor of Van Diemen's Land, was another client chosen for his status as well as his access to influence, rather than his creditworthiness. He negotiated a loan with the directors of the Royal Bank in London in April 1843. Similarly unbusinesslike priorities were applied: 'we have by ... judicious Liberality secured a firm friend to the Bank', wrote one director with satisfaction, adding that he had impressed on Sir Eardley that Boyd was 'a Man from whose powerful intellect [he] might derive most effectual aid and support'.[25] Unfortunately, Wilmot died with his debt unpaid. Because of an oversight, the bank had not renewed the insurance policy on his life and, to increase the bank's chagrin, the Royal Bank does not seem to have gained any material advantages in Van Diemen's Land as a result of its sponsorship of Wilmot.

Boyd's loan to the New Zealand government was a more significant affair, which brought the bank clearly into the political arena and gave Boyd a degree of influence with the New Zealand government that he never achieved with the governments of New South Wales or Van Diemen's Land. Ultimately the Boyd family benefitted from this influence, although the Royal Bank, once again, was the loser.

When Boyd arrived in Sydney the New Zealand government was in its infancy. In early 1840 New Zealand was annexed as a dependency of New South Wales. Captain Hobson proclaimed himself Lieutenant-Governor on 29 January, and it was as lieutenant-governor, under the *de jure* authority of the Governor of New South Wales, that he met with the New Zealand chiefs to negotiate the Treaty of Waitangi on 5 February. Despite numerous ambiguities, the Treaty ceded a prescriptive right over all

3 *First Speculations* 41

Maori land to the new colonial government. This land could be purchased by the government for re-sale to European settlers, and the profits of these land sales, together with customs duties, constituted virtually the whole revenue of the New Zealand government.

The following year New Zealand was proclaimed a separate Crown colony. The new government had inadequate funds, an inadequate income, and had been obliged to take over the debt incurred on its behalf by the New South Wales government. Gipps was forced to draw unauthorized bills on the Treasury to pay for the new colony, in order to relieve the New South Wales revenue which was earmarked for the immigration fund. The Lords of the Treasury reluctantly authorized the bills, 'assigning as a reason the fact that Gipps had not been apprised of their intention to make the New Zealand Government repay the advances'. Hobson was ordered by the British government to repay this debt of £44 000 in addition to all local demands. This proved impossibly unrealistic.[26]

To make matters worse, Governor Hobson was incapacitated by a stroke shortly after his arrival in Auckland, and the civil officers who took control lacked the necessary financial skills to administer the new colony. Faced with a severe economic crisis, they adopted desperate, and possibly illegal, methods.

The government depended financially on the equally fragile New Zealand Banking Company. The history of this bank's formation parallels, in miniature, that of the Royal Bank of Australia. Established in Sydney in 1840, the bank's original prospectus promised 10 000 shares of £10 each. The bank might have survived the rigours of the 1840s had this capital been raised, but only 4239 shares were subscribed, for an initial payment of £1 per share. The bank began business with this meagre capital in September 1840. A later call of £1 only raised a further £3747, and the bank was soon in trouble. Nonetheless it served a useful function in Auckland and the New Zealand government, when not itself relying on it, attempted to support it.[27]

During 1841 and 1842 the New Zealand government was close to bankruptcy. It was expected to finance its operations from the sale of lands and from customs dues, but land sales fell during the depression and were complicated by the need to conciliate the original Maori landowners. Customs duties also dropped, partly in response to depression and falling consumption, partly because of increased smuggling which had the added effect of destroying the trade of New Zealand's oldest port, Kororareka. In 1841 government expenditure exceeded £80 000, while revenue was only £37 000, of which £28 000 came from land sales and £6407 from customs dues.[28]

Government expenses were considerable. The extension of government to New Zealand involved the appointment of large numbers of petty officials—too many, according to the merchant community—and their salaries were another drain on the revenue. In March 1842, faced with a burden of debt, Governor Hobson, like Gipps and Governor Gawler of South Australia, took the desperate measure of funding government expenditure with bills drawn on the Treasury which had not been authorized by the Colonial Office.

Five months later the New Zealand government decided to use this expedient again. In August 1842 the Executive Council authorized the drawing up of £15 000 in government drafts on the British Treasury and sent them to New South Wales with George Cooper, Customs Officer and director of the New Zealand Banking Company. Cooper was directed to discount the bills in Sydney so that cash could be obtained urgently to cover current expenditure. Shortland, the Colonial Secretary, justified the illegal action:

> draw[ing]...attention to the following Extract from His Excellency's Instructions from the Secretary of State for the Colonies, in which, speaking of Public Revenues, His Lordship Remarks *'Extreme cases may* of course arise, to which every such general rule must yeild [*sic*]' by which you will perceive that in *emergencies* like the present Governors are authorised to adopt any financial measures they may with the advise of their Council consider necessary.[29]

Cooper arrived in Sydney at a time of depression. Credit was tight, and there was massive and entirely warranted suspicion of the New Zealand government's financial position. By October he had found no financial institution prepared to handle the Treasury drafts, unauthorized as they were by the British government. That month the New Zealand Banking Company asked the government to repay its overdraft. The government was desperate. In New Zealand, Bishop Selwyn agreed to lend it £5000 from Church of England funds, at what was, given the government's credit rating, the generous terms of 5 per cent per annum. For further funds, the government turned to Cooper in Sydney.

Shunned by the orthodox financial institutions, Cooper turned to Boyd and Robinson. They had been in Sydney only a few months, but the terms on which they agreed to accommodate the New Zealand government were so harsh that it is clear that the bankers were fully aware of the speculative nature of the undertaking and the poor financial standing of their new client.

On 12 October 1842 Boyd and Robinson agreed to provide the government with cash in exchange for £15 000 in Treasury bills, discounted by 15 per cent, which would be sent to England for payment. As collateral security they would take £15 000 in debentures on the revenues of New Zealand, to pay 15 per cent. On 31 October the size of the loan was reduced to between £6000 and £7500. Meanwhile, on 10 September, Hobson died and the Colonial Secretary, Willoughby Shortland, an ambitious young naval lieutenant, became Acting-Governor. When the news reached Sydney, Boyd wrote to Cooper asking whether or not the contract was to stand, and was reassured that it would remain intact.

During these weeks the immediate plight of the government had eased slightly. The New Zealand Banking Company, despite its fragile condition, managed to raise £2000 to lend to the government. On the basis of this temporary respite, Shortland decided, perhaps not understanding the nature of Cooper's contract with Boyd and Robinson, not to send the debentures to Sydney.

As yet, Shortland had not drawn on the Royal Bank of Australia loan, but the government's improved situation proved transitory. At the end of 1842 the New Zealand Banking Company requested the return of its £2000. Otherwise, it warned, it might have to shut its doors. A run on the bank would precipitate a financial crisis in Auckland, and the Colonial Treasurer, Alexander Shepard, was faced with a dilemma. As both Shortland and the Attorney-General, Swainston, were absent from Auckland, Shepard found himself dependent for economic advice on men who were directly involved in the crisis—the directors of the New Zealand Banking Company. On 15 January 1843 Shepard met William Connell, the Acting Colonial Secretary, and George Cooper and Felton Mathews, directors of the New Zealand Banking Company, to discuss the financial crisis of the bank and, consequently, of the New Zealand government. Jointly they agreed to fall back on the earlier negotiations of Cooper with Boyd and Robinson. On 27 January 1843 Shepard wrote a cheque for £2000 to Alexander Kennedy, manager of the New Zealand Banking Company, payable at thirty days sight on Boyd and Robinson.[30]

The promised debentures, which were to provide security for this loan, had not yet arrived, so Boyd and Robinson paid the £2000 grudgingly. However, their acceptance of the cheque made the treasurer less cautious. On 13 March 1843, with the government still in financial trouble, Shepard wrote a cheque for a further £3000. By now aware that some indication of good faith was required, the New Zealand government instructed G. R. Griffiths, of Griffiths, Gore and Co. of Sydney, to offer Boyd and Robinson debentures to the value of £3500, with instructions to pay the remaining £500 into the Bank of Australasia.[31]

Boyd and Robinson would have none of it. Apart from the failure to fulfil the original contract, the New Zealand government was now offering debentures dated from 13 March 1843, rather than the original contracted date of 31 October 1842, a loss of five months interest on the loan. On 8 April they told Griffiths that they considered their contract had been breached by the non-arrival of the debentures. They would agree only to the terms of the original contract. If the debentures were backdated to 31 October 1842, and if a further £4500 in debentures were delivered 'by return of post from Auckland', they would meet the present £3000 cheque and make available a further £2500 'which with Two thousand already advanced will make up the full sum of Seven thousand five hundred Pounds as arranged on the 31st October, and from which time the money has been unproductive at the call of the Government'.[32]

Griffiths was not empowered to fulfil the original contract. A fruitless search ensued as he sought alternative creditors in a desperate attempt to prevent the dishonouring of the government cheque. He even approached Gipps, but without success[33]

3 *First Speculations* 45

and the cheque was duly dishonoured. In effect, the New Zealand government was bankrupt.

In Auckland, the local newspaper, ever hostile to Shortland and his associates, criticized his arrangement with Boyd and Robinson as 'not only the most injudicious but the most injurious as to the interests of this Colony that could be entered into'. Angry at the harsh treatment the government had received, it railed:

> Obliged to sell Bills upon the British Treasury at a discount of 15 per cent., giving Debentures upon the Colonial Revenue as security besides!! Was the British Government ever before at such a discount in any other part of the world?![34]

Was the Royal Bank of Australia's treatment usurious? Fifteen per cent was a high, but not an extreme rate of interest in 1842, when loans were being negotiated locally for 10 to 12 per cent. Loans secured by British Treasury bills should, of course have been a different matter. Boyd told Sutherland that 'dealing with the Government puts all risks out of the question, and would give the Bank the highest position in the Colony from such a connection'.[35]

Unauthorized bills were a different matter. The speculative nature of the loan was apparently well understood in Sydney. No one, apart from Boyd and Robinson, would touch the New Zealand government's paper at any price. As Boyd and Robinson themselves made clear:

> [Mr Cooper] never applied to us until he had tried every other Channel not excepting the Government here, but such was the low estimate of New Zealand credit that he was unable except through us, to raise a shilling, and it was entirely from the knowledge that we had offered assistance that the Government again got credit.[36]

Credit was indeed extremely tight. The New South Wales government was hard pressed to meet its own commitments for the immigration fund, and all financial institutions were anxious to avoid large loans, especially after the collapse of the Bank of Australia in March 1843.

In the event, this caution was fully justified. On 7 August 1843 news arrived in Sydney that the Treasury bills for £15,000, sent to London by Boyd and Robinson for payment, had been refused by the British government the previous March.[37] At a stroke, the tables were turned. Now Boyd and Robinson were faced with the need to retrieve from the New Zealand government the £2000 they had already lent, preferably with interest or, as a last resort, accompanied by the government debentures they had spurned so scornfully the previous April.

This was to prove difficult. The British government, in refusing to honour New Zealand's unauthorized Treasury bills, advised the colonial government that outstanding loans should be changed to 5 per cent non-transferable debentures on the government revenue.[38] This was unacceptable to Boyd, for the earlier debentures had promised 15 per cent. Moreover, these new debentures were to be dated from 15 January 1843, the actual date on which the government cheque for £2000 had been met by the Royal Bank. While this was an improvement by two months on Griffiths's earlier offer, it was still unacceptable to the Royal Bank since the money for the New Zealand government had, they said, been set aside since 31 October 1842, and interest should be paid from that date.

In December 1843 the new Governor of New Zealand, Robert FitzRoy, arrived in Sydney to discuss the consequences of the loan with Boyd and Robinson, and with Gipps. By this time a good deal of anger had been generated between the parties to the original contract, and the real intentions behind those negotiations had become blurred by subsequent argument.

FitzRoy, for his part, blamed Boyd and Robinson for entering into an unequal contract and claimed that 'the Lords of the Treasury had refused to accept these bills from a Knowledge that the Transaction was one of so extraordinary & unheard of a character as to stand ... on a pedestal of its own'. The Treasury, he claimed, had been alerted to the arrangement in a despatch from Gipps. In an interview with Boyd, Gipps denied that he had done this, or 'had considered the transaction ... discreditable', or, indeed, had known anything about Boyd's negotiations with Cooper until Griffiths's arrival in Sydney six months later. Something, however, must have led the Treasury to treat the transaction with such suspicion that the Royal Bank's London manager, 'on making the third application for them' to the Treasury was fobbed off: 'the answer is "that they are under the consideration of Lord Stanley"'.[39]

Boyd, too, was shifting his ground. He now denied that the contract had been a loan at all:

> it was not an arrangement for a Cash credit... but a direct bargain of Sale of certain Debentures bearing 15 Pr Cent Interest.... We receiving as collateral security for the due payment of said Debentures at maturity certain Bills of Exchange upon the Lords of the Treasury the proceeds of which if accepted in London, were to be held by us at the credit of the New Zealand Government.

By treating the Treasury bills, rather than the debentures, as the collateral security, Boyd hoped to avert the prospect of losing the bank's money entirely through a bad debt. The debentures might retain some value in the future. More interesting is Boyd's statement to FitzRoy that 'We fully explained to [Cooper] that we were not Purchasers of Bills upon England, at all, our business being the employment of Capital in the Colonies'.[40]

If such an assurance was given to Cooper, it was certainly not entrusted to print. It is a startling statement in the light of the bank's indenture, where the purchase of bills for conveyance to London is a clearly defined aspect of the bank's operation. Boyd's claim, unlikely as it is, is the clearest statement of the shift in the operations of the Royal Bank of Australia from the intentions of the original founders to the wider colonial activities favoured by Boyd.

The dishonouring of British Treasury bills caused a minor sensation in London. George Wray wrote despairingly: 'the statement that the [New Zealand] government there is in an insolvent condition is alarming our Directors as they, & all here, are not only ignorant in this case but also as to our position in respect of Murray's dfts.' First reports indicated a loss of £15 000. As the bank had not paid the full amount negotiated, the case was less disastrous, but the loss of £2000 was still a serious blow. Coupled with the news of Murray's default and death in Borneo, it caused questions to be raised, both inside and outside the bank, about Boyd's acumen. Both loans had, by their very nature, attracted a blaze of unwelcome publicity for the bank, soon to hold its first shareholders' meeting.[41]

Boyd's other banking activities were limited and informal. He quickly gained the reputation of bankrolling numerous people and organizations in New South Wales, manipulating those who were in his debt as a way of gaining political and economic influence. In the straitened circumstances of the early 1840s, it was comparatively easy to exert pressure in this way. Many of the leaders of society were overextended and vulnerable to offers of financial help. The radical *Sydney Chronicle* asserted in 1846:

> The house of Boyd has long been known as a Refuge for the Destitute. Bankers, and Customs House Clerks, Merchants and Superintendents of Police, if they become *unfortunate*—which means, of course, if they become *insolvent*—are received with open arms and tears of joy.[42]

The *Chronicle* was successfully sued for libel for printing this article, but the contention was essentially true. Such loans can only marginally be reckoned as banking, for they were not based on a rational assessment of the creditworthiness of the client, but on vulnerability and susceptibility to financial pressure.

Boyd's first year in New South Wales was a time of transition. During this period he was erratically engaged in banking business, nearly always with unhappy results. The New Zealand loan, in particular, did nothing to enhance the reputation of the Royal Bank or of its chairman. The failure of his flirtation with government banking may have added to his determination not to continue with orthodox banking in New South Wales, although, by the time news of the full disaster of this loan reached Sydney in August 1843, the decision had already been taken. The other aspects of Boyd's colonial enterprises, already foreshadowed before his arrival, increasingly took precedence, and the Royal Bank of Australia became merely a source of funds for his other activities.

Boyd extended the non-banking activities begun by his employees, buying sheep, accumulating squatting runs and operating a steamship run. The extent of these operations, the publicity with which they were promoted and, perhaps, the covert influence he was able to exert through his careful, selective offers of financial assistance, combined to make Ben Boyd a power in the land within eighteen months of his arrival.

3 *First Speculations* 49

His more ill-considered projects, such as the New Zealand loan, were disregarded as he moved beyond banking to pursue new activities. The Royal Bank of Australia was left to bear the brunt of his unlucky ventures: his fertile brain was already conceiving new schemes.

4
A Lust for Land

IN 1844 WILLIAM WESTGARTH undertook a trip through the Port Phillip District, visiting the many squatting runs of his employer, Benjamin Boyd. He went first to Colac, the station north of the Barwon River, on Lake Colac, that Boyd had purchased in July 1842. Westgarth noted the beauty of the mid-winter landscape, the pelicans flying above the lake and yellow-crested cockatoos roosting so thickly 'as to give the look of a cap of snow'. One day, there would be a town of Colac, but in 1844, 'excepting the partial post-and-rail barricade of my friend William Robertson's ... 5000 acres of purchased land, there was nothing all around but free and open squatting. On every side was the hardly yet disturbed indigenous aspect'.

From there he rode west to Boyd's station at the Eumerella River, north of Portland Bay where the first squatters had settled. 'My nag was more than ever "in clover," and we wandered on through marvels upon marvels of remarkably rich and fertile country. The country was all but empty as I now coursed through it'. The station covered an area of perhaps 200 000 acres, and was managed by 'a versatile youth of the name of Craufurd, of a good Scotch family'.[1]

At the neighbouring station of Dunmore, owned by Andrew Lang, Westgarth had reached the western frontier of European settlement and was accompanied by a station detachment to protect him from possible attack by the Aborigines. He passed through safely, but heard about the 'strong mutual antipathies' that had led to massacres within recent years.

He then set out 'north for the Wannon', where he spent a night with 'a solitary shepherd in an out-hut, so far and away from all companionable life but that of his sheep that I could well realise ... the dolorous side of squatting'.[2]

His last Boyd station was in the Pyrenees district. This run, unnamed, was under the charge of James M. Hamilton, and was probably located near the present town of Hamilton. A year later, Sir Thomas Mitchell was to describe Hamilton and his partner as 'two intelligent young gentlemen—blue eyes and yellow-bearded like the Boyd himself'. Boyd's overseers, it seems, were usually Scottish, and seem to have included several men connected by family to the Royal Bank of Australia.[3]

So extensive and so scattered were Boyd's properties that Westgarth's journey took many weeks, stopping briefly at each station. Yet his trip took him to only a small portion of the squatting stations then controlled by Boyd. By 1844, Benjamin Boyd had become one of the leading squatters in eastern Australia.

Whatever may have been the initial objective of the Royal Bank of Australia, Boyd's intention to invest in land was confirmed within a week of his arrival on Australian soil, when he bought his first sheep, and the run to put them on, at Colac. Robert Fennell, the bank's agent in Melbourne, who shared a house with Westgarth, accompanied Boyd on his buying expedition, and Boyd probably took Fennell's advice on the prospects of the wool industry; nonetheless his purchases seem remarkably hasty at a time when depression was widespread throughout the Port Phillip District. Perhaps the new arrival, relying only on advice from his subordinates, was overwhelmed by the apparent cheapness of both land and livestock, for these early purchases illustrate the extravagance which was to be characteristic of his actions in Australia.

To understand just what Boyd was purchasing, it is important to bear in mind the nature of squatting in the 1840s. During the early years of settlement in New South Wales, land grants by the governors to appropriate settlers had been the rule. These grants gave the new proprietor freehold title to his land, qualified only by the existence of a quitrent, a small tax on the land common to many parts of the British Empire. Land granted under these titles could be bought and sold in the normal way, and because most of it was close to Sydney and the coast, settlers coming after the original grantees, or others consolidating their holdings, provided a constant demand. The size of land grants to some extent determined their use; they were relatively small (up to about 2000 acres), and accompanied by generous amounts of convict labour. They were designed for, though not necessarily devoted to, agricultural production. With security of tenure and plenty of labour, steady capital improvement was possible, and the value of land in the county of Cumberland increased.

The governors' criteria for selecting recipients for land grants were based on wealth and respectability, for the potential employer of convict labour must be an appropriate instrument of reform. Under this system, many men, particularly those whose origins were dubious, were denied a grant of land—the main source of income in New South Wales. If, nonetheless, they hoped to make a living from the land, they 'squatted', taking livestock—purchased or poached—on to Crown Land, from which they could rarely be evicted. They were perceived to be disreputable, associated in the public mind with convictism and theft.

In 1831 the new Whig government in Britain changed the system. Under the Ripon Regulations, land would in future be sold rather than granted. The new policy was intended to encourage concentrated settlement (as well as provide a revenue), but in practice it had a very different effect. By 1831 the pastoral industry had become, with whaling, the major export industry in New South Wales. The economics of colonial sheep farming required extensive, not intensive, pastoralism, and neither the original land grants nor the new land sales made allowance for the amount of land demanded by the sheep men. At five shillings an acre, the cost of a block of land large enough to sustain a flock was prohibitive. Meanwhile, beyond the slowly moving surveyors, gradually cutting 640 acre blocks out of the wilderness, lay the 'waste lands', where only 'native blacks', their own land tenure denied, roamed free.

The sheep men chose to squat on the Crown Lands. The new squatters of the 1830s were men of a different social class from their predecessors and respectable according to the values of their day. They were also successful. By 1836 wool had replaced whale products as the major export of New South Wales, and the squatting movement was an economic, and therefore a political, force in the colony. Under these circumstances, the British government could do little to hold them back. In 1829 Governor Darling had proclaimed nineteen counties, which comprised the 'limits of location' of the settlement. Beyond were the 'waste lands'. In 1836, acknowledging the reality of the squatters' movement into these waste lands, Governor Bourke legitimized the situation by introducing an Act 'to restrain the unauthorised occupation of the the Crown Lands'. Occupation of Crown Land within the nineteen counties was to be strictly discouraged, but Bourke's Act introduced a £10 licence fee under which a squatter beyond the limits of location could hold his land as an annual tenant of the Crown. The waste lands were subdivided into squattage districts, and in 1837 commissioners of Crown Lands were appointed to each district to exert some control; they attempted to arbitrate in disputes amongst the squatters, and between squatters and the Aboriginal population they were displacing.

Meanwhile, loyal to the precepts of Edward Gibbon Wakefield and the systematic colonizers in London, the Colonial Office raised the upset price of Crown Land, to 12s an acre in 1839, then to £1 per acre, first in the Port Phillip District in 1841 and then in other areas in 1843. The rising cost of purchase further reduced the likelihood that the squatters would either buy their runs or be replaced by more legitimate proprietors. The revenue from the sale of Crown Lands reached a peak in 1840, when sales amounted to £316 626, then fell dramatically to £9387 in 1841, £14 574 in 1842 and £11 297 in 1843.[4]

The situation was unsatisfactory to all parties. The main source of revenue for the colonial government was the sale of Crown Land, which was subverted by the squatting movement. Instead, the land was being alienated without recompense to the government which, nonetheless, had a responsibility to maintain control over these waste lands. Government authority was too easily flouted, and the Crown Land commissioners, often socially inferior to the squatters they were appointed to police, proved unable to keep the peace between squatters and Aborigines, or amongst the squatters themselves. In the 1830s wool became the main export and source of foreign exchange in the colony, and this dominance gave the squatters greater influence, as did the general belief, however fallacious, that they 'include[d] many of the most educated, the most intelligent and the wealthiest of the Inhabitants of the Colony'.[5]

For the squatters the situation was equally unsatisfactory. Fortunes were made in the pastoral industry in the early 1830s, but the squatters were highly geared and very vulnerable to any contraction in the market for sheep or wool. The pastoral industry of the 1830s was established on credit; new arrivals put their borrowed money into flocks and drove them into the interior in search of new land. But the squatters had no tenure in their runs, only an annually renewable licence. When the price of wool and the productivity of sheep dropped simultaneously at the end of the 1830s, the squatters' lack of equity in the land left them ill-equipped to ward off bankruptcy. Many had established their runs on credit, but the terms on which they borrowed were unfavourable. The obverse of the high interest rates which had attracted Boyd was the difficulty, for the working squatter, in meeting repayments out of diminishing returns.

A distinction must be drawn between the real property of the landowner, and the *personal* property—in stock and other moveables—of the squatter. To borrow money, the squatter could offer as security only his flocks and, after August 1843, their unshorn wool. That month, in a response to the difficulties besetting squatters during the depression, William Charles Wentworth introduced a bill which gave them the right to borrow against their anticipated wool clip. The Colonial Office viewed the measure unfavourably and called for its withdrawal, but in practice the wool clip remained an important factor in the squatter's capacity to raise money, and similar legislation was periodically enacted until more secure forms of land tenure made such collateral less significant.[6] To borrow money on the basis of future wool prices and sheep productivity, neither of which could be accurately predicted, added a considerable element of risk to the squatter's relations with his creditors.

The price of wool first droppped in 1836; drought began in 1839 and further cut profits by reducing the fertility of sheep as well as setting limits to pastoral expansion. By the early 1840s the price of sheep had dropped dramatically as flocks were off-loaded to meet debt repayments. Without title to the land, the squatters could not, legitimately, sell their squattages, but such sales were

common and reflected the quasi-legal status that land claims had
acquired since the introduction of licences in 1836. The flocks
were sold attached to a station, and it was assumed, in these
transactions, that the purchaser would replace the vendor as
licensee.[7]

Boyd, like other speculative purchasers, took advantage of the
low prices created by the depression to buy runs. The regulations
governing squatting licences required that the licensee should be
an individual rather than a company. For this reason, it is impossible to tell from the gazetted licences in what capacity Boyd was
purchasing: whether individually, or as chairman of the Royal
Bank of Australia, or on behalf of the Australian Wool Company,
whose £100 000 in borrowed funds was to be invested in pastoral
and other property.

Boyd accumulated his properties very rapidly. By early 1843 the
Hobart Town Courier already referred to him as 'the proprietor
of immense flocks in New South Wales', and reassured its readers,
with a certain wariness, that

> Notwithstanding the varied and ill-natured reports respecting
> the intended speculations about to be commenced by Mr.
> Boyd, we have every reason to believe that the prosperity and
> welfare of the colonies is a subject which that gentleman has
> duly considered, and would wish to promote as well as his own
> personal interest.[8]

The uncertainty with which his speculations were viewed was
understandable. In a society where so many were in financial
trouble, his ability to command a seemingly endless source of
credit gave Boyd great leverage in his quest for cheap stations,
and his reputation for ruthlessness began around this time. While
the Royal Bank of Australia failed to develop more legitimate
banking business, Boyd used the threat of foreclosure to accumulate runs. One observer reported bitterly:

> The state of the Colony has been such that men who have
> been unfortunate, to enable them to have a little money in
> their pockets prior to their passing the Insolvent Court, have
> flown to Mr. Boyd and to obtain money, have sold him the
> whole of their cattle at a reckless price, with the extensive runs
> given in, such will clearly shew why Mr. Boyd was not inclined
> to purchase Land at 1£ per acre, he having obtained a Million

of acres for nothing independent of being in possession at a very low price of a Quarter of a Million of Sheep and Tens of Thousands of Cattle.⁹

Within two years of his arrival, Boyd was, in Governor Gipps's estimation, 'one of the largest Squatters in the Colony'. Just how large, neither the Governor nor Boyd himself could have said for certain. Gipps outlined Boyd's claims in mid-1844:

> He holds fourteen Stations ... in the Maneroo District, and seven Stations ... in the District of Port Phillip. The fourteen Stations in Maneroo are estimated to contain 231 000 acres of land—the seven at Port Phillip 150 000 acres, the whole of the land being well watered and in the best parts of the Colony.¹⁰

For these stations Boyd paid licences amounting to £80. Gipps's estimate gained wide currency, leading Mark Boyd to demand of the Colonial Office 'a refutation to a statement so unjust towards my Brother'.

The Colonial Office referred the complaint to Gipps, who in due course replied that his first estimate was indeed wrong; in fact, it had *under*estimated the Boyd empire. He now estimated that the real acreage in Maneroo was 240 000, and in Port Phillip 186 000 acres. Moreover, Boyd and his partner Robinson also held land in six other districts: Wellington, Murrumbidgee, Lachlan, Bligh, Darling Downs and New England. For these he paid £140 in licences. Boyd himself told the Legislative Council's Select Committee on Crown Land Grievances, in June 1844, that he had stations in every one of the sixteen squatting districts, with the single exception of Gippsland.¹¹

The vagueness of all these estimates hints at some of the problems associated with squatting as an investment. Since it was livestock rather than land that changed hands, a 'squattage' was technically personalty, not realty. And squatting land was not surveyed, so estimates of the size of squatting runs varied widely. Essentially the focus of a run was its waterfrontage; the backblocks were roughly drawn on the basis of the length of waterway the run commanded, and measurements of acreage were then estimated. The run was then licensed from the government in the name of an individual. Ultimately, the Royal Bank and its creditors found it very difficult to identify such amorphous property, bought with Royal Bank of Australia money, but purchased in the name of Benjamin Boyd or Joseph Phelps Robinson.

Because of the depression, runs were cheap, and Boyd entered the market for squatting land with enthusiasm and lack of discrimination. His investments took two forms: productive and speculative. Most of his sheep stations were purchased for speculative purposes. Depression in the wool industry at the time of Boyd's arrival had reduced the price of holdings to such a degree that they constituted a major temptation to men with Boyd's appetite for speculation. That, and the hope that if one day a new and more generous system of land tenure should be introduced, the squatter with possession would be well placed to attain a more permanent right to the land he occupied. Hence the interest of speculators, such as Boyd, in land which might offer windfall profits if the land laws changed.

The temptation to purchase runs for speculative purposes was considerable. It was accompanied by a lust for land based on a misconception regarding colonial land. As F. G. Clarke points out:

> Land was regarded in Victorian England as possessing an intrinsic worth of its own, and Englishmen [and Scots!] found it extremely difficult to adjust to the antipodean situation where land was abundant and only appreciated if it could be put to use.[12]

Boyd shared this error in evaluating the land he laid claim to with such abandon. The rental value of land he knew, in his own parish of Penninghame near Newton Stewart, was quoted in 1838 at between £1 and £3 per acre, depending on location and fertility. Australian land, by comparison, appeared startlingly cheap to a newcomer to the colonies. For the year beginning 1 July 1843, Boyd and Robinson paid £140 in licence fees with another £387 0s 1d for assessment on stock, rising by 1 July 1845 to £619 10s 0d in licences, and £847 13s 8d for stock. While it is not possible to know the prices for which Boyd purchased these runs, it may be assumed that they were bought at little more than the price of their stock. As the price of sheep dropped, so stations became ever cheaper. While in July 1842 Boyd had bought Colac at the rate of seven shillings per head, by 1844 the price of flocks had dropped as low as one shilling per head, with the run thrown in.[13]

In this way Boyd collected squatting runs like so many postage stamps on a map. The full tally must remain uncertain, not least because his knowledge of his new possessions was often so slight that he was uncertain how to spell their names. And the true ownership of the runs was sometimes uncertain too. Boyd claimed to own squattages in all but one squatting district, but the ones he had in mind in New England and Darling Downs were owned, at least nominally, by his partner and his cousins. Robinson was the licensee of Canal Creek and Clifton on the Darling Downs, Beaudesert and Laidley Plains in Moreton Bay District, and Yarrowitch and Shannon Vale in New England. Archibald Boyd was licensee of Newton Boyd in the Clarence River District, and Whitmore and Boyd's Plains in New England, while his brother, William Mitchell Boyd was his partner at Boyd's Plains, and separately owned Broadmeadows in the Clarence River District.

All these runs were funded by Royal Bank of Australia, but the bulk of the purchases were held by the bank's chairman. In the Port Phillip District, in addition to those runs visited by Westgarth, Boyd also owned Strathmerton, just south from Tocumwal on the Murray, with an estimated area of 192 000 acres. On the northern side of the Murray, in the Murrumbidgee District, Boyd's largest runs were along the Edward River. These runs, sometimes referred to under the general heading 'Edward River', included Poon Boon, the Woolshed, Nyang, the Edward River run itself, and Deniliquin, not yet a town, but the site of Boyd's head station on the north bank. Hundreds of miles from the sea, the Wanderer Inn, at the emerging township of Deniliquin, bore witness to the variety of Boyd's activities.

In the Maneroo District[14], in the high snow country which formed the watershed for so many rivers, Boyd's runs included a headstation at Mafra [later Maffra], on the Snowy River south of Cooma. To the south-east were the three adjoining stations of Boco Rock, Gennong and Wog Wog, and further south the large spreads of Bibbenluke, Cambalong and Matong. Moving north from the Riverina, in the Lachlan District Boyd owned Wallawalla and Jemalong (or Gemalong), while along the Lachlan

4 *A Lust for Land* 59

Boyd's land holdings were unsurveyed: their extent and in some cases their location can only be guessed at.

River, in the huge district of Wellington stretching to the Darling River, were a whole series of stations, some of which are now little more than exotic names: Brimadura, Gonoo, Gulgo, Coolee, Condabolin, Minore, Memildra, Timnee, Warraberry and Garra.[15]

Many of these stations have disappeared; some are no longer identifiable. A squatting run had no surveyed boundaries, and its location was identified by its head station, or by the water courses that ran through it. Its extent was determined as much as anything by the season: in a poor season, the sheep and cattle strayed further in search of feed. Boundaries between stations then became more tenuous than ever, especially where, as in Boyd's case, he owned neighbouring runs.

It is doubtful whether Boyd ever visited many of these outlying stations with their exotic, obscure names. The stations changed hands in Sydney, in deals between absentee landlords, 'who could not point their runs out on a map'.[16] In the midst of depression, however, the land that Boyd acquired had, in reality, little intrinsic value. At a time of low wool prices, sheep were worth little. However, the introduction of tallow production, the so-called boiling-down works, provided a base line below which the price of sheep would not fall; if their wool was of little value, and the season's lambs were unsaleable, at least the tallow boiled from their carcasses could be sold for soap and candle production. For Boyd, as for other squatters, boiling down offered a temporary respite in the face of the depression in the wool industry.

Boyd bought freehold as well as squatting runs, but as might be expected he was more selective in these purchases for, at £1 per acre upset price, the land had to have productive rather than speculative value. He had told Lord John Russell in 1840 of his wish to acquire land for ports for his steam ships, and Gipps followed the Secretary of State's instructions to help Boyd obtain appropriate land. Soon after his arrival, Boyd chose Twofold Bay as the base for his shipping and whaling activities, and by Christmas 1842 a special survey was undertaken so that land on the harbour site could be auctioned.

The privilege of a special survey, undertaken at Boyd's request within months of his arrival, was indicative of the influence he could command in government circles. The Surveyor-General, Sir Thomas Mitchell, was the older brother of John Mitchell, one of the directors of the Royal Bank of Australia—but there is no evidence that he gave Boyd extra help. It is more likely that, once more, Boyd's social standing, ambience of wealth and, perhaps, the sympathies of a fellow Scot, were sufficient to ensure that his wishes would be attended to by any government department to which he turned. However his request for a similar special survey at Indented Head, Port Phillip, was disregarded.[17]

Boyd's purchases in Sydney itself were less extensive, but still considerable. His agents had already leased business premises at Church Hill, but these could not do for a gentleman's residence. On the north shore of Sydney Harbour, at Neutral Bay, he purchased land and began to build Craignathan, apparently named for Craignathan Castle, a ruin some miles south of Glasgow. Despite the speculative nature of so many of Boyd's endeavours, his house had an air of permanence, combining grandeur with functionalism. There were large cellars cut out of the solid rock, baker's ovens built in the underground walls and a well cut in the cellar and fed with rainwater caught in a large depression in the roof. Beside the house he built warehouses and a private wharf along the water's edge, and a dammed reservoir on the foreshore, so that his wool could be washed before loading in his ships.[18]

Despite the financial troubles of 1843, Boyd participated in the social rounds of Sydney, and gained a reputation of a generous, ebullient and entertaining companion amongst his peers. He spent much time aboard *Wanderer*, either supervising his building projects at Twofold Bay, or travelling between the various ports with his companions. Apart from J. P. Robinson, his associates included some who had come from England in his train, such as Oswald Brierly and his younger brothers Curwen and James. Colonial associates included Adam Bogue, whom Brierly had known in London, Stuart A. Donaldson, a pastoralist and shipping agent, and the merchant Thomas W. Campbell, one of Curwen Boyd's Campbell relatives, who became a general factotum on behalf of the Boyd interest in New South Wales. Perhaps the relationship between Campbell and his patron can be gauged from the fact that Campbell named his eldest son Boyd, while Benjamin gave the name Campbell to his favourite horse!

On the whole, Boyd's relationships with other men appear to have been functional rather than friendly, and his relationships with women, other than the transient one with Emma Green, remain a mystery. Only his ties to his family were truly deep, and these too were based on his role as patron, rather than brother or son. As a bachelor, Boyd lacked a hostess, so much of his hospitality was exclusively male; but there is little doubt that he cut a dashing path through Sydney society. The contacts he made were useful, but Boyd also clearly revelled in a society of which he automatically became one of the most prominent members.

Joseph Robinson also became involved in the affairs of the colony, though in a quieter and more serious way. In March 1844 Robinson was elected to the Legislative Council unopposed for the Borough of Melbourne. In his acceptance speech, he stated:

> in the broad path of politics I am decidedly liberal,—an advocate for liberty in its most extended form, civil as well as religious—and for the Institution of a system of Education upon a basis the most extended,—to be of service to all classes of the community.[19]

Thereafter, until his untimely death in August 1848, Robinson was a conscientious member of the Council. True to his pledge, and his Quaker principles, he devoted much time to the fight for a non-sectarian system of education, a cause he shared with the lawyer Robert Lowe and the journalist William Augustine Duncan. He acted as a reliable representative for his constituents in Melbourne and the Port Phillip District generally, presenting numerous petitions on their behalf, and loyally supporting their demands for separation from New South Wales. He also fought a solitary battle against capital punishment: each year he moved 'that the disgusting item for two executioners, and the equally disgusting charge for coffins, rope, &c, be struck out' of the estimates—though his amendment sometimes failed to find a seconder.

Many of Robinson's Council activities were associated with his interest in shipping, and some undoubtedly reflect the Royal Bank's shipping activities. He presented a petition from 'certain owners of coasting vessels trading to Port Adelaide, complaining of port charges', for instance, and pressed the Colonial Secretary for the appointment of a revenue officer at Twofold Bay 'to prevent the extensive practice of smuggling which prevailed there'. He was one of the more industrious and able members of the Council, and also, at a time when the Port Phillip representatives had a particularly rapid turnover, one of the most durable.[20]

Robinson's political activities were a mixed blessing both for Boyd, and for the longsuffering shareholders of the Royal Bank of Australia. He was always the dominant partner in matters relating to shipping, and the day-to-day running of the business, but the application and devotion to duty that Robinson brought to the Legislative Council distracted his attention from his directorship of the bank. Instead, too many of the bank's activities were left to employees who lacked direction or responsibility, or to Boyd, who had flamboyant charm and extravagant vision, but lacked the capacity for painstaking detail which his partner, had he been less preoccupied, might have provided.

On 26 January 1844 Ben Boyd attended a regatta in Sydney Harbour to celebrate the fifty-sixth anniversary of the founding of New South Wales. It was a fine day, with a southerly wind 'sufficient to cool the crowds ... and especially favourable to the sailing matches'. As the most prestigious yachtsman present, Boyd was in his element, though the two boats he entered lost their races. The regatta, as the *Sydney Morning Herald* was eager to report, was 'a sport which all classes may enjoy ... Governor, judges, bishops, officers, merchants, tradesmen, mechanics, and labourers'. As so often since, Sydney was enjoying a summer day in the way she knows best, on the Harbour.

At dusk, however, the general festivities were followed by a more exclusive gathering for the top three hundred men and women of the colony aboard the flag ship of the day, the *General Hewitt*. Ben Boyd took the chair, flanked by Governor and Lady Gipps. After dinner, 'a very excellent one', but served in relays because of lack of space on the gun deck, Boyd proposed a toast to the Queen, observing, with profound originality, that New South Wales would soon become 'one of the brightest gems in her crown'. He commented in particular on the new constitution just introduced to the colony, and 'trusted that it would be handed down intact to our posterity'. He then moved on, by way of Prince Albert, the Prince of Wales, the Princess-Royal and all the royal family, the army, and the navy, to propose a toast to the governor.

It was in many ways a generous speech, one that met the

requirements of a public and a festive occasion. He treated his audience to a brief résumé of the governor's past career, noted that Sir George had been a 'brilliant ornament of the profession to which he belonged', and referred to the delicacy of his previous appointment in Canada. But Boyd's reference to Gipps's background also highlighted the differences between the two men; unlike Boyd, the governor owed his position 'not to the adventitious circumstances of high birth, but had won it by his own talents, his own assiduity'. The grandson of a landowning clergyman was patronizing towards the son of a landless one.

Boyd also drew attention to their different political loyalties, for though

> [h]e would not talk politics ... he could not help remarking that Sir George Gipps was elected to his present office by the Whigs, and there was no doubt that the Tories when they came into office would have been glad to have filled up the office, but they did not do so because they could not find a man better fitted to fill it. But without any reference to Whig or Tory, he believed the Governor was a man determined to do his duty, and when he [left] the colony, however persons may be opposed to particular acts, he was sure that all would agree that he would leave clean handed and perfectly free from corruption.

Damned with such faint praise, the governor responded with the blandest of platitudes. He, too, referred to the 'hard knocks of late', but hoped that the future would be fair.

Boyd then proposed a toast to Lady Gipps who, 'without being aware of it, had done much towards drawing together parties of different opinions, and had thrown oil upon the waters of political strife'. Boyd's yachting enthusiasm briefly surfaced with an encomium on the importance of regattas as an encouragement to shipbuilding—'there being no doubt that the models of ships have been much improved by the regattas and yacht clubs of England'—and the ceremony was over. As the toasts and speeches continued, the guests began to drift away, to dance quadrilles on the quarter deck, or, like the governor and his lady, to leave. Within three months of this celebration, the veiled provocation of this formal byplay had been replaced by open hostility between Boyd and Gipps.[21]

By 1844 Boyd was established as a landed proprietor in New South Wales. His squatting runs and his flocks were numerous, and potentially of great value if the price of wool, and consequently of sheep, returned to the high levels of the 1830s, or if a more secure form of land tenure confirmed the squatters in possession of their runs. At present, however, their value was largely speculative. His other investments, in shipping and in the infrastructure associated with Twofold Bay, had yet to show a profit, and he had meanwhile been beset by several serious financial problems.

The New Zealand loan, and the smaller loan to Murray, had left the Royal Bank with bad debts amounting to at least £5000. In June 1843 *Sea Horse*, the largest and most expensive of Boyd's ships, went aground in the Tamar River in Van Diemen's Land, damaging its engines; the subsequent fruitless battle for insurance compensation was costly. The banking business of the Royal Bank was at best desultory, but very large sums of the company's money had been sunk in Boyd's quest for speculative profits which, in the atmosphere of depression then pervading Sydney, seemed unlikely to show a quick return.

Until his arrival, the accounts had been kept by the bank employees, Rennie and Laurie, but from July 1842 Boyd and Robinson took over responsibility for keeping the books. Rennie was already seriously ill and died in late 1843, while Laurie was sent to Hobart. Subsequent reports of the Bank's operations became irregular and inadequate in detail. 'You will, I am satisfied, see the necessity of Accounts being sent us', George Wray wrote to Boyd in March 1843, 'as the want of them is productive of disagreeable remarks at the Board as to the unbusinesslike conduct in not being able to show a statement as to the disposal of the Funds sent out'.[22]

A month later the board discussed the possibility of sending someone from the bank to check on his operations. They decided against it, but worrying rumours of mismanagement in New South Wales proliferated. The failure of the loan to the New Zealand government became publicly known in April 1844, but by then financial circles were already well aware of the Royal Bank's general malaise. Wray's jeremiads became a regular feature of his correspondence with Boyd and his agents in New South Wales. In September 1843 he wrote plaintively to Webb:

the continued arrivals of bad news from Sydney as to the Banks, lead to much speculation among those who *profess* to be our *Friends* as to the fate of the R. B. and which unfortunately, in the absence of accounts, we are unable to settle— many infer that we have lost considerably by bad debts,... others again affirm that our Chairman is losing by his Steam Ships & that we are also involved in these *desperate* speculations all these reports I of course flatly deny stating that our *letters* are most satisfactory—If Mr Boyd only knew our situation here with the Shareholders, who in many cases write us most impertinently, attacking the Characters of all he would I am sure see the necessity of our having accounts, even bad ones in preference to none... [23]

Despite such exhortations, however, Boyd remained dilatory in his correspondence and hostile to the possibility of interference. 'I... can be silent no longer', he wrote to Sutherland defiantly in October 1843,

when I hear through indirect channels... that even some of my Brother Directors have suggested other persons being sent out. To these I do not pay the slightest attention, feeling assured that I was too well acquainted with my colleagues to suppose that any such interference would be proposed, I should be delighted to have the advice and cooperation of any of themselves in the Colony, but with regard to the interference of a third party they must be well aware that I would not submit to such a thing for a moment.[24]

The first, tentative suggestions by board members that he should be replaced were successfully rebuffed by Boyd; short of admitting their disquiet and replacing him, there seemed little that the directors could do to control their over-mighty director from half-way around the world. Boyd had told Sutherland on his departure to tell the bank's shareholders as little as possible; he further impressed on his fellow directors the need to conceal from the British government the bank's profitability since there was 'every disposition on the part of Lord Stanley to impose additional burdens upon the Squatters'.[25] However by the time the directors became suspicious of these imagined profits, the habit of secrecy had become too well entrenched. Their tendency to resist the criticisms of shareholders seems to have led them to resist self-criticism too. Besides, the security of the bank relied on its creditworthiness, and this could too easily be injured by rumours of irregularities.

Boyd's early procrastination was beginning to catch up with him. The indenture of the Royal Bank of Australia had specified that the first shareholders' meeting must be held within five years of the establishment of the bank. That date was now rapidly approaching, and the bank's capital was tied up in investment that had yet to show a return and was in many cases virtually unsaleable. The ensuing battle between Gipps and Ben Boyd must be seen against this background of Boyd's rising anxiety, of pressure from his associates in England, and of his need to convert his land speculations into a profit which would confound his critics within the boardroom of the Royal Bank of Australia.

5
The Squatting Interest

AT THE BEGINNING of 1844 there were many groups in New South Wales who disliked the social and political implications of squatting, even while they recognized the economic advantages that squatting had brought to the colony through the expansion of wool exports. The old gentry, men such as James Macarthur, considered the squatters a rapacious and barbaric lot, whose behaviour ill-fitted them for the responsibilities of citizenship rightfully devolving on the landed interest of the colony. New immigrants and the urban middle classes also resented the squatters, for their opportunity of attaining land was jeopardized by the squatters' claims. Even Edward Hamilton, a working squatter and member of the Legislative Council, shared this concern:

> Is the prescriptive right of the squatter ... to prevail against the interests of thousands? Is he to say the wealth of nature was intended for the monopoly of men, and not for the benefit of mankind?[1]

Meanwhile Gipps was under pressure, both from Britain and in the colony, to change the present unsatisfactory situation regarding the Crown Lands. At present, licences to squatting runs were changing hands as if they were freehold, yet brought no return to a colonial government desperately short of revenue, especially to pay for assisted immigrants sent by the home government. The squatters themselves were unhappy with the present system. Without security of tenure they were unwilling to improve the carrying capacity of their runs—by capital investment in fencing or other improvements—since such investments might be lost, without compensation, to a new owner if the land were sold. All groups, it seemed, were united in their wish to change the present system of land tenure. None, however, could agree on the means to accomplish this, and the governor's attempt to introduce an equitable solution to the problems of colonial land policy was lost in acrimony, an acrimony in which Boyd played a considerable part.

In August 1843 a new, partially elected Legislative Council met for the first time in New South Wales. The first elections to the Council sharpened divisions within the colony, and focused attention on the twin issues of land and immigration, with their attendant revenue implications. The qualification for election to the Council was freehold property to the value of £2000 or of £100 annual rental value, while the qualification for electors was freehold property of £200 or of £20 rental per year. Those who only held licences to Crown Land were thus excluded from the franchise, and other country dwellers, living in areas where few houses would attract such a rental value, were similarly excluded. Yet in a colony so dependent on a single product for its wealth, it was only to be expected that most rich men would, to some degree, be involved in the pastoral industry. The consequence was that those who were elected to the Legislative Council were either professionals—one doctor, several lawyers, one clergymen—or they combined an interest in sheep farming with the possession of town property. Most were to at least some degree squatters, either within the boundaries or beyond. Their numbers were such that Gipps would inevitably be thwarted if he attempted to introduce measures to control squatting through the Legislative Council. Instead, acting executively, he published two sets of regulations which attempted to meet some of the problems of the squatting system.

The first set, the 'occupation regulations', were published on 2 April 1844. The governor's first concern was to introduce a greater degree of equity between large and small squatters, and for that purpose the occupation regulations introduced restrictions on the size of squatting run that could be covered by a single £10 licence: a station was now defined as an area of not more than twenty square miles, capable of carrying 4000 sheep or 500 cattle.

Explaining the occupation regulations of 2 April to the Secretary of State, Gipps emphasized the inequity of the system under which squatters, large and small, paid the same £10 licence irrespective of the size of their run.[2]

His second concern, shared by the officials of the Colonial Office, was to prevent the squatters from converting their squatting claims, by right of occupation, into *de facto* freeholds. This possibility had already been recognized by James Stephen, the Permanent Under-secretary of the Colonial Office, when he predicted:

> It is, I apprehend, sufficiently clear that the titles of these Squatters will rapidly ripen into indefeasible proprietory claims unless the authority of Parliament shall come to the aid of the Govr.; nor is it evident to me that even Parliament will be able to overcome such a combination at such a distance.[3]

For this reason, too, Gipps opposed the idea of leaseholds, favoured by many squatters, because 'a lease for 21 years would in New South Wales, be in the majority of cases, a Lease for ever'.[4] One indication of this tendency for squatters to treat their runs as private property was the growing practice, in more closely settled districts, of subletting portions of their runs for agricultural purposes, sometimes at a higher price than their own licence fee of £10. This caused understandable resentment, as did the emergence of a class of absentee squatters such as Boyd. 'Can it be just', asked one disaffected settler, 'that the property of the Queen should be taken possession of by Individuals, who have scarcely ever seen the place they hold, and consider themselves freeholders, Selling, Jobbing, and Bartering the same'?[5]

To avert this process, the 'homestead regulations', published unofficially on 13 May, were designed by Gipps to offer encouragement to squatters to settle as freehold proprietors on the land. Every licensed squatter would, after an occupation of five years, be given the opportunity to buy a 'homestead', a block of 320 acres of his run, offered at auction at the upset price of £1 per acre, which would secure his occupation of the whole run for the next eight years.

Both sets of regulations had some defects. Nonetheless, they represented a genuine attempt by Governor Gipps to deal with a variety of needs: to offer some equality to squatters of different sizes, to grant a measure of tenure without compromising the principle of a distinction between freehold and occupation, and to increase government revenue through the anticipated sale of Crown Land.

Gipps erred, however, in his timing. What might have proved acceptable to working squatters during normal times was unacceptable in depression. As one of the commissioners of Crown Land remarked: 'the profits will certainly admit of a much heavier tax than is at present demanded, but the present time is most inauspicious for the imposition of it'. A later historian has pointed out that Gipps was certainly unwise to announce the two sets of regulations six weeks apart for, by the time squatters heard of the possible benefits offered by the homestead regulations, they had already been antagonized by the occupation regulations. Besides, since the occupation regulations were designed to introduce some equity into the cost of licences, for large and small squatters alike, they inevitably caused dissatisfaction to those squatters with many runs, who would now have to pay much more in licence fees. These were not a majority of squatters, but they were the most vocal. Besides, the dominance of wool in the colonial economy meant that few individuals or groups were prepared to oppose the squatting interest, for bankruptcy in the pastoral industry would result in the bankruptcy of all.[6]

Finally, the manner of the announcement caused grave and widespread dissatisfaction amongst all groups in society, because Gipps bypassed the Legislative Council. His action was probably necessary in practice, for the composition of the Council was such that it was unlikely the regulations would have gained majority support, but by denying the Council any input into the issue, Gipps brought down on himself the anger of constitutionalists such as the lawyer, Robert Lowe, and the radical, John Dunmore Lang, who might in other circumstances have had little sympathy for the squatters' cause. The landowning gentry, too, was disaffected by Gipps's concurrent attempt to raise revenue by the collection of quitrents which previous administrations had allowed to fall into arrears. The result was the emergence of a widespread coalition of forces in opposition to the governor.

Ben Boyd, confronted by financial problems within his own commercial empire, and threatened by the extra costs entailed in Gipps's proposals, was one of the leaders of this opposition, and other members of the Boyd interest were also prominent. On 9 April a meeting was held at the Royal Hotel in Sydney 'to take into consideration the New Regulations respecting the Squatting interest, which, if carried into effect, must inevitably increase the existing difficulties of the colony to a most fearful extent'. The meeting expressed its unanimous opposition to the occupation regulations. The outcry against the resolutions was well orchestrated and showed, as Gipps himself conceded, 'how completely the occupiers of these Lands have accustomed themselves to look upon them as their own'.[7]

Boyd was more extreme than other speakers in voicing his objections. Unlike more moderate squatters, he claimed that 'so long as he continued to pay the price of his License, £10 per annum, he had a freehold in the Lands he occupied, and that from it the Government could not eject him'. Other speakers tended to frame their opposition in constitutional terms: because Gipps had not taken the regulations to the Council, and because those regulations would have the effect of raising revenue, they complained that 'the right of imposing Taxes by the Representatives of the People' had been removed.[8]

On the motion of J. P. Robinson, a committee of seventeen was formed to pursue the objectives of the meeting. Subsequently, on 23 April the *Sydney Morning Herald* announced the formation of the Pastoral Association. The Royal Bank was closely identified with the new association: Ben Boyd was Chairman, Joseph Phelps Robinson became Treasurer, and Charles D. Logan, described by the *Australasian Chronicle* as 'that very nice man Mr. Logan, Mr. B. Boyd's factotum and amanuensis', was appointed Secretary. The Legislative Council was also strongly represented, with fourteen of its members on the new body. As well as Robinson, they included William Charles Wentworth, Charles Cowper, Hannibal Macarthur, and the lawyers Richard Windeyer and Robert Lowe.

Under Boyd's leadership, the Pastoral Association proved to be an extremely effective lobby group. Within weeks, further meetings were held in the inland centres of Windsor, Penrith, Camden, Goulburn, Yass, Bathurst, Maitland and Mudgee, at which similar resolutions were passed, though in 'language ... more moderate than that which was used at the Sydney Meetings', and petitions against Gipps's regulations were forwarded to the Colonial Office.[9]

On 13 May, however, Gipps published his second set of regulations, and splits began to appear within the opposition. One division, noted by Gipps, was between large and small squatters: 'The greater Squatters are ... by no means pacified, on the contrary, and not unnaturally, they become more irritated as they see moderate men beginning to desert them'. Many of the smaller, resident squatters, whose main objective was greater security of tenure, were likely to be appeased by the terms of the homestead regulations, published in the *Herald* on 13 May. Problems still remained. If the homestead were sold at auction, at an upset price of £1 per acre, a squatter ran some risk of being outbid and consequently of losing the entire run without compensation for his improvements. Nevertheless, the purchase regulations did offer a realistic prospect for security of tenure.[10]

The regulations were aimed against the large and the absentee squatters who formed the bulk of the membership of the Pastoral Association. Even the country meetings in support of Pastoral Association resolutions were held in areas relatively close to Sydney and did not penetrate the real squatting districts. As Hamilton, a working squatter as well as a tenant of the Australian Agricultural Company, trenchantly pointed out:

> the only flockmasters who are at hand to attend public meetings, and to act as the mouthpiece of the settlers, are the absentees from their stations—those who never will be successful, and never would have been if the assignment system, and the high price of wool, had not rendered failure almost impossible.

He insisted that sheep farming could still be profitable, 'when followed in earnest as a pursuit, and not merely indulged in as a speculation. . . . I wage war on the absentees—the drones, who would have it believed that the working bees can cull no honey in the forests of this country'. Hamilton spelt out in great detail the costs and the profits involved in the pastoral industry, and singled out Boyd as 'just one of those speculators in stock who will burn his fingers, and then blame the fire for being hot. . . .

My opinion on the details and profits of the Banking establishment would be about as valuable as Mr Boyd's on stock-farming'.[11]

Boyd's claim, at the Royal Hotel meeting, that he regarded his holdings as equivalent to freehold, set many critics against him, both in New South Wales and in Britain. 'For a squatter to regard his stations in the light of "an inheritance," or "a freehold," appears to us the most impudent, not to say the most dishonest, pretension ever put forth', wrote the radical journalist William Augustine Duncan in the *Weekly Register*. At the Colonial Office, Lord Stanley was equally taken aback, telling Gipps,

> I am well aware that the language used by Mr Boyd cannot justly be assumed as that of all those whom he represents; but it is not only by the expressions used by him that I have been startled.
>
> I am equally so by the general arguments which have been adopted, and the grounds upon which the opposition to your measures is based.[12]

However others were less careful in their generalizations, and Boyd, as Chairman of the Pastoral Association, and as one of the most clearly identifiable absentee squatters, was commonly used as an example of the type.

A further division existed between the squatters and the old established pastoralists, those who characterized themselves as the colonial gentry. The gentry had a greater stake in the country; most had acquired the freehold of their lands through land grants before 1831, or by purchase in the following years. As such, they were subject to quitrents, and Gipps's attempts to collect quitrents, often many years in arrears, gave them for a time common cause with the squatting interest in opposition to the governor's revenue-raising schemes.

There was also considerable overlap between the two groups: men like James and William Macarthur owned land within the boundaries but had also purchased stations in the squatting districts, partly as a speculation and partly to provide grazing land for their expanding flocks. Socially, the two groups were comparable. Even Gipps conceded that the squatters included 'great numbers of young men every way entitled to be called gentlemen, young men of Education, and many of good family and connexions in Europe'.[13]

The distinction between the squatters and colonial gentry lay in their attitudes to the wider issues. The landowners shared Gipps's concern to maintain the integrity of freehold property as a legal principle. On the whole, men like James Macarthur saw their future in the colony; many of those squatters who made most noise about the squatting regulations were, like Boyd, interested in short-term exploitation of the colony, and a profitable return to their 'family and connexions' in Europe. There was also an economic question involved; as it became clear that the squatters desired to hold their lands by licence fee alone, without purchase from the Crown, the gentry became alarmed. For this would give the squatters an unfair advantage over earlier settlers, whose land tenure had been acquired at considerable cost, by purchase, by quitrent, or by the maintenance of convicts.

Differing economic interest thus became entangled with ideological divisions. Many moderate men were distressed by Boyd's intemperate language at the Royal Hotel and, like Hamilton, were suspicious of his claim to represent their interests. Others feared that the dominance of the large squatters would prevent that concentration of settlement and development of agriculture which was still, despite the failure of Wakefield's theories, seen as ultimately desirable. The squatting system had led to dispersal and barbarous conditions on the frontiers, for squatter and employee alike. With secure title to the land, on the other hand, 'towns will spring up, trade will flourish, and the arts of civilised life will make "the wilderness blossom like the rose"'.[14]

While attitudes in the general community towards the squatters varied, within the Legislative Council there was a widespread sympathy for the purpose of the Pastoral Association. On the committee, nominated by J. P. Robinson on 9 April, the conjunction of interests was very evident: of the seventeen, nine were elected members of the Legislative Council, including Robinson himself; a tenth member of the Council had seconded another resolution at the meeting, and an eleventh, Hannibal Macarthur, was a signatory of the original advertizement which called the meeting. Eventually fourteen councillors joined the Pastoral Association. Inevitably, then, the Council became the focal point of anti-governor opposition.

On 30 May the Legislative Council appointed a Select Committee 'to enquire into, and Report upon all Grievances connected with the Lands of the Colony, with an instruction to distinguish between the grievances which can be redressed in the Colony, and those which cannot'. Chaired by Charles Cowper, the membership of the committee was carefully selected, for all seven members were in the Pastoral Association, including Joseph Phelps Robinson.

The select committee became the forum for a concerted attack on Gipps's land policy, and a special plea of behalf of squatters for security of tenure on their own terms. Prominent amongst its carefully selected witnesses was Benjamin Boyd. He argued, as did others, against any fixed price for land, and in particular that the upset price of £1 per acre was absurdly high compared with the real value of the land. This high price had checked 'the spirit for emigration, and desire to invest in this Colony...amongst people of Capital'.

> If you ask me as a grazier what I do want, I answer water—and it is unnecessary for me to inform the committee, that from the nature of the country I must measure my stations, not by the number of acres they contain, but by the situation and supply of water upon them.

Only leases 'for, at least, 21 years' would satisfy the needs of squatting. With such security of tenure, civilization could at last be brought to the inland, and landholders could 'draw about them a well conducted and respectable peasantry'. On the other hand, Boyd warned that if Gipps's regulations continued in force,

> I shall have no alternative left... but to give notice to all those to whom cash advances have been made [by the Royal Bank of Australia or by Boyd personally], to liquidate their debts; and the immediate effect of this will be to force, taking into account my own stock, very nearly a quarter of a million of sheep, and many thousand head of cattle, into the melting pot; annihilating not only the present, but the prospective wealth of many persons in the Colony, and ruining those individuals indebted to me.[15]

It was a grim threat, and one which few capitalists—urban or pastoral—could afford to ignore.

The committee's final report recommended that the licence fee be abolished, or reduced to a nominal sum, and that the British government should abandon its policy of a fixed minimum price of land. It argued that control of the Crown Lands should be transferred to the governor *and* Legislative Council. Once vested in local hands, that control should be used to establish a system of leases, incorporating the rights of pre-emption and compensation for improvements for the present occupants of Crown Lands.

The demand for local control of Crown Lands, and, in particular, hostility towards Wakefield's prescription of a fixed price, had already been voiced during previous years.[16] The select committee went further, however, displaying its squatting origins in its recommendation to replace licences by Crown leases. Nor did it reach any conclusion regarding an appropriate price at which to sell Crown Land, a question on which the present unanimity would eventually founder. Instead, the committee stressed its impotence to implement these recommendations directly while control remained with the imperial government. Many of the issues raised could only be resolved in a wider imperial context. This was indicated in the committee's final paragraph, where the members expressed their gratitude to Charles Buller and the Honorable Francis Scott, members of the House of Commons, for their efforts on behalf of New South Wales. Gipps's efforts to reorganize the system of land tenure in the colony ultimately proved irrelevant; real power resided at Westminster, and by the time the Select Committee on Crown Land Grievances printed its report in August 1844, the squatting lobby in Britain had acquired a momentum of its own.

Boyd's importance in the cause of the Pastoral Association was not confined to his activities in New South Wales, for it was his ability to command influence in British political circles that was finally of most consequence. The first stage of this lobbying process began when, immediately after the issuing of the occupation regulations, Boyd wrote on behalf of the Pastoral Association to Lord Stanley asking the British government to withhold consent to Gipps's regulations until the petitions being organized throughout New South Wales could arrive in London.[17]

He also wrote to his cousin, Archibald Boyd (of Broadmeadows, New England, and formerly of Broadmeadows, Selkirkshire) who had returned to England in late 1843 on a trip, possibly to find a wife,[18] and asked him to act as a lobbyist for the squatters. And he wrote to the Royal Bank of Australia and his brother Mark explaining that the financial problems of the bank were a consequence of two specific difficulties of squatting in Australia: land and labour.

Archibald Boyd had arrived in England in October 1843 and his advocacy of the squatting interests began before Gipps's regulations added urgency to the squatters' agitation. By his own report, he seems to have agreed, at Boyd and Robinson's request, to lobby for the squatters' cause as soon as he arrived. The major issue in late 1843 was not the price of land but the shortage and, consequently, the cost of labour. To accomplish his objective, he formed an alliance with 'one... whose talents and high character, I have been acquainted [with] half my life—my old friend the Hon. Francis Scott, M.P., for Roxburghshire',[19] and Scott's elder brother, Lord Polwarth.

Through Polwarth, Archibald Boyd approached Stanley, the Secretary of State for the Colonies. In an interview of three-quarters of an hour, he described the privations of the squatters in the current depressed state of affairs in New South Wales, and argued that the remedy for these conditions lay in cheaper labour and security of tenure. He expressed himself satisfied with Stanley's response.

Other members of the Boyd clan now rallied to the squatters' cause. Edward Boyd, now an old and ailing man, nevertheless used his political influence to good effect. On 14 March 1844 Scott, primed by Archibald Boyd, spoke on the affairs of the squatters in the House of Commons. Edward Boyd had five hundred copies of the speech printed and distributed 'with a very clever leader on it, by our indefatigable friend Mr. Weir, the editor of the *Colonial Gazette*'. The old man also wrote 'to his numerous Parliamentary friends, and engaged 6 or 8 of the more intimate to speak on the subject' in parliament. He also introduced his nephew to the member for Lymington, W. A. Mackinnon, one of the commissioners of South Australia. Archibald Boyd met Mackinnon in company with 'our mutual friends Mr. Marsh of New Zealand, and Mr. Browning', one of Ben Boyd's employees in the Royal Bank of Australia, who had returned from Australia on 16 May 1844.[20]

Mackinnon was delegated to ask Stanley to establish a parliamentary committee to enquire into the condition of the squatters, but by 10 July he reported failure. Despite the Boyds' combined efforts to whip up public support for a committee, and a debate in the public press, Stanley remained unpersuaded: 'it does not appear that Sir George Gipps is unfavourable to the squatters, it seems on the contrary that he contemplates some arrangement involving compensation to the squatters for their improvement'—apparently a reference to the forthcoming homestead regulations, news of which had not yet reached London.[21]

Despite this setback, Archibald Boyd remained optimistic. As he wrote to Ben:

> We have success in our hands if we persevere. I have received pledges from our joint connexion, that upwards of forty members [of Parliament] will support us, besides the auxiliaries who may do so, on the principle of abstract justice, and William [Sprott Boyd, another cousin] goes into Parliament for the purpose on the first vacancy.[22]

Archibald Boyd left for Australia by early August. His advocacy of the squatting cause therefore cannot be linked specifically with reaction to Gipps's initiatives of April and May 1844. His correspondence with Mackinnon, with covering letters to Ben Boyd, was printed in the *Sydney Morning Herald* and the *Atlas* at the end of December, and greeted with approval in editorial comment from these two pro-squatter newspapers. Archibald Boyd, said the *Herald*, had 'met the despatches of Sir GEORGE GIPPS on the only vantage-ground whereon they could have been effectually grappled with—the audience-chamber of Downing-street, and the floor of the House of Commons'.[23]

This emphasis on the priority of London in changing land policy was very pronounced. One indication of this was the decision by the New South Wales Legislative Council, in October 1844, to appoint Scott as Parliamentary Agent for the Council, a decision made on the basis of Scott's speech in the House of Commons the previous March.[24]

Meanwhile the role of lobbyist-in-chief on behalf of the squatters remained with the Boyd family. So effectively had the Royal Bank promoted the public perception that its problems were a result of the difficulties of squatting, that in October 1844 a small shareholder in the bank wrote to Wray:

> The recent augmentation of the colonial taxes [occupation and purchase regulations] on Squatters... have... occupied the attention of the Bank Directors as it is calculated to injure the colony generally, & in its abrogation the Royal Bank is reported to be particularly interested. Colonists being as such without political influence, little can be expected from their efforts. It is here therefore that efforts afford the best chance of success. Would it not be desirable therefore to organise a small committee through which memorials & other influence of the proprietors of yours & other Banks & of others might be made available?[25]

That process was already underway. As early as 24 June 1844, G. Mackillop of Edinburgh had written to Wray, the manager of the Royal Bank, suggesting that they co-ordinate their efforts to influence members of parliament.

> You may have it in your power to induce some member of parliament to move in the matter. I am now in correspondence with several influential Gentlemen in London on this subject, & if I find you are inclined to interest yourself on the occasion, I shall be glad to communicate further with you.

From such negotiations, a pressure group, consisting 'of firms engaged in wool-importing, exporting, shipping, banking, and woollens manufacture, together with such colonial graziers or their friends as happened to be' in London, was formed in time to reassert its influence in the 1845 session. Further support came with the formation of the Glasgow Association for the Protection of the Squatting and other General Interests of New South Wales, with Boyd's uncle, Mark Sprott, one of the committee members.[26]

On 22 May 1845 a meeting of 'Noblemen and gentlemen' was held at No. 4, New Bank Buildings, an address leased by the North British Insurance Company on behalf of the Boyd brothers, and hence the address of the Royal Bank of Australia, to draw up and sign a petition on behalf of the squatters of New South Wales.

Four days later Mark Boyd, 'entrusted by the Pastoral Association of New South Wales with a large number of petitions to both Houses of Parliament', led a deputation of about twenty-five to the Colonial Office, to discuss with Lord Stanley the prospect of replacing annual licences with leases.

In his *Reminiscences*, Mark Boyd's recollection of this meeting was sanguine:

> The question was entered upon seriously, and it proved a source of extreme satisfaction to me to find that no point was mooted by the illustrious statesman (and none escaped him) which some member of our deputation could not elucidate and explain. His lordship gave us an attentive hearing, extending over two hours, and, at its conclusion, intimated his willingness to grant leases to the Australian squatters, 'but *not* for twenty years, as Mr. Boyd asked—being more than is granted in this country—but on a footing to be subsequently arrranged, and which nothing would be wanting on his part to render satisfactory'.

At the time, however, the two-hour discussion cannot have been entirely satisfactory, since Stanley questioned him closely on the size of Ben Boyd's holdings, 'making it appear that [he] did not contribute his proportionate quota to the Licence Fund'.[27]

Of the thirty-two men who met to sign a petition on behalf of the squatters, fifteen can be linked directly with Benjamin Boyd and the Royal Bank of Australia. They included Polwarth and Scott, who were friends of Archibald Boyd—Scott was a beneficiary of Archibald Boyd's life insurance policy.[28] The Royal Bank's deputy chairman, John William Sutherland, one director, Adam Duff, and the manager, George Wray, were there, as was one employee, Samuel Browning, who had just arrived from Australia. J. P. Robinson's brother Anthony was there, and Captain Thomas Bushby, a friend of Mark Boyd, who had sailed with Boyd on *Wanderer* in 1841 as far as Rio before turning back after a stroke. Two of Ben Boyd's brothers, Mark and Edward Lennox Boyd, and no less than four cousins, William Sprott Boyd, Archibald Boyd, Maitland Boyd and Frederick Maitland, completed the list.

As a measure of Mark Boyd's ability to rally support for his lobbying effort, the petition was impressive; as a commentary on the power of a family network to express its opinion forcefully to government, it was remarkable. Its influence is less easy to gauge. The Secretary of State's vague assurances, in any case, remained unfulfilled; during the next few months the Tory Party began, for internal reasons, to break up, and Stanley was replaced by Gladstone at the Colonial Office in December 1845.

Mark Boyd's activities continued unabated and, as his skill as a lobbyist increased with experience, he extended his area of concern, looking at questions of steam communication and emigration to Australia in addition to the particular problems of the squatters.

Meanwhile, back in Australia, Ben Boyd set out to mobilize public opinion on behalf of the squatters. He took three separate initiatives: he encouraged a particular public attitude by supporting a pro-squatting newspaper, the *Atlas*; he discouraged opposition to that position by destroying the main anti-squatting newspaper, the *Weekly Register*; and he entered the political arena more directly by standing for the Legislative Council.

In November 1844 the *Atlas* newspaper was established by the Pastoral Association as a vehicle for the squatting interest. Funds were subscribed by Boyd, Robinson, Windeyer, Wentworth, Nicholson and others, and Robert Lowe, a brilliant but vituperative lawyer, became editor.[29]

The importance of newspapers did not only lie in the influence they could exert on public opinion in the colony. They also represented an alternative source of information on the colony, and what purported to be public opinion, in Britain. As such, they could modify the arguments presented to the Colonial Office by the governor in his despatches. By sponsoring newspapers, and forwarding them to the Colonial Office, Boyd and the Pastoral Association were able to promote an alternative view of the squatting question.

The first issue of the *Atlas* stated in its platform:

> The prosperity of New South Wales is so intimately, so completely dependent upon its export of wool, that the first question which would naturally suggest itself to a wise Governor in entering on the duties of his high office, ought to have been the condition and prospects of the wool growers.[30]

Subsequent issues pursued this theme. The *Atlas* reported with approval the efforts of Archibald Boyd and his associates in London. On his return, it advertized a series of public meetings throughout New South Wales, and later reported the enthusiastic thanks and subscribed testimonials he received at these meetings

Benjamin Boyd as a young man
Oil, artist unknown

The Wanderer, RYS
Engraving, from a sketch by Oswald Brierly

The Sea Horse
Engraving, from a sketch by Oswald Brierly

Favorites   *Boyd's six imported stallions*
Lithograph, artist unknown

Mafra Homestead, Maneroo
Sketch by Oswald Brierly

from the squatters. The *Atlas* supported the recommendations of the Select Committee on the Crown Land Grievances. It sympathized with the squatters in their financial difficulties, and bemoaned the high price of labour. And always, on every occasion that presented itself, it criticized Sir George Gipps.

On the other hand the *Weekly Register* was unsympathetic towards the *Atlas*, constantly alluding to the subsidies it received from the squatting interest:

> The Squatters are in this condition,
> Their leader is a politician
> Though Low[e], a pillar of the state
> B[u]oy'd up but sinking 'neath his fate
> Suppose then Atlas ne'er so wise;
> Yet, when the weight of Squatting lies
> Too long upon his single shoulders,
> Sink down he must or find UPHOLDERS.[31]

Through the editorials of the *Atlas*, the opposition to Gipps was given its most rational form, but the brilliance of Lowe's style papered over cracks which were forming within the squatting party. Moreover the virulence of Lowe's personal attacks on Gipps in the pages of the *Atlas* may ultimately have proved counterproductive. In 1845, for instance, Lowe attempted to organize a boycott of the annual May ball, held at Government House in honour of the Queen's birthday, and a campaign to this effect was pursued in the *Atlas*. Boyd and Robinson stayed away, but most colonists were not prepared to insult the governor in this way, particularly as a boycott could be interpreted as an insult to the Queen. If anything, more people than usual attended, some coming 'from a considerable distance to pay their homage who never came before'. Even Charles Logan, the Secretary of the Pastoral Association, attended.[32]

Conservatives increasingly found Boyd's aggrandizement and Lowe's poisoned pen offensive. James Macarthur, for instance, sponsored the *Australian* during 1844 and 1845, largely as a counterweight to Boyd's manipulation of the press. The editors of the *Australian*, dependent on this bounty, were naturally eager to encourage this rivalry: 'Your yourself', they told Macarthur, 'have a more bitter foe in Boyd than perhaps you are aware of, but the public will soon be alive to the grasping nature of his schemes, and his hollow pretensions for the public weal will be seen through'.³³

The most influential newspaper, with the largest circulation and a growing reputation as a newspaper of record, was the *Sydney Morning Herald*. Throughout 1844 the *Herald* pursued an editorial policy which was favourable to the squatters. Towards the end of the year there were rumours that 'Boyd's party' intended to purchase the *Herald*, and that, in any case, 'from the tenor of their articles we feel pretty certain they are *Boyd* up'.³⁴

This innuendo is impossible to prove but if, on the one hand, Boyd and the Pastoral Association offered financial support, overt or covert, to newspapers which supported the squatters, they were ruthless in their efforts to suppress papers which offered an alternative viewpoint. Only the *Weekly Register*, a small newspaper owned and edited by William Augustine Duncan, offered a pro-Gipps *critique*. Colonial newspapers were vulnerable; they relied on advertising and job-printing to eke out the scant return they gained from sales. Within two years of the establishment of the Pastoral Association, the *Weekly Register* had folded and Duncan was bankrupt. Gipps was in no doubt of the reason: 'It is within my knowledge', he told the new Secretary of State, 'that large offers were made to Mr. Duncan by the Pastoral Association, or its agents, to induce him to alter the Politics of his Paper; and that on his refusing to do so, it was determined, if possible, to ruin him'.³⁵

In August 1844 Sir Thomas Mitchell, one of the members for Port Phillip, resigned his seat in the Legislative Council. He had found difficulty reconciling his dual roles of elected member and public servant, since he sympathized with many of the aspirations of the squatters. Boyd put himself forward for election in his place.

Boyd listed his policies in a public statement to the electors. He supported the separation of Port Phillip and the appropriation of its revenue to local improvements, a necessary pledge for any aspiring candidate in the Port Phillip District at that time. Possibly as a sop to his friend Robinson, he supported the extension of a system of general education applicable to all classes. In true political style, he called for a reduction of the 'monstrous' government expenditure and reform in the system of police. It was clear, however, that his major objective was the

5 *The Squatting Interest* 85

promotion of the objectives of the Pastoral Association: support for fixity of tenure, and opposition to the governor's squatting regulations 'so pregnant with abuse'. Unlike other policy statements by colonial politicians, Boyd's speech was republished in the 'leading metropolitan journals', an indication that the Boyd machine in London was backing his efforts.[36]

Duncan satirized Boyd's pretensions in verse:

> Electors of Port Phillip, I,
> None of your 'small' and unknown 'fry,'
> Would wish just now my hand to try
>   A legislation.
>
> ... I'll open my most puissant lips,
> Against that naughty tyrant, G ...,
> I'll dog his heels, and *if* he trips,
>   I'll keep him under.
>
> I *was* his friend, you know—till he
> Levelled his April-fool's decree,
> Against the high 'Squattocracy,'
>   Of this fair land.
>
> Fool that he was to brave *our* wrath,
> To stand a moment in *our* path,
> As if *we* were mere things of lath—
>   Mere ropes of sand. . . .
>
> He wants to wring from us '*ten pound*,'
> For *twenty thousand acres round*,
> Of miserable grazing ground,
>   Alas! poor Squatters . . .
>
> The evils of this government,
> Its crying evils I'll resent;
> I'll *shake* the British Parliament,
>   If *they* support it . . .[37]

Boyd did not visit his electorate at Port Phillip, but the District's electors, far from the seat of political power, were inured to such neglect. The District found it virtually impossible to persuade a local candidate to travel to Sydney for Council meetings, and was forced to rely on political opportunists like Boyd to represent its interests. Local feeling was sufficiently assuaged by Boyd's twenty guinea donation to the Melbourne Mechanics Institute.[38] Boyd was duly elected unopposed, not on the basis of his personal qualities or particular election promises, but because he was clearly identified with the squatting interest, and would increase opposition strength in the Council. And besides, there was no one else.

At this juncture, Boyd's political career devolved into bathos. On 7 October fifty gentlemen sat down at Petty's Hotel, near his business premises on Church Hill, to celebrate his return as member for Port Phillip. That same day the attorney-general and solicitor-general were attempting to unravel a muddle. Although Boyd had been elected unopposed on 10 September, the writ announcing his election disappeared on its journey to Sydney, apparently when the 14 September mails from Melbourne were lost in flooded rivers. Eventually the matter was resolved, and Boyd took his seat on 28 November 1844.[39]

He sat only briefly. On Christmas Eve, when the attendance was thin, the colonial secretary moved 'that the House resolve itself into committee for consideration of the Governor's message on the appropriation bill'. Wentworth, the leader of the opposition, moved an amendment questioning Gipps's competence to propose any new grant of public moneys. The amendment was not seconded, but before the Speaker could put the original motion, the leaders of the squatting faction, W. C. Wentworth, Dr Bland, Hannibal Macarthur, W. Walker, Major Wentworth, Dr Lang and Benjamin Boyd, walked out, denying the House a quorum.

This was Boyd's first and last statement on the parliamentary form of government! He seems to have been exceedingly irregular in his attendance during early 1845, and in May 1845 the Council was prorogued pending the arrival of the new governor, Sir Charles FitzRoy. On 27 August 1845 Boyd placed a motion on notice in the Council 'that a Select Committee be appointed to enquire into, and report upon the operation of the present laws affecting seamen and others engaged in whaling'. The next day Robinson withdrew the motion, and Boyd never again appeared in the Council chambers.[40]

In an open letter, Boyd set out to justify himself to his electors in Port Phillip. He denied that his objective had been to support the large squatter at the expense of the small, or that he had claimed a freehold in his landholdings, or opposed the legitimate authority of government: 'For my own part I can distinctly state that I have never offered a factious opposition to any Government'. He wrote with some complacency of his efforts in the cause of other issues such as immigration and the separation of Port Phillip: 'if I have made some sacrifices of time and money in the struggle, I trust neither have been thrown away'.[41]

In terms of his relationship with his electorate, such complacency was misplaced. The new member, Thomas Elder Boyd, a Melbourne merchant, was at pains to emphasize that he was *no* relative of Benjamin Boyd, and when Archibald Boyd also stood for election in the same district, he was rejected by the electorate 'in a pretty intelligible demonstration on the part of the people of Port Phillip that they would no longer support the Council in their extreme measures of opposition to Her Majesty's Government'. Shortly afterwards, Robert Fennell was approached by Boyd's friend Stuart Donaldson to help raise money for Archibald Boyd's testimonial in the Port Phillip District. He refused, 'for fear of its proving a complete failure [and] mentioned the fact of the way he and Boyd had been treated when standing for one of the vacant seats for the representation of the District as evidence of the estimation in which he was held' in Melbourne.[42] The tide was turning and the Boyds were no longer popular in Port Phillip, or elsewhere in New South Wales.

Boyd made clear his disillusion with local politics in the explanation that he gave to his electorate for his resignation:

> I do not disguise from you my belief that all appeals to the local legislature will be made in vain, and that it is only by sedulously petitioning the Throne and Parliament, and bringing the injustice of your thraldom before the British public, that you can ever hope to attain your object.

In fact, much of the heat of the agitation provoked by Gipps's regulations in April and May 1844 had died down by late 1845. The occupation regulations, first announced in April 1844, came into effect in July 1845. Henceforth a separate licence had to be taken out on each squatting run. This was a costly procedure for large squatters like Boyd, but one which most finally acquiesced in: 'as the Licences were almost in course of payment, few could be found who would risk the chance of losing their runs, when they found that their home appeal had had no effect'.[43]

A better season and better prices for wool reduced the fervour of the squatters' opposition. The remaining issue to be resolved was the future tenure of squatting runs. Gipps's homestead regulations of May 1844 were not to come into effect until approved by the Colonial Office, and pressure in Britain seemed to be having an effect. By September 1845 Boyd was optimistic that the end was in sight:

> although we have not as yet got all we wish nor in fact any security but the word of a tricky Governor, still he has had such a lesson of the power of the Squatting interest, that he will I think be glad to propitiate it, not only for his own peace & quiet, but to attempt through it to form a strong party who will assist him in opposing the democratic faction in the Colony who have no real sympathies with the Squatter but on the contrary only joined our party to more effectually annoy the Government.

He was critical of the efforts of his friends at home, and impatient for results:

> We have been all much disappointed that the petitions had not been at once presented to the House—as it would have given the squatters confidence in having had their grievances known at home, but instead of that method the reiterated 'Sic Nolo'— 'Sic Nolis' ['I do not want it; you may not want it'] recommendations of Sir George confirmed by my Lord Stanley—and the squatters became quite disheartened that the result of all their demonstrations had not been more effectively taken up. had they been so, we could have made any terms we liked with Sir George. But he was equally aware with ourselves that the opportunity had been lost by the delay . . .
> I see that Mr Scott is at last about to take up the question— but he has allowed the golden opportunity to slip.[44]

His disappointment was unwarranted, however, and his complaints unfair to Scott and the other lobbyists. By mid-1845 responsibility for the resolution of the issue had moved from the Colonial Office to parliament, where the Parliamentary Under-Secretary, George Hope, first introduced a Bill proposing to offer the squatters seven-year leases without competition. Further action on the matter was temporarily halted by the change in government which brought Gladstone to the Colonial Office, but the essential concession of leases without competition for the squatters in possession had been accepted. Further representations from the squatting interest argued for the length of leases to be extended, rather than for any change in principle.

In New South Wales, Boyd watched these developments with considerable satisfaction:

> If the extended leases are granted it would alone double the value of all the Stock in the Colony For in fact a Crown Lease almost at a nominal rental may be looked upon as a fee Simple ... It is true that if Sir George keeps faith, the most valuable concessions have been made—and in my opinion if we go on as prosperously as we are now doing no Government will be able to stand that does not go hand in hand with the Squatters.[45]

Earl Grey replaced Gladstone in July 1846, and the Australian Lands Act was finally passed the next month. The following March, an Order-in-Council confirmed the achievement of the squatters' party. The lands of the colony were now to be divided into three parts: the settled, intermediate and unsettled districts. The settled districts encompassed the area of the old 1829 limits of location, and here land sales were expected to be the norm, for Crown Land leases were of only one year's duration. In the intermediate districts, leases were for eight years, but the lands could be offered for sale at any time, provided the lessee received sixty days notice. In the unsettled districts, where the great majority of Boyd's runs were located, renewable leases of up to fourteen years were to be issued, and the squatters in possession were allowed to apply for leasehold to their runs without competition.

The resolution of the land question, with the granting of fourteen-year leases, represented a potential windfall profit for the speculative squatters. In Boyd's words, it would 'in the course of a few years render the value of a Crown lease equal to a freehold at home'. It was a major achievement for the squatting lobby in London. The degree to which British government policy was altered to fit the requirements of Boyd and his associates may be debated; what cannot be disputed, however, is that Mark and Archibald Boyd, and their parliamentary associate Francis Scott, had some input into the new policy.[46]

The squatting party had judged correctly that the ultimate source of decisions regarding Australia lay in England, not in the colonies. It therefore directed its activities towards the Colonial Office and the British parliament. An effective network of influence had been formed to address the issue of colonial land policy. With the success of this engagement, the same individuals extended their activities into the inter-related areas of emigration and shipping, continuing to use the facilities of the Royal Bank of Australia, and the co-operation of Francis Scott, Parliamentary Agent for the New South Wales Legislative Council.

Boyd probably never had any intention of continuing in the Legislative Council for any length of time. His original plan in coming to Australia had been to establish the Royal Bank and its various business enterprises, then to return to London and his rightful position as chairman of the bank.

In November 1844, in an address to his electorate, he warned

> that it would be out of my power to devote much of my time to the business of the Council, and in announcing to you, therefore, that it is my intention at no distant period, to proceed to China for a short time, it will be for you to consider whether you should continue the trust which you have done me the honour already to confide in me.[47]

This Chinese trip had long been foreshadowed. As early as December 1842, when the end of the first Opium War made travel possible, the manager of the Royal Bank had sent Boyd information on the London market for tea, silks and other Chinese products, in the expectation that he would visit China on his return voyage. Boyd had contacts in China, through Jardine, Matheson and Co., and his cousin, W. S. Boyd had worked in their Canton agency. Samuel Browning, a Royal Bank employee, visited China in 1843, coming back 'full of information', and Boyd talked 'of going to China at some indefinite period'.[48]

Boyd told his electors that he planned to seek a market for Australian wool in China, and on 1 November 1844 Brierly wrote excitedly in his diary: 'Hurrah!! The Wanderer going up to China—orders to get up to Sydney quick as possible and get ready for a cruise to China'—but the trip never eventuated. Boyd also told his electors that 'my departure for England cannot be long postponed'. Yet he failed to return to England, though the death of his elder brother in India in late 1844 had left him heir to the Boyd estates at Merton Hall. Instead he remained in New South Wales, and this procrastination seems to be an early symptom of a tendency to sudden and erratic swings in Boyd's behaviour, of plans incompleted, schemes unfulfilled.[49]

Boyd had been expected back to report to the first annual general meeting of the Royal Bank of Australia. Instead he left his fellow directors to carry the burden of an extremely difficult meeting with the bank's puzzled, and increasingly irate, shareholders. In a letter which was read at the meeting, he told the shareholders that he had intended to return by July, but had decided to wait until the present financial crisis in the colony had been resolved.[50]

It seems likely that Boyd had become too closely involved in the colonial political scene to draw back at this stage. His decision to speculate in land, rather than pursue legitimate banking business, was a risky gamble which had not so far paid off. However a change in colonial land policy, to give security of tenure to the purchasers of squatting runs, could yet change the fortunes of the Royal Bank. Otherwise his speculations seemed doomed. Boyd therefore was deeply committed to the efforts to change that policy, for his bank's money was irrevocably tied up in squatting runs. His threat to withdraw that money, and thus precipitate ruin in the colony, possibly reflects a secret fear that such a course would eventually be inevitable.

Confident in his brother Mark's ability to lobby in Britain, he apparently decided to wait in New South Wales at least until the new governor arrived. Gipps's retirement had been long foreshadowed—it was referred to aboard the *General Hewitt* in early 1844—and Boyd possibly hoped that a new governor, less inflexible in his opposition to the squatters than Gipps, would be easier to manipulate.

It is also at least possible that Boyd feared a return to England, given the failure of so many of his plans. It was tempting to remain in Australia instead where, if disliked by many, he was too influential a personage to be ignored by his neighbours, and where few people guessed the depths of his financial difficulties. So he closed his mind to the increasingly anxious chidings of Wray, responded even less regularly to requests for information from London, and concerned himself with political, rather than economic, decisions. A consequence of this paralysis of will in economic matters was that Boyd sought alternative, less threatening, areas of activity to absorb his energies. He lavished money on his favourite project, his private town, Boydtown. And he found a scapegoat for his impending financial disaster in the high price of labour in the colony.

6
Boydtown

B OYD'S ARRIVAL in Australia was preceded by the arrival of his steamships and other vessels. These ships, and his projected shipping activities, lay at the heart of his enterprise in the colonies, and accounted for a large proportion of the capital investment of the Royal Bank of Australia. The failure of these projects foreshadowed his wider failure, and serves to illustrate many of the problems associated with his colonial adventure.

The first ship in his incipient fleet to arrive in Australian waters was the paddlesteamer, *Sea Horse*. She was worth £30 000, claimed Boyd, and 'entirely my own property', of which at least the second claim was demonstrably false. *Sea Horse* was 150 feet in length, with 600 tons burthen, and was capable of carrying seventy passengers in the saloon, together with cargo. Newly overhauled and heavily coppered, she was only three years old when she left Gravesend on 2 September 1840. She carried £1000 in sovereigns and £10 500 in notes, together with ten employees of the bank who were to establish agencies for both shipping and banking business in the different colonies.[1] *Juno*, a somewhat larger and stronger ship, sailed in 1841, and the smaller *Cornubia*, with Robinson aboard, followed in January 1842.

The steamers were dogged by ill-luck: *Sea Horse* was run down by another ship off Cape Finisterre, and had to be repaired in Lisbon, delaying her arrival in Australia by some months; *Juno* lost her rudder off the Cape of Good Hope.[2] *Sea Horse* finally arrived in Sydney at the beginning of June 1841, and the other ships in the following months.

One of the first functions of the agents of the Royal Bank, who arrived with the ships, was the establishment of a shipping run between the southern ports. Boyd's ships were the first ocean-going steamers to reach Australian waters, as opposed to the many smaller ships built locally for the coastal trade. They therefore aroused considerable interest. 'A large concourse of persons assembled', in mid October 1842, to see *Sea Horse* leave Hobart on her voyage to Sydney, reported the *Hobart Town Courier*, and the *Sydney Morning Herald* assured its readers that 'Mr Boyd has undoubtedly laid the colony under great obligation by the introduction of these two splendid vessels [*Cornubia* had not yet arrived], ... and we should regret exceedingly to hear that he did not obtain a fair profit upon his outlay'.[3]

In fact the colonial government went out of its way to make the new service a success. The steamers were given the conveyance of mail between the ports, with the incentive of a charge of 1s 3d (the land postage rate) instead of the normal sea-mail rate of fourpence, in acknowledgement of the greater reliability and speed associated with steam.

A steady traffic in government business also supported the steamers. In December 1842, for instance, Boyd and Robinson tendered to carry passengers to Van Diemen's Land for the government at the rate of nine guineas for cabin passengers, and £4 17s 6d for soldiers, their wives, and convicts. A tender by a competitor, Samuel Lyons, was significantly lower, but the government gave the contract to Boyd and Robinson, 'considering the advantage of Steam Conveyance, and the expediency of encouraging it'. The first Maori War began in 1844 and Boyd and Robinson won contracts to ship soldiers to New Zealand, again despite their higher charges.[4]

Even with public and private support, however, the steamships proved a costly failure for Boyd. One reason was the inelasticity of the carrying trade: 'it requires high rates of freight and passage money', the *Herald* pointed out, 'to remunerate the proprietors of steam boats, on account of the comparative paucity of the persons travelling from one port to another and ... the rate of passage money makes very little difference in the number of passengers'.[5]

Moreover the reason for supporting the steamships was their greater reliability: 'next to speed, regularity is the great advantage of steamers over sailing vessels'. But *Sea Horse* and *Juno* were not reliable. Following their inauspicious voyages from England, they were often laid up for repairs. They were just too large and expensive for the small trade between Sydney and the southern ports. The Hobart crowd was happy to watch *Sea Horse* start for Sydney, but the *Hobart Town Courier's* shipping lists tell the real story: with capacity for seventy passengers, she carried 'stock and sundries; 3 women, 3 children, 1 man'. *Shamrock*, a smaller, colonial-built steamer owned by the Hunter River Navigation Company was an adequate if less luxurious alternative.

At first an attempt was made to divide the colonial market. An unofficial agreement in 1842 between Boyd and Robinson, and the Hunter Steam Navigation Company, agreed that the two shipping lines would keep clear of each other's business, with Boyd's ships staying south of Sydney. However Boyd's competitors had a further advantage in their access to coal supplies. From 1842 the company began to use coal mined at Limestone (now Ipswich), upstream from Brisbane, while Boyd's ships remained dependent on coal bought from the Australian Agricultural Company under the terms of the old coal monopoly.[6]

Beyond these problems of competition and new technology lay mismanagement. The irritation of one port officer at Port Phillip is typical of the frustrations repeatedly expressed by lowly bureaucrats in their dealings with Boyd. Apparently in reponse to a complaint from the owners, he assured La Trobe:

> So far from having thrown any unnecessary difficulties in the way of the *Sea Horse* or her passengers, I beg to state most distinctly that I have on all occasions acted with the greatest indulgence; overlooking her invariable breaches of the Act of Council with regard to her lists of Crew and Passengers and the difficulties and impediments that have repeatedly been thrown in the way of the proper search and Clearance of the Vessel; although I had no authority for so doing...I do not consider that I should be justified in altogether setting aside the Water Police Act which I am appointed to enforce, out of regard to the trifling pecuniary loss of Mr Boyd which he insists upon so strongly.[7]

Boyd always took a cavalier attitude towards regulations and the sensibilities of those beneath him socially whose unfortunate duty it was to enforce such rules. He preferred to rely on the force of his personality and the power of his wealth and connections to avoid normal pathways.

The single most serious blow occurred in June 1843. By then, the Royal Bank's steamers had been in operation for nearly two years, long enough to show how inappropriate they were for colonial conditions. Consequently, an accident to one of the steamers was possibly fortuitous. At 3 p.m. on 4 June 1843 *Sea Horse* left Launceston with a full crew and a licensed pilot. That night she moored in the Tamar. At seven the next morning, just as the tide was changing, the crew weighed anchor. The paddle-steamer was caught in the current and driven on to the bank. Several hours later she was refloated on the rising tide, and subsequently completed the journey to Sydney.[8]

Boyd later claimed that the ship's engines had been seriously damaged while the ship was aground, and that as a result, *Sea Horse* had to be written off. But the insurers, Royal Exchange Assurance, were suspicious. By mid-1843 *Sea Horse* had already proved uneconomic, and they suspected that Boyd was trying to recoup his losses by exaggerating the consequences of the accident. They refused to pay the full amount of £5000 for which *Sea Horse* was insured, apparently well below her market value which was now estimated at between £22 500 (Boyd) and £15 000 (Royal Exchange Assurance). The insurers paid out only £1250, and the Royal Bank sued for the remaining £3750. The bank lost the case in mid-1845 and lost again on appeal in 1846.

Several factors contributed to that loss. The defendants claimed that 'She rather sailed or floated than steamed [to Sydney in] ... twice, or more than twice, the time of the ordinary voyage', but *Sea Horse* had, in fact, completed her voyage in good time. Her own log attested this, and the *Sydney Morning Herald* shipping report noted that 'having taken the mud in the Launceston River ... [she] completed the passage in 73 hours (allowing for her detention in Twofold Bay)'. A further voyage was advertized two days later, before she was abruptly withdrawn from service. Boyd claimed that the steam engines had been severely damaged by the efforts to refloat the ship and that, while the structural damage could be repaired in Calcutta, there was nowhere closer than Europe where the engines could be repaired.

But the English attorney-general, representing Royal Exchange Assurance, queried whether the deterioration which by then was in evidence resulted from the accident, or from Boyd's decision 'to let her lie and rot there day by day, exposed to every weather, before his eyes'.[9]

To substantiate his case that *Sea Horse* was irreparably damaged, in early 1845 Boyd invited about thirty-five people to look over the ship as she lay in Sydney Harbour. As usual lavish in his hospitality, Boyd wined and dined these witnesses so comprehensively that his hospitality was used as evidence against him in the case. The court found in favour of the insurance company. Boyd appealled against the decision, and the case was re-heard in 1846. Once again he lost, and costs were awarded against him. The information which won the case for the insurance company was provided by a rival shipowner, Robert Towns, who, it was later claimed, received 'a *valuable silver salver and a purse containing* FOUR HUNDRED SOVEREIGNS... in special appreciation of the value of his evidence!'[10]

Sea Horse continued to lie, indubitably rotting, in Sydney Harbour until the end of the decade. The fate of *Juno* was similarly unhappy. When the St George Steam Packet Company failed in 1843, Boyd was instructed, as part of the resolution of the bankruptcy, either to sell *Juno* in Australia, or to send her back for sale in England. In May 1845 the *Atlas* advertized that *Juno* would be auctioned.[11] This first attempt to sell her was unsuccessful, but instead of returning her to England as instructed, he kept the ship moored in Sydney Harbour.

In January 1844 Boyd's importance within the shipping world had been marked by his prominence in the Anniversary Regatta; a year later newspaper reports ignored him, but *Juno*, moored and out of operation, was used, ignominiously, to mark the extremity in the races. She was in and out of service for the rest of the decade. Too large to be economic, by 1848 she was not even paying the crew's wages. Another attempt was made to sell her locally, but the Hunter River Steam Navigation Company was deterred from buying her 'because in case of accident there is no place in these Colonies where she could be repaired', and an attempt to sell her to an Adelaide company for £10 000 failed when the price of copper fell. By then, she was in such poor condition, with shrinking planks and dry rot in the stern, that Robinson would not consider sending her back to England, as he feared she would not survive the voyage. She eventually passed out of Boyd hands in 1849, and was sold subsequently to the Spanish government. *Cornubia*, which was registered in the name of J. P. Robinson, was finally sold for £1485 in early 1849.[12]

From late 1842 Ben Boyd attempted to co-ordinate his shipping and pastoral interests by developing a port at Boydtown on Twofold Bay, a short distance from the already established township of Eden. Twofold Bay lies on the far south-east corner of present-day New South Wales. Matthew Flinders visited the area in 1799 and found the skeleton of a right whale on the beach, and in 1817 Phillip Parker King noted the quality of its anchorages.[13]

The Imlay brothers, Peter, Alexander and George, arrived in the area during the mid-1830s. Using mainly Aboriginal labour, they developed a rudimentary industry catching whales in the bay to be boiled down for the blubber on the beach. The brothers also kept cattle and, with the expansion of settlement to New Zealand by the end of the decade, a trade in cattle and sheep developed across the Tasman.[14]

Boyd chose Twofold Bay as the site of his whaling operations and as a port for his steamships. Oswald Brierly recounted in his journal the travels of Boyd's party to see the area. They sailed south to Twofold Bay, then travelled inland through the Monaro hinterland. On 2 January 1843 they reached 'Pampoola' [Pambula], where they met the government surveyor, 'whose attention we had already experienced at the Bay' before returning to Twofold Bay:

> During our absence the people had been very active in clearing away a portion of the Scrub on the south side of the Bay, which had been fixed upon as ... the site of the intended Township, comfortable bark huts had been built, a large marquee which we had brought down in the Steamer had been set up within a short distance of the beach, and with the feelings of ... the founders of a new City we hoisted a blanket, nailed to a pole as our standard and with all the proper forms named the town Boyd Town.[15]

Cartoon of Ben Boyd and 'Quaker' Robinson
'Gallery of Comicalities, No. 5', from Bell's Life in Sydney, *March 1847*

It was another two months before this land, already tacitly claimed as his own, was put up for auction by the New South Wales government in twenty sections of 640 acres each. Boyd was then the only purchaser, of a single section, at the upset price of £1 per acre. He also bought some town blocks, but the revenue which the colonial government derived from the sale, a bare £640, can scarcely have covered the costs involved in the survey.[16]

By early 1843 Boydtown was emerging. Brierly was appointed manager of the whaling station, for which patronage he was effusively grateful. Boyd, he wrote, was

> a second Pericles who made Phidias superintendent of the Public Works of Athens... Like Pericles in the greatness of

his undertakings—the singular address with which they are carried out—Like him he has fitted out Fleets—Like him he is raising Towns.[17]

Boydtown was Boyd's most ambitious project, planned on an extensive scale to contain a village of four hundred workmen's cottages, a church, an inn, and a lighthouse for the use of Boyd's ships. He also planned to provide the infrastructure to establish Boydtown as a whaling station and a port.

In September 1843 the town's first child was born—stillborn. The baby was immediately buried without Christian rites for, despite the unfinished church, the town was without priest or parson. Within a few days, rumours began to spread culminating in accusations by some of the other women that the child had not been stillborn, but killed at birth by its mother. The body was exhumed, and no evidence was found of any interference—but then, the town also lacked a doctor, a mid-wife or a magistrate. In such a small settlement, gossip and innuendo thrived, but the incident was an ill-omen for the new town.[18]

The facilities of Boydtown were advertized regularly in the colonial press to attract visiting whalers:

> Ships can Refresh or Refit at this Harbour free of all Port charges, Pilotage, and can obtain Wood, Water, fresh and salt Provisions, Vegetables, Ship Chandlery, Stores and Slops of every kind and description, and if required the services of Shipwrights and Boat-builders upon the most reasonable terms. N.B.—Oil and Bone taken in exchange.[19]

A blubber works was established to process whales caught locally by Boyd's, and other, crews. Boyd invested in both bay whaling and deep-sea whaling, with varied success. By 1843 he had two boats employed in bay whaling, and his fleet expanded in subsequent years.

However during the 1840s, whale numbers were depleted. Brierly, with his artist's eye, described bay whaling with a bloodthirsty attention to detail:

> nothing can be more exciting than to join the pursuit and be in at the death of one of these Enormous animals... one morning, when we had begun to dispair of seeing any... there was a call from the Lookout under which we lay, after about

three quarters of an hour hard pulling we... first caught sight of the whale—a large Black one—There! it has struck one of the headsmen and knocked him out of the Boat in an instant he was hauled in again and sends a Lance deep into his side— the sight gave us redoubled energy—'Spring' was the word... and the gig darted forwards with increased velocity, and in a few minutes we were within a Boats length of the animal (Huge mass)—it spurts Blood mingled with water which was now in its last agonies. Blood pouring from gashes in its sides and Back and discolouring the water around—what a scene the shouts and men the splash of the Whale the more Languid motions where the Fish comes up to Blow becomes exhausted... sometimes a sudden rush to rid itself of its pursuers the Boat flying along with terrific rapidity. Oars peaked Water boiling on each side—the Hollow Burst when compelled to return to the surface to Blow then all the Boats tailing away after him to fasten if he should get Loose.

Bay whaling was self-limiting and exploitative. Although Brierly described this whale as 'he', most of those killed were the pregnant females which came into coastal bays each season to give birth. Inevitably the constant slaughter of cows and their calves took its toll. At Boydtown, moreover, Boyd's whalers had to compete with the older established whalers of the area and, as whale numbers declined, competition with other whaling crews grew fiercer. This led to a degree of secretiveness. On 28 October 1844, for instance, Brierly reported:

> a man came stealthily down from the lookout to say there was a whale... the difficulty was to shove the Boat off without being perceived by the Vessels—two men only got into the Boat while the rest of the Crew walked round and were taken in at a little nook out of sight of the shipping.

Despite such precautions, this whale, at least, got away.[20]

Boyd's ships were also employed in the deep-sea fisheries, where sperm whales were the main catch. *Terror* and *Velocity* came from England; *Edward, Margaret, Rebecca, William* and *Duchess of Kent* were purchased during 1844 and were later joined by *Portenia, Fame, Lucy Ann, Prince of Wales* and *Juno* (barque).[21] As well as whaling, they were also involved in the important carrying trade; Boyd employed ships on the trans-

Tasman and inter-colonial trade, carrying livestock and general cargo. Some ships also made trips to the Pacific islands, but whaling was the focus of most activity.

The depletion of whale numbers was beginning to take effect in the deep-sea fisheries, too, but despite increasing problems, Boyd's ships could be productive. It has been estimated that they earned £42 000 from whale oil during 1848, though this figure probably includes oil purchased or bartered at Boydtown from other ships as well. The amounts involved were very great: a single consignment of sperm oil sent to London on 20 September 1848, when the operation was being wound down, amounted to 19 851 gallons.[22]

Boyd's intention was to develop Boydtown as a port for whalers and other shipping, and to combine the activities of shipping and squatting. Nineteenth-century New South Wales had two frontiers, an inland one, and one reaching out into the Pacific. By Boyd's time, the relative importance of the Pacific frontier was declining, but 'whenever there seemed to be a quick profit to be made to the east, or whenever inland expansion was temporarily blocked, opportunities to the east gained a correspondingly greater amount of attention'.[23]

Boyd went beyond this established pattern of choosing the more profitable pathway according to the economic situations on the two frontiers. Unlike other colonial entrepreneurs, such as Samuel Marsden, John Macarthur or William Charles Wentworth, Boyd tried to integrate elements from both the pastoral and the ocean frontiers into a rational economic whole. At Twofold Bay, he set up a conglomerate enterprise which included whaling, trading and pastoralism. Boydtown was developed to capture the whaling activity of the area, and to become a port for the coastal shipping between Sydney and the southern ports. His private town was to service both the port and the hinterland.

The town was raised on a monumental scale. The Sea Horse Inn, the church and the lighthouse were built in stone, and Boyd employed a surveyor to lay out a road to the Monaro to tap the resources of that rich area for his port. The 'settlers of the Back country', noted Brierly, 'will be able to ship their wool and cattle within a distance of fifty miles instead of having as formerly to send it nearly three hundred to Sydney. Twofold Bay will also be the port where whalers may get their supplies instead of being obliged to go up to Port Jackson'.[24] The Monaro hinterland would be linked to the township of Boydtown by mutual interests—as well as by the new road, which began construction in 1843.

The salting works, which produced corned beef and mutton for the New Zealand trade and for visiting whalers, was a practical example of this co-ordination between ship and shore. Both livestock and salt meat were sold to New Zealand, where, in 1846, military expenditure raised the price of cattle to between £12 and £15 a head. A boiling-down works, to convert the oversupply of sheep into tallow, also operated in the port, and tallow could then be shipped cheaply to Sydney. Seven hundred tons of tallow were produced in 1847, but the very existence of such a boiling-down works was an admission of wool's unprofitability.[25]

Despite this, Boyd continued to accumulate squatting runs in the area. Mafra [later Maffra], near Cooma, was one of his head stations and there, and at Gennong and Matong, he ran sheep, while at Bibbenluke, near Bombala, as well as at Myalla Downs, Wog Wog, Cambalong and Boco Rock, he concentrated on cattle production.[26]

The close relationship between sea and land is illustrated by Boyd's plan to transport the increase of his flocks in the Monaro to Van Diemen's Land, where prices were higher (9s to 18s per head), using his steamers to move the flocks. With the accident to *Sea Horse*, this plan was abandoned, but later in the decade he shipped cattle to New Zealand in *Juno* and his sailing ships. Horses, too, were shipped from Boyd's runs, and a trade developed supplying remounts for the cavalry of the East India Company.[27]

Boyd lavished funds on his namesake at Twofold Bay. Yet, with all its geographical advantages and the extravagance of its owner's support, Boydtown failed to thrive. One problem lay in the rivalry between the two townships, Boydtown and Eden, on opposite sides of the bay. At the end of 1842 Brierly described Eden as a desolate spot:

> some posts and boards among the trees on the top of the hill marked the different directions in which the streets were to run, and near the beach were the sheds and huts of a whaling station; bones of whales that had been taken at different times

lay scattered on the beach, a few crows walked about among the deserted huts and the whole place looked as desolate and uninviting as any I had ever seen.[28]

Nonetheless Eden was selected as the government settlement, with the various advantages that government preference offered. In 1843 land was offered for sale at both townships. Although he favoured the southern settlement, Boyd covered himself by buying land at Eden as well. At Boydtown he was the only purchaser, but at Eden bidding was vigorous, and Boyd paid £24 3s for three town lots while Robinson bought two lots for £29 4s 3d.[29]

Boyd fought a continual battle to promote his township against the supposed advantages of its rival. Eden lacked fresh water, he said, which had to be rafted across from Boydtown by permission of the proprietor.[30] The road from Monaro, built under Boyd's direction, fed its traffic from the hinterland into Boydtown. And Boyd was determined that his lighthouse would shine only for his own ships. Yet, to Boyd's chagrin, the government settlement remained obstinately at Eden, a constant brake on the development of the rival port.

The ultimate failure of Boydtown, however, was managerial. Brierly was an inadequate manager of the affairs of the whaling station. Aware of deceit amongst his men, and of rumours of smuggling in the port, he was unable to control the situation. Prone to boredom and restlessness, he—and probably Boyd—conceived his appointment as a sinecure in which to develop his undoubted artistic talents. The self-styled Phidias (to Boyd's Pericles) was soon involved in conflict with Boyd's associates, in particular Joseph Phelps Robinson: 'you are now opposed to one', Brierly soliloquized in his diary,

> who is most crafty and perservering—of a disposition the most wary and ambitious and who is ever on the watch to seize the smallest opportunity of increasing his own importance by sacraficing [sic] the interest of those around him—covering a want of Education by an affected eccentricity and bluntness of manner—and combining with all this the most unblushing impudence—he is endeavouring to remove from around Mr Boyd all who are attached to him by ties of Gratitude—duty—or Blood and in contradiction to his most positive orders keeps those of his own party in his immediate Employ!![31]

One of Robinson's appointees was W.S. Moutry, who was appointed manager, to take over control of all non-whaling activities at Boydtown. Brierly refused to acknowledge his authority or co-operate with him, and rivalry reached such an absurd level that all communication was reduced to exchanges of notes, before Brierly finally left, disillusioned, in 1848.[32]

Moutry presided over the gradual decline of Boydtown, helpless to rescue the enterprise from the increasing apathy of its owner towards it. Boyd blamed the failure of his project on the high price of labour, but many other factors were involved. When Moutry complained, persistently, that supplies were not being sent to the store and hotel, the problem lay in poor management rather than labour costs. Lack of organization at the top demoralized the middle managers, Brierly and Moutry: 'I am sorry to hear you say Mr. Boyd has such bad servants', Moutry told Robinson tartly; 'I have always been given to understand that where they are constantly quarrelling among themselves it is a sign of bad management in the Household'.[33]

Boydtown was well placed for the maritime trade for which it was designed. Twofold Bay was an excellent bay, well positioned half way between Sydney and Port Phillip. The hinterland had potential, and it was still frequented by whales. But the geographical advantages of Boydtown for the purposes of shipping and trade were not advantages for those employed at the bay. It was four hundred miles from Sydney, accessible only by sea, and this isolation, together with the total control of Boyd's managers over every aspect of economic life, made workers and their families very vulnerable. 'The chief exports of Eden', remarked *Bell's Life in Sydney*, 'are wool, tallow, sheep, cattle, train-oil, blubber, and bolting wives'.

But Boydtown was also a company town, with tied housing, a company store, and its own currency. 'The monetary circulation ... is efficiently provided for by the two great Banking Establishments of "Boyd" and "Walker", whose issue of "five bob" notes, payable at their respective stores, or, par preference, PUBLIC HOUSES! has entirely superseded the current coin of the realm'.[34]

Of course Boyd was not the only large employer of labour to operate on the 'truck' system. That 'Most people manage to pay a great part of the expense of their stations by the profit on stores and slops' was a cynical reality. But inefficient and thoughtless management made the situation of the individual under such a system very much worse. When Boyd failed to keep his stores supplied, he hurt not only his workers, but himself as well. 'No prospect of Beef for Christmass', Brierly noted in 1843, and added, on Christmas Day itself, that there had been 'unpleasantness with the men—in con[sequence] of some little work'. It is suggestive that Moutry asked Robinson to 'hire a Butcher . . . if possible . . . who has never been at the Bay and knows nothing of its concerns or people'.[35]

An ideal free market for labour requires both the equal negotiating power of the two parties to the contract, and a full knowledge of the working situation for those entering into an agreement. Neither of those conditions held for Boyd's employees. Their powerlessness was reinforced by their total isolation. A single fare from Sydney to Twofold Bay was £2 cabin, £1 steerage, on *Sea Horse*,[36]—a prohibitive rate for ordinary workers, especially if accompanied by a family—and Sydney was too far to reach by any other means. Those who arrived to work for Boyd had few alternatives but to stay, whatever the conditions under which they were employed, or to get away by whatever means presented themselves.

Under these circumstances, men trapped at Boydtown were unwilling workers, who revenged themselves on their employer in various ways. Brierly knew that the whaling crews sometimes allowed whales to escape:

> it strikes me more than ever that there must be some understanding between at least some of Imlays Boats and ours (davis said that his crew while in chase peaked their oars and said they were tired of pulling after the B—dy whale and allowed Imlays to go on.[37]

Brierly also believed Moutry was cheating the management, adding 30 per cent to invoice prices, and selling inferior flour in the company store. The most widespread corruption, however, was aimed against the government. In 1846 Robinson finally achieved his request for a customs officer to be stationed at Twofold Bay. By then, however, the habit of smuggling was too well entrenched to be rooted out. Boyd's port was an ideal location for the illicit landing and distribution of tobacco and spirits.[38]

Brierly suspected that the Imlay brothers were involved, or at least that they turned a blind eye. Boyd probably did the same. One letter to John Sutherland in London suggests more active involvement, for Boyd apparently considered importing '"Brandy" a neutral Spanish spirit sent out by Cockburn and Co., and chiefly purchased by the smugglers for relanding on the coast'.[39]

Though much smaller than Hokianga in New Zealand, Apia in Samoa, or Levuka in Fiji, Boydtown came to share many of the characteristics of these other Pacific beach communities. Attracting sailors and whalers with promises of 'refreshment', it became a community of drifters, where all races and nationalities mixed in a roisterous, anarchic diversity. Boyd hoped to attract an international shipping traffic to Twofold Bay by offering free wharf facilities. He never succeeded to any significant degree but, nonetheless, Brierly's diary is scattered with references to 'Yankee Lads', 'Mowries', and someone known as 'Otaheiti Bill', who may, or may not, have been a native of Tahiti.[40]

Conflict developed between Boyd's vision of a private town, based on an almost feudal relationship between Boyd and his workers, and the wayward, drifting population on which the whaling industry was based. Violence lay not far from the surface, and relations between workers and employers were rubbed raw by too close proximity. In early October 1843 Brierly overheard murmurs of a plan by discharged whalers to seize *Wanderer*. He had the arms cleaned, and he and two others sat up all night on watch. On another occasion, Brierly asked some 'Idlers lounging about' to help move *Wanderer*, and was told in no uncertain terms that 'the yacht might go to H—l'.[41]

Boydtown was in several ways a tied town. Boyd had his own store, his own currency and, from 1846, his own law. During 1846, Oswald Brierly and Thomas Winder Campbell, another of Boyd's employees, were appointed magistrates. The appointments were contentious. Brierly was respectable enough, and appears to have treated his new office seriously but Campbell, related by marriage to Curwen Boyd, was a recently discharged bankrupt. Both men were clearly employees of Boyd, without the financial independence to act against his interests on the bench. Yet, because of Boydtown's isolation, their office would be more powerful than that of justices of the peace in more closely settled districts.

The office of justice of the peace was particularly important in negotiating and arbitrating agreements between employer and employee under the provisions of the Masters and Servants Act. Boyd was almost the only employer of labour in Boydtown; he was also the employer of the two local magistrates. It is not surprising that the appointments therefore raised questions about the private nature of Boyd's town. The appointment of 'these two fawning sycophants' was questioned by 'Robin Hood' in a letter to the *Sydney Chronicle*:

> There is no British Colony, I believe, of which it can be said, that one of the wealthy inhabitants is almost, if not entirely, the sole owner of the township—*his own servants the population*—AND HIS CLERKS THE MAGISTRATES!

'Robin Hood' questioned how Boyd's influence had accomplished the appointment, and implied that pressure had been exerted on Sir Maurice O'Connell, the officer administering the government following the departure of Gipps. He claimed that O'Connell's son, Captain Maurice O'Connell, a member of the Legislative Council, had been saved from bankruptcy by Boyd money. 'A few hundred pounds, perhaps, was not too much to pay for a sure vote on the squatting question, and the appointment of two magistrates.'[42]

'Robin Hood' had gone too far. In the following days, criminal and civil proceedings were launched by Boyd's solicitor, George Cooper Turner, on behalf of Captain O'Connell, Boyd, Campbell and Brierly, against the printer of the *Sydney Chronicle*, the radical but impecunious Edward John Hawksley. 'Robin Hood' offered a tendentious apology—'My opinions of Mr. Campbell render it unsafe for me to allude to that gentleman's claim for damages. The loss of one's character is sometimes a boon for which we ought to be grateful'—but failed to reveal his name, which remains unknown. The case involving Brierly and Campbell did not proceed; they had been at Boydtown during the period when the writs were issued, and could have had no part in the subsequent legal proceedings. O'Connell, however, pursued the matter, claiming £2000 damages. The jury awarded him only £50, 'as much cause for mortification as for triumph', but still sufficient to bankrupt Hawksley.[43]

The *Sydney Chronicle* managed to survive under a new proprietor, Charles St Julian, despite the belief, aired in its editorials, that the destruction of the newspaper had been the prime objective of the litigation. It is noteworthy, however, that from the beginning of the new year the amount of advertising fell sharply, and at the end of September 1847 the newspaper finally failed.

The *Sydney Chronicle* had walked into a trap of its own making in its dealings with Boyd and his associates. Like the rest of the Sydney press, the *Chronicle* had sympathized with the squatters, or at least with the constitutional issues raised by Gipps's regulations during the great agitation of April 1844, but by 1845 it had shifted to a stand of firm opposition. By the time of the 'Robin Hood' correspondence, Hawksley's position was typical of that of the urban radicals, who saw Boyd, and the situation he had created at Boydtown, as the quintessence of the system they opposed.

The anxieties expressed to such disastrous effect by 'Robin Hood' were widespread in Sydney by 1846. Boyd intended to make Boydtown a private town. He built the church, the inn, the workers' cottages, the whole industrial and social infrastructure of his community, aspiring to control both the spiritual and the physical life of his workers. His experiment was unprecedented in Australia. It raised political questions about the rights of employers to control their workers, the right of a landlord over a tied tenantry, and the rights and responsibilities of the state to intervene in the relationship between master and servant. These were pertinent questions in the highly charged atmosphere of New South Wales in the mid-1840s. Boyd's challenge to the free market for labour was extrapolated to the rest of his class, and caused anxieties, particularly amongst the increasingly articulate middle classes. As another correspondent to the *Sydney Chronicle* said of 'Mr. Boyd and his confederates':

> The Squatters have no community of feeling with us. Their grand aim is to revive the feudal system, with all its attendant horrors, as it existed four or five centuries back, and thereby perfectly demolish the middle classes of society. Should this wicked attempt ever be accomplished, then farewell to the domestic happiness and comforts of the working classes, such as they now enjoy.[44]

Stripped of its rhetorical flourishes, this concern was shared by many during a year when the possibility of convict transportation to New South Wales was again a topic of debate.

7
Labour Problems

TWO SEPARATE ASPECTS of Boyd's attitude towards labour came to be questioned in colonial New South Wales: first, his recruitment of labour from increasingly contentious sources, and second, his treatment of that labour once contracts had been signed. The two issues were related. Boyd's background was that of a financier. As a stockbroker, he had dealt with profit and loss, speculation and capital, but he had little experience of dealing with people. He treated his employees as particularly intransigent factors in his economic calculations, and in consequence his labour relations were exceedingly bad. Boyd's attitude towards the recruitment and employment of labour was not typical of all employers. However because of his wealth, the scale of his operations, and his high profile as an articulate capitalist with British connections, that attitude had consequences for labour relations generally in New South Wales.

The size of his enterprise made it necessary for him to use a great many middle men and he had little direct association with his workforce. The Royal Bank of Australia employed a small group of educated expatriates as agents, clerks and middle managers, whose salaries were fixed in England, but the majority of workers were recruited in New South Wales at whatever rate the labour market would bear. Neither Boyd nor his managers were interested in long-term colonial objectives such as the formation of a stable labouring class. As a sojourner rather than a colonist, Boyd responded to the perceived problem of a shortage of labour with short-term solutions based purely on the profit motive. Boyd accepted the introduction of kanakas, the reintroduction of convicts, and the preferential employment of single men unhampered by the inconveniences of wives and children without regard to the social consequences of such actions, or the need for future generations of capitalists to ensure the reproduction of the labouring classes. He did not suffer the soul-searching of native-born employers such as James Macarthur or Charles Cowper who faced the same labour shortages, but also saw Australia as their future home and therefore were obliged to weigh up the economic benefits of such labour against its social costs—sometimes with ambiguous results.

Boyd wanted to establish a pool of labour. Not 'sufficient', but more than sufficient labour was needed, both to bring down the price of that labour and to ensure that the threat of unemployment prevented workers from becoming recalcitrant. The social implications of such a pool of labour did not concern him, since he did not intend to stay in New South Wales. However they were of deep concern to the government which could ill afford the potential social unrest arising from large-scale unemployment, to the urban middle classes who would live with its effects, and to free immigrants faced with competition pushing down wages.

Boyd did not even recognize the basic requirement of capitalism that labour should be able to reproduce itself. His credo was interpreted in simple terms by the colonial public: single men were better than married, despite the fear of sodomy or social instability; convicts were better than free men, despite the fear of criminality; coloured men were better than white, despite the fear of miscegenation.

Much of Boyd's activity was speculative rather than productive. When he did produce goods for sale, these products—wool, oil, salt beef and livestock—were sold in an export market where he had no control over prices, and his profits therefore depended on outside forces. His response to this uncertainty was to concentrate on reducing the costs of production to ensure a profit on his exports. Some of his non-labour costs, such as government charges and licences, were fixed, or could be changed only by political agitation in which he was also active. He does not appear to have considered reducing his management costs. Possibly some of these were also fixed, for many of his managers were appointed in England and their salaries had been determined there. There is little doubt, however, that greater managerial efficiency would have reduced his costs. Boyd's problems were later revealed by his cousin, who reported 'the most extraordinary bad management, partly owing to the system on which Mr. Boyd has been going and partly to the ineficiency [sic] of his Managers'. It was generally recognized that absentee squatters, who could not personally control the activities of their subordinates, faced higher management costs.[1] Such problems were difficult to resolve, especially for a man like Boyd who probably had little specific knowledge of the work of distant managers. Perhaps a class element was also involved. Managerial costs could only be reduced by tightening the controls on men who were his social equals, some of whom were related to his fellow directors. No such social solecism was involved in reining in the aspirations of unskilled labourers. In his efforts to reduce costs, Boyd consistently concentrated on the most vulnerable of his factors of production—his unskilled workforce.

In Boyd's estimation, the price of labour was the most elastic element in his costs, and the high price of labour in the colonies the cause of all his woes: 'Labour is more than 4/5ths of the expense of Wool-growing & is the greatest difficulty we have at present to contend with'. Many employers shared his point of view but at times his emphasis on labour costs was simply unrealistic. In 1843, for example, he blamed the increased cost of settling the most distant areas of the colony on the higher wages required to persuade labourers to work in the interior. Yet the problem of increased transport costs, both for supplies and to transport wool to the ports, must have been at least as significant a factor. But labour costs, and various schemes for reducing them, remained the basis of all Boyd's arguments.[2]

An investigation of his recruitment of labour and of his treatment of his workmen reveals Boyd at his most ruthless and his most controversial. His obsessive search for cheaper labour had political implications, for it embarrassed his fellow capitalists, even though they sometimes profited from it. Boyd's extreme position was used, unfairly but understandably, by the urban radicals to exemplify the rapaciousness of all his class; in their efforts to distance themselves from him, more moderate men such as Cowper and Lowe became allied with the radical cause.

On 19 September 1845 Boyd told Sutherland that 'if monarchical institutions are to be supported in this Colony... it will be alone through the Squatting party... those men may almost to an individual be ranked amongst the conservatives'.[3] Yet even as Boyd was writing this the squatting party was already fragmenting. Despite their widespread fear of democratic tendencies, the pastoralists failed to form an effective political alliance during the crucial years between 1846 and 1850. One cause of that failure was the rift caused by Boyd's labour policies, which challenged the social views of more orthodox conservatives.

Boyd arrived in New South Wales at a time of depression. The financial crisis which had begun in the pastoral industry rapidly spread to urban areas as well, and during the next two years there was considerable unemployment in Sydney. The depression had its origin in falling wool prices, drought, and the contraction of credit, but one factor which was most clearly evident to the wool growers was the change in the labour market brought about by the end of convict transportation in 1840. Convict labour was no longer available, and free labour was more expensive and less servile.

Assisted immigration to New South Wales had begun in 1831, funded from the sale of Crown Land. After a slow beginning it became considerable by the end of the decade, influenced both by poor economic conditions in England and Ireland, and by the anticipated end of transportation, which made New South Wales a more desirable destination for respectable lower middle-class families. Convicts not only lowered the tone of society; they lowered the demand for free labour as well.

In 1841 free immigration reached a peak of 22483.[4] The considerable cost of assisted immigration to the land fund was a major factor in Gipps's attempt to increase the squatters' contribution to land revenue through the occupation and homestead regulations. The pastoralists objected, however, not only to the expense involved, but to the subsidizing of a class of immigrants which did not meet their labour requirements. Most immigrants came from the cities and many were married, whereas the squatters wanted unskilled, single men to replace convicts as shepherds. Accustomed to employing convict labour, the pastoralists were notoriously slow to provide any amenities for free workers and their families. An impasse was reached. By the early

Boyd's Light *The lighthouse at Boydtown*
Watercolour by Oswald Brierly

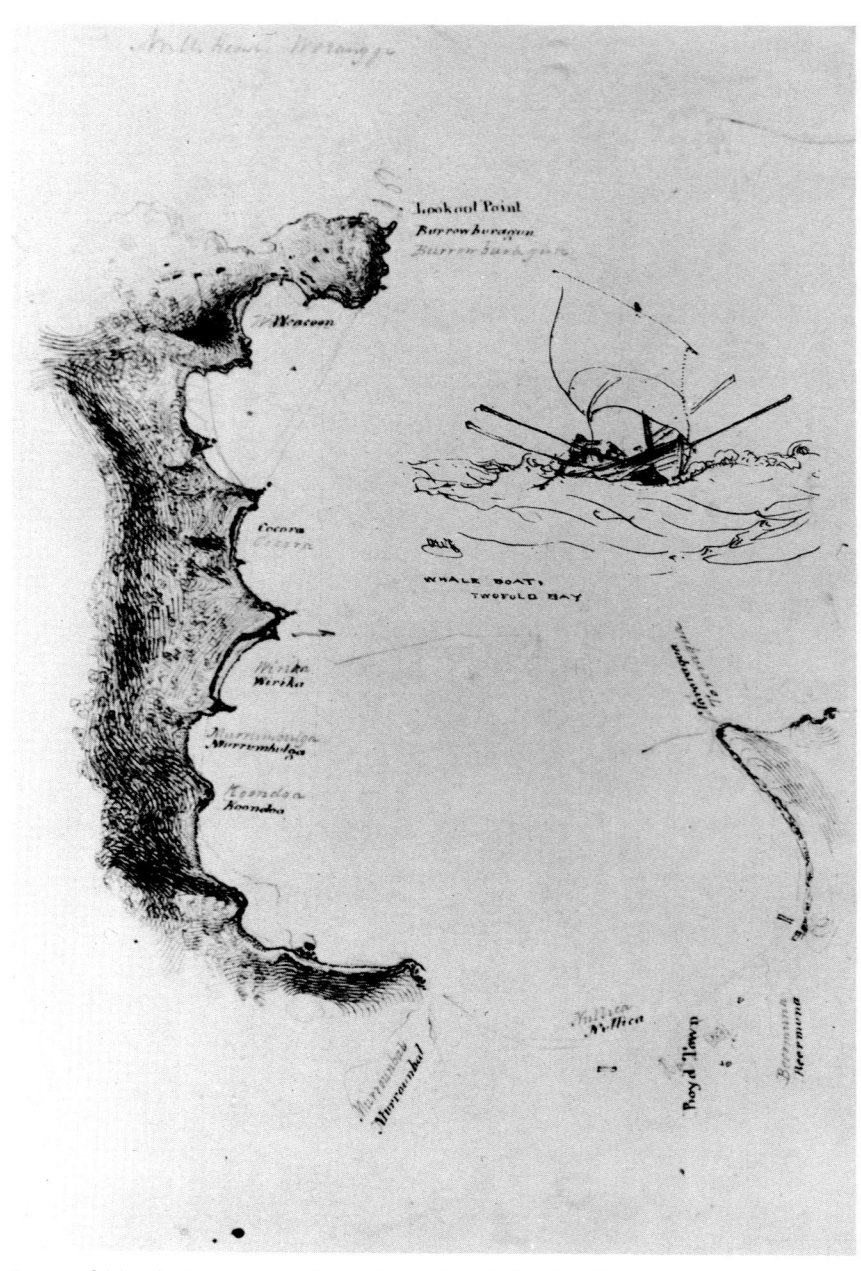

Map of Twofold Bay, with Whaleboat, Twofold Bay *inset
Pen and ink sketches by Oswald Brierly*

Portrait of Benjamin Boyd
Sketch, artist unknown

Whaling off Twofold Bay
Watercolour by Oswald Brierly

Craignathan 'Residence of the Late Benjamin Boyd, North Shore, Port Jackson'. Engraving, reproduced from Australian Picture Pleasure Book, Sydney, J. R. Clarke, 1857

1840s unemployment in Sydney co-existed with a shortage of labour in country districts, a paradox which led to bitter recriminations: the squatters argued that the immigrants were work-shy and self-indulgently luxuriating in the fleshpots of Sydney, while urban workers pointed to the poor wages and conditions offered in pastoral areas.

In September 1843 the Legislative Council established a Select Committee on Immigration. By then, assisted immigration had stopped, partly in response to the growing problem of unemployment but largely because falling land sales had dried up immigration funds. The objective of the committee was to demonstrate that labour rates were too high and that, consequently, more assisted immigration was needed to provide a pool of labour which would force wages down.

One of the witnesses called by the committee was Benjamin Boyd. Neither he nor Robinson was yet a member of the Legislative Council, nor had Boyd yet emerged as a leading spokesman for the squatting movement, but he was already one of the largest employers of labour in New South Wales. In his evidence, Boyd referred to many of the general arguments of the pastoralists, giving specific details from his own enterprises. He emphasized the perceived conflict between the productive economy of the rural areas and the 'occupations of convenience, luxury, and pleasure' of the city: 'I am inclined to think that the symptoms of the dawn of returning prosperity, will be the grass on many of the streets of Sydney'. He acknowledged the difficulty of persuading city dwellers to face the rigors of bush life, but his main complaint was not the difficulty of recruiting workers, but of keeping them:

> if I give them money for the expenses of the road, it is immediately spent in Sydney public houses; and on the other hand, if they undertake to find their way to the interior at their own expense, a very small proportion of them ever reach their destination, as an offer of an extra pound of wages from another party will always induce them to break their engagements.

Boyd's complaint highlighted two problems: the impotence of the Masters and Servants Act, despite its apparently draconian measures to force workers to adhere to their contracts with employers, and the imperfect knowledge of the labour market shown by workers when they signed such agreements. Far from being a free labour market, the system under which contracts were negotiated between master and servant was based on ignorance on the part of the servant, with knowledge of wage rates sometimes deliberately suppressed by the employer.

Boyd drew comparisons with the poorer situation of agricultural labourers in England and Ireland. In 1838 wage rates in the parish of Penninghame, where Merton Hall was situated, were 1s 4d to 1s 6d per day in summer, and 1s 2d in winter, for unskilled labour, and from 2s to 3s for artisans. But by the mid-1840s rates there, as elsewhere throughout Britain, had dropped to famine levels. Boyd told the Select Committee on Immigration in 1843:

> the bush here admits of comforts far superior to what the peasantry are accustomed to at home; butcher's meat and flour they have in abundance, and dairy produce too, for the trouble of milking the cows, which, on my stations, they seldom take the trouble of doing.[5]

Inevitably, as a new arrival, Boyd drew such comparisons, but they were essentially false. While conditions at home were undoubtedly poorer for the rural workforce, there were social compensations in a more settled society. Ironically, squatters like Boyd made disparaging comparisons between the expectations of their workers and those of a recollected peasantry, but they were not prepared to provide the social structure which might have established such a 'peasantry' on their lands. Milking cows, for example, and other dairying activities, were traditionally women's work, but Boyd avoided employing married men—and the cows remained unmilked. He was equally critical when the same workmen responded to the consequent sterility of their social environment by drinking their wages.

Boyd observed that there was 'no mystery in shepherding'. It was, in fact, tedious, lonely work, for which few traditional rural skills were required. The colonial system of shepherding had originated in the early years of the wool industry. Since fencing was uncommon, the sheep were sent out to graze during the day, under the care of a shepherd who was required to live with his flock. At night they were enclosed in folds, or 'hurdles', while the shepherd slept in a hut nearby. He was responsible for the care of his sheep, protecting them from dingoes and from scab and other diseases which could decimate a flock. If he lost sheep through carelessness, they were paid for out of his scant wages. It was a 'lonely, monotonous, and indolent life', but the amount of work involved depended very largely on the size of the flock. During the 1820s that flock had averaged 300 to 350 sheep, but from the late 1830s falling profits and a shortage of labour led employers to increase their flocks to between 500 and 1000 or more. At the same time, as pastoralism moved to the less fertile backblocks, the shepherd was expected to graze his flock over a larger area of pasture each day.[6]

In the 1840s Boyd was one of the first to introduce the new system of 'camping'. Instead of being folded at night, sheep in open country were now left unconfined and unattended except for the shepherd, who was required to take up a completely nomadic life, sleeping out with his flock. The new method had its attractions to capitalists because it saved labour, but it was thoroughly unattractive to the shepherds forced to abide by it, and it was only in times of high unemployment that men could be induced to accept work under such conditions. As an historian has explained: 'Camping sheep could save labour but paradoxically it was only possible when there was little need to save labour ... as practised in the 1840s camping sheep could only be put into operation by ruthless employers such as Boyd'. Boyd embraced the new system wholeheartedly, and was critical of more old-fashioned methods. He often employed sailors, he told the Select Committee on Immigration, 'and find their flocks as well tended, (if not better) than those of the old hands, who are full of a great many of the absurd prejudices, which grew up under the old system of small flocks, hurdles, &c.'.[7]

The increased productivity offered by the new system was not passed on to the shepherds. In his evidence to the committee, Boyd quoted from labour agreements signed at a time of flux, when wages were falling, but he was clearly paying the lowest wages that the market would bear. The most distant areas commanded the highest rates, and on the lower Murray, Boyd said, he paid on average £30 per annum, with a weekly ration of 10 lb flour, 12 lb meat, 2 lb sugar, ¼ lb tea. Closer to civilization, in the middle district, the wages were 'until very recently' £20 per annum with a similar ration, and in Port Phillip, £25 per annum. These wages were dropping. As unemployment bit, so men were forced to accept lower rates, and at Twofold Bay, within the previous three months, the wages agreed had ranged between £18 5s and £10 per annum with rations. By November, Robinson was engaging men for the Lachlan, in the unsettled districts, at £10 a year with the usual rations.[8]

Ten pounds per year was their objective. For this wage, Boyd's employees were required to look after larger flocks, staying out with them at night and deprived even of the marginal comfort of a shepherd's hut. Because of the greater difficulty of looking after larger flocks, the shepherd also ran the risk of having his wages docked if sheep were lost while in his care, and Boyd's method of camping sheep made such losses much more likely. Workers were wary of rural contracts because of their fear that they would be cheated out of their wages in just this way.

On his own evidence, Boyd was a less generous employer than other squatters. While many of his comments and attitudes towards the laziness, truculence and general perfidy of the lower orders may be typical of his class, his difficulty in retaining labour indicates that the men he employed found they could do better elsewhere. They voted with their feet, and only the legal constraints of the Masters and Servants Act prevented more of them from leaving. In small ways, Boyd showed his parsimony towards his workers. When he could, for instance, he cut tea and sugar from their rations as a cost-cutting measure, though other employers found that these 'luxuries' could be more effectively used as an incentive to encourage better work from their men.[9]

By contrast, the next witness to the select committee was Charles Campbell. He had been paying his men between £20 and £24, but had recently given notice that wages would be reduced to £18 for shepherds and £16 for watchmen—'I should hardly like to see them lower'. He opposed the reintroduction of immigration during the depression which, while 'indispensable to the success of the land speculator', was inadvisable at the present moment. Phillip Parker King, another concerned employer who was manager of the Australian Agricultural Company, also reduced wages in 1843, to between £10 and £16 'according to circumstances...and I believe we shall not be short of hands at that reduced price', but he also stressed that 'men with small families are to be preferred', and provided a clergyman, a school and other facilities to meet their needs.[10]

Shepherds constituted the greatest number of Boyd's employees, but the operatives of Twofold Bay, in the whaling and onshore, were also a large group, and less is known about their lives as Boyd's employees. Least of all is known about the whalers. Boyd was involved both in bay whaling and deep-sea, otherwise known as pelagic, whaling. The pelagic whalers were under the immediate control of their ship's captain and, within this constraint, had considerable independence. Their pay was based on their catch, for each received a fixed proportion of the oil, known as a lay. They signed on for a voyage, and the period surrounding their discharge and possible rehiring could be tense. Pelagic whaling appealed as a risk-taking venture to some men, for a good catch could pay well, but it was also a dangerous and isolated job.

The bay whalers were more restricted, but they too had a habit of independence, especially at Twofold Bay where several employers competed for their labour. Nonetheless, the bay whalers were at a disadvantage in their dealings with their employers, especially ticket-of-leave convicts who could be threatened with legal sanctions. Brierly could assert considerable authority, even before he became a magistrate: 'Discharged some of our whalers to day', he wrote in 1844, 'guaged [sic] the oil in order to make out those four mens accounts—one of the Ticket of Leavers refractory, had him called out and threatened to take his ticket from him when he became very penitent and begged to have another chance in the Boats'.

Boyd used Aborigines and Pacific islanders in both pelagic and bay whaling. Of the two boats employed in bay whaling during 1843 'one [was] composed of natives—who are very expert'.[11] A tradition already existed at Twofold Bay of employing Aborigines, just as they had earlier been used in the coastal sealing trade. Boyd extended this tradition, using Aborigines much more extensively in his operations than was usual in colonial New South Wales at this time.

In April 1844 a Sydney newspaper noted that he had 'brought up with him from Twofold Bay a crew of aboriginal seamen, who appear to be a finer and more intelligent race of men than any of the native tribes on this side of the Continent. We congratulate Mr. Boyd on his successful application of aboriginal labour to the purposes of navigation'. From then on, Boyd seems to have had a black crew aboard *Wanderer*. Amongst them were men from Rotumah and Ocean Island, as well as Australian Aborigines.[12] However, as the Navigation Acts forbade the use of non-British labour aboard British ships, many Pacific islanders employed in colonial shipping were called 'New Zealanders', even when they came from other parts of the Pacific.

There was often conflict amongst the different groups in the bay. The whalers despised the landlubbers, and there was hostility amongst the various racial groups. Boyd deliberately manipulated racial tension to keep his workforce from acting in a concerted manner against him. In 1847, for instance, the crew of *Juno* went on strike, refusing to obey their captain's call to leave the local pub. In somewhat rollicking detail, Mark Boyd recounted what happened next:

> My brother had a party of South-Sea Islanders working for him at his wharf—for such is the scarcity of sailors that a large portion of every crew consists of New Zealanders... The captain was asked if with twenty picked men of those at the wharf the steamer could put to sea. He said 'yes,' and in the course of a few minutes the owner was seen at the head of a band of fine athletic South-Sea Islanders, hurrying to the vessel. This was too personal for Jack... as the movement had been observed from the public-house, and the party there started off at last, only just beating their wild competitors, and the steamer went out of harbour with her proper but overindulged crew.[13]

The potential for conflict was increased by the different levels of wages paid to different ethnic groups: 'the majority of the crew are from South Sea Islands, consequently have a very small lay', Boyd told Sutherland, describing the colonial whaling fleets. Aborigines, too, were restricted to the least skilled and lowest paid jobs. They were 'remarkably useful during the whaling season, and if only led on by a white person, form excellent boats' crews'. As early as 1843 Boyd was also considering importing labour from China; 'I have been offered many Chinese families for little more than the cost of their rations', he told Sutherland.[14]

Such deliberate use of coloured labour to divide and rule a multi-racial workforce has been an effective tactic for employers in many times and places. Boyd's policy served as a warning and an example to white labourers, who correctly inferred that he would use coloured workers to reduce their standard of living when he could, and whose own racism made them vulnerable to such manipulation.

Workers ashore enjoyed far less independence than the whalers. Between July and September 1843 Boyd signed on mechanics to work on the building of Boydtown at between 1s a day or £18 5s per annum, and £10 per annum, both with rations. Unlike the shepherds, these were skilled tradesmen, some of whom had worked as carpenters, joiners, bricklayers, stonemasons or blacksmiths on the major building projects in Sydney.[15] Yet their wages were comparable with those of shepherds, an indication that, during the depression, trade skills were of little value.

Concurrently, benefiting from the unemployment of Sydney, Boyd arranged for one hundred people to be given a free passage to Twofold Bay aboard *Velocity*. On arrival the single men were divided into groups of twenty, provided with a ration (200 lbs of pork, 200 lbs of flour, 40 lbs of sugar and 5 lbs of tea) and an Aboriginal guide, and told to walk the forty-five miles to Monaro to find work before their ration ran out. The married men were provided with a similar ration, with half rations for their wives, and left to their own devices to seek employment in the bay area. A critic later claimed that those who refused to accept £10 wages were refused a passage back for less than £5, and 'those who remained created such a feeling in the country that Mr. Boyd could not venture to visit his stations until the time of the year when the police magistrate, with a guard of policemen, took his annual round'.[16]

The 1843 Select Committee on Immigration recommended an elaboration of Boyd's rough and ready method of bringing labour and employers together. It suggested that in future immigrant ships might be sent directly from England to various setttlements along the coast, such as Portland Bay, Geelong, Melbourne, Twofold Bay, Jervis Bay and Moreton Bay.[17] This would also have the advantage of keeping new immigrants from making contact with the Sydney working class and consequently reaching an informed knowledge of the state of the labour market in New South Wales. They would thus be willing to accept wages and rations which were high by British standards, but low in colonial terms.

Boyd and other employers constantly complained about the shortage of labour in New South Wales. The problem for capitalists, however, lay not only in a shortage of labour but in the lack of submissiveness of the colonial workforce once the worst rigors of the depression began to abate. In Britain, where there was endemic unemployment in an immobile working class, employers were accustomed to a submissive, if not servile, workforce. In New South Wales, the experience of convict labour had led to an expectation that labour could be controlled by legal means. Power rested with the employer when he could threaten to cancel a ticket of leave, or return an insubordinate convict to government service. Now, however, those solutions had gone, but the problem of finding and keeping an effective workforce remained.

In the absence of large-scale immigration from Britain, two solutions were mooted by Boyd and some other employers in the mid-1840s: the colony might reintroduce convict transportation, or it could seek labour from non-European sources. Both solutions sacrificed long-term social goals to the short-term economic advantages of their class, and caused political conflict in New South Wales.

In 1840 convict transportation to New South Wales ended, and the worst depression for more than a decade began. Many employers saw more than coincidence in these two events. As the labour shortage continued during the following years, and government efforts to promote free immigration were condemned for their cost and ineffectiveness, many in the colony began to think wistfully of old convict days, when profits were high and working men knew their place. James Macarthur, who had supported the end of transportation in his evidence to the Molesworth Committee during 1837, changed his mind, and in 1843 his brother Edward presented petitions from the Legislative Council to the secretary of state for the colonies, calling for the renewal of transportation. The issue was complicated by concurrent proposals that coloured labour should be imported from India or

China. Boyd considered importing Chinese workers during 1843, and Robert Towns, William Charles Wentworth's brother-in-law, brought in coolies via Hong Kong.[18]

The Colonial Office disapproved of the introduction of coloured labour, but recognized that a problem existed. In 1844 Britain began to send 'exiles' to Port Phillip, men who had undergone their initial punishment at Pentonville penitentiary, and were now considered sufficiently rehabilitated to be given a ticket of leave. Then, in April 1846, William Gladstone, the newly appointed Secretary of State for the Colonies, wrote to FitzRoy hinting that transportation was being reconsidered, and asking for an expression of opinion on the subject from the Legislative Council.[19]

Gladstone's request led to the establishment of a Select Committee of the Legislative Council, under the chairmanship of William Charles Wentworth, to inquire into the possible renewal of transportation in New South Wales. Amongst the witnesses called were Boyd's cousin, Alexander Sprott, who reported on the successful employment of Pentonville exiles at Port Phillip, Charles D. Logan of the Pastoral Association, who reported on conditions in Van Diemen's Land, J. P. Robinson, who gave statistics on penitentiaries in Britain, and Benjamin Boyd.

In its final report, the committee chose to treat Gladstone's suggestion as being in the nature of a *fait accompli*. This being so, they argued, since Britain planned to go on sending convicts to Van Diemen's Land and exiles to Port Phillip, New South Wales would suffer the disadvantages of a convict society without the accompanying economic benefits unless she agreed to the reintroduction of convicts.

The report caused grave offence in Sydney. Public opinion, led by the *Sydney Morning Herald*, was firmly opposed to the reintroduction of convicts. Three days after Boyd gave his evidence, on 22 October, a public protest meeting in Sydney condemned his suggestions and rejected transportation as a solution to the colony's problems. The meeting elected a committee to prepare a petition to this effect, and appointed Charles Cowper to present the petition to the Council. Further meetings were held throughout the colony, and the flood of petitions to the Council was such that Wentworth avoided tabling the report until the closing minutes of the session. He then moved successfully for the report to be printed, but the report was neither debated nor voted on.

Like the report itself, Boyd in his evidence gave lip-service to the concerns of colonists about the moral and social implications of convictism, and mouthed platitudes about reformation, while keeping an eye to the main chance. This is clear, for instance, in his recommendation that convicts should not be landed at Sydney or Melbourne, but be disembarked at Portland, Twofold Bay and Moreton Bay, 'thus avoiding the contamination of the large towns, where idleness and profligacy prevail, and former habits would be renewed'.

He stressed the shortage of labour in New South Wales, and its consequent high cost, and argued that the economy would thrive again if convicts were available to ameliorate the labour shortage. Boyd agreed with the chairman that female convicts should be included—'the disparity of the sexes led to a great many of the evils in the colony'—and emphasized that the assignment of convicts as shepherds would hasten their reformation 'by its very solitude giving time for reflection'.[20]

In 1847 Boyd arranged for his evidence to be republished in England, and it appeared together with a copy of the report, lending stature to a document which in fact had no mandate. He had learned from his experience of lobbying for changes in land policy that concerted effort by his friends in Britain was more effective than any action he might take in New South Wales. 'I hope you & Mark will push the Transportation—Exile or Emigration scheme (provided we are not to pay for it) in every channel', wrote Robinson to Sam Browning in June 1847; 'you cannot do better than follow up the Transportation report & our BB's evidence is considered by all practical men to be one of the most able digests of the question ever given—& you will redily [sic] see that it was intended to have its effect at home'.[21]

He followed this publication with an open *Letter to His Excellency Sir William Denison, &c., &c., &c., Lieutenant-Governor of Van Diemen's Land, on the Expediency of Transfering the Unemployed Labor of that Colony to New South Wales,* which was published in Sydney in 1847. Inevitably the pamphlet reached London and it was reviewed by the *Economist* on 18 March 1848. In his *Letter* Boyd continued his arguments in favour of convict labour, but specifically he asked Denison to release ticket-of-leave convicts from Van Diemen's Land, where there was insufficient work to occupy them, and send them to New South Wales—Boyd offered to provide the ships—where the demand for labour so outran supply. 'The approaching shearing-season is really looked forward to by the Australian sheep farmers with dread and perplexity'. Boyd admitted that Wentworth's committee had received a bad press in New South Wales, but he dismissed the groups opposing transportation. The emancipist party's opposition was most illogical, since 'the present gratifying position of the majority' of emancipists was 'the most powerful argument in favour' of the convict system's capacity to reform. Nor should immigrants complain, for they benefited from the advantages of a convict economy, which had paid for their passages out, and they were themselves unprepared to accept work in the pastoral districts.

One objector was dealt with more specifically, though not by name:

> In respect to the opposition offered by another small section of this community to our reception of the laborers in question, I do not deem it necessary to trouble Your Excellency with any lengthened remarks. Of the sincerity of their *fears of contamination*, they themselves have offered the strangest proof, in *importing*, AT THEIR OWN EXPENSE, *Expirees from Van Diemen's Land*, whose importation, as a comprehensive public measure, they oppose on the score of *morality*; yet justify their own *private* arrangements, on the ground of expediency![22]

The reference was to Charles Cowper. In 1844, as Chairman of the Select Committee on Crown Lands Grievances, Cowper had worked for a common end with Ben Boyd—to reject Gipps's squatting regulations. But within a year the alliance between landowners such as Cowper, and squatters like Boyd, was breaking down. In 1846 he remained, in his biographer's words, 'almost obsessed' with the problem of acquiring sufficient rural labour, but he also spoke at the 22 October meeting, and subsequently became a leader of the anti-transportation movement.

Cowper's position was tendentious, however, in taking a high moral stand against convicts, for a year earlier he had allowed J. P. Robinson to import on his behalf seven ex-convicts from Van Diemen's Land. Inevitably, Robinson leaked the story: 'I feel perfectly convinced that if all the members of the "Vandemonian-cheap-Labour and Questionable-Moral-Importation-Company" were tried for their acts, Charles Cowper, Esq... would be found guilty by any jury in the Colony, not only as an accessory before the fact, but as a receiver'. *Little Ingenuity* managed to escape with only minor embarrassment, but the experience left an enduring enmity between Cowper and Boyd, which surfaced on several further occasions, and culminated in the challenge to a duel.[23]

The most notorious example of Boyd's obsessive quest for cheaper labour was his decision in 1847 to import Pacific islanders. This incident became a part of Australian folklore. Thus, for instance, in August 1863 when a ship carrying indentured Melanesians arrived in Brisbane, a member of the Queensland parliament drew on Boyd's example to criticize the new trade: 'call it what you will, it simply resolves itself into a branch of the ... slave trade under a milder name. We perfectly remember that Mr. Benjamin Boyd deluged the colony of New South Wales with South Sea Islanders to the disgust and horror of the colonists'.[24]

Boyd's use of coloured labour did not begin in 1847. As has been seen, he used Aborigines as sailors, whalers and stockmen, and both Maoris and other Pacific islanders in the whaling industry. His use of islanders as strikebreakers set the scene for conflict between his white and coloured workers, and suggests that he was paying these islanders at lower rates than his European employees. Lurking in the background, too, was 'Dick', Edward Boyd's Black African family retainer, and a family history of involvement in the slave trade. Boyd's action, dramatic and contentious though it appeared to his colonial contemporaries, was merely the most extreme example of his labour relations which he based on the principle of divide-and-rule: contracts were made under conditions of imperfect knowledge by the worker, and enforced against their later and more experienced judgment; single men were chosen in preference to those with

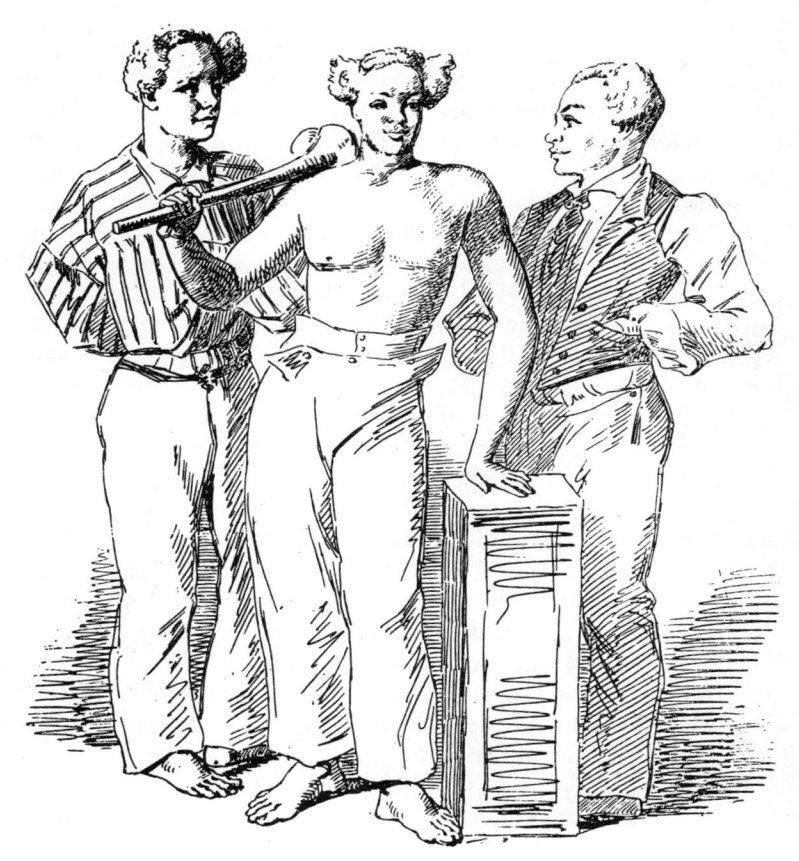

'Panyella, Etoidsi and Sabbathahoo', three islanders recruited by Boyd
From Heads of the People, 1 May 1847

dependents; and men were deliberately isolated from the opportunity to sell their labour elsewhere. All these features characterized Boyd's experiment with indentured Melanesian labour.

Boyd was not the only colonist at the time investigating the prospect of importing coloured labour. In March 1846, for instance, the shipowner Robert Towns, who was exporting horses to India, used the return voyage to bring in coolies from India, but they 'turned out a parcel of worthless rubbish and refused to work under their agreement'.[25] But indentured Asian labour fitted into a general pattern of labour movements within the British Empire, one which Australia had avoided as long as the alternative of convict labour remained. It was based on legal, if one-sided contracts, and proceeded in a regulated way. Boyd's venture into the procurement of Melanesians was a much more irregular affair.

By the beginning of 1847 New South Wales was emerging from its depression, and wage rates were rising. For the Boyd enterprises, however, the improved economic climate had little impact. Boydtown stagnated, with the road still uncompleted, whale numbers dwindling, and Boyd's squatting runs, bought with the objective of a quick speculative profit, still awaiting the rising land values that changed land legislation was expected to bring. Meanwhile, as productive sheep farms they were unsuccessful. Boyd left the management of his runs in the hands of subordinates, and failed to follow through a breeding programme with his livestock. He sold some horses in Singapore and India, but profits were marginal, and salt beef was, he admitted, a 'drug from one end of the world to the other'.[26] The trans-Tasman trade declined with the gradual restoration of peace during 1846 and 1847. Meanwhile Boyd's objective remained to lower wages to £10 per annum, a rate usually exceeded even during the depths of depression in 1843. His search for cheap labour now took a new and more insidious direction.

On 20 January 1847 J. P. Robinson wrote to his brother, George, who was managing Mafra station in the Maneroo (Monaro) District:

> We start the *Velocity* in a day or two for a cargo of South Sea Islanders for shipboard they will be landed at Twofold Bay & will go to Maneroo & the Murray... The present high price of Labor & low price of Wool will ruin one half of the settlers & we must take some decided steps to save our property.[27]

Less than three months later Captain Kirsopp arrived back at Twofold Bay with sixty-five Melanesians from Lifu in the Loyalty Islands and Tana and Aneityum in the New Hebrides (Vanuatu). On 9 April Brierly went on board *Velocity* to meet the new arrivals, accompanied by Captain Nagle, the clerk of the local bench of magistrates in Eden: 'none of the natives could speak English, and all were naked', he recalled; 'they all crowded round us looking at us with the utmost surprize, and feeling at the Texture of our clothes... they seemed wild and restless'.[28]

The pressures which led sixty-five islanders to board *Velocity* and to put their mark to a document which bound them to five years' indentured labour, remain unclear even in a century which claims a greater understanding of anthropology, and a more disinterested curiosity, than characterized the various parties which subsequently tried to unravel the mystery.

The contract which each of the islanders marked was as follows:

> I [blank] native of [blank] in the Pacific Ocean, have this day agreed with [Captain of the ship] on the part of Mr. Benjamin Boyd of the City of Sydney, New South Wales, to serve the said Benjamin Boyd, in the capacity of a seaman on any of his ships, or as a whaler either on board or on shore, or as a shepherd or other labourer in any part of the colony of New South Wales, and to make myself generally useful for the term of five years.

In return for this they were to be paid 26s per year, with a weekly ration of 10 lbs meat, and would receive two pairs of trousers, two shirts, and a kilmarnock cap.[29]

At Twofold Bay, Brierly and Nagle recopied the agreements under which the islanders were bound, 'which they all signed'. However Brierly was clearly unhappy about the arrangement, and refused to sign the contract in his capacity as justice of the peace. His refusal precipitated an argument with Moutry, who promised to tell Boyd of his refusal, and led to the final disintegration of relations between the two men. Thereafter, communication between Moutry and Brierly was reduced to an exchange of notes.

Within the week Moutry started inland with the party of islanders. His intention was to distribute them to Boyd's managers, Daniels at Strathmerton on the Murray, and George Robinson at Mafra. Some of the bewildered Melanesians immediately 'bolted and came back to the Town'. On 2 May Brierly recorded the first death amongst those remaining at the bay. The man was buried at sundown, and Brierly read the Christian burial service over his grave.[30]

Winter had begun. One of the most constant criticisms levelled against this experiment in indentured labour was the decision to send these men from the tropics straight into the depths of winter in the Southern Highlands. Robinson, his Quaker conscience perhaps pricked by their plight, sent his brother parcels of warm clothing for the men, but they continued to drift back to the coast. 'Morning went over to Boyd Town', noted Brierly on 3 June, 'more of the natives returned. Sixteen now in all some of them crying to go back to Lieaffoo. Stupid and will not work'.[31]

Moutry, too, was by now entirely disillusioned with the scheme. On 20 June he wrote to George Robinson, asking him to return all the islanders' contracts, for 'Suffice to say they have all run away via the Sea Coast for Leefoo. as I leave here for Sydney by the Shamrock I wish to take their agreements with me in case they make for Sydney'.[32]

However Boyd was not prepared to admit the failure of his experiment, so evident to his foremen. Towards the end of May *Velocity* again left for the New Hebrides, this time with a second ship, *Portenia*, to recruit more workmen in the islands. The newspapers reported this new expedition uncritically; the Sydney correspondent of the *Port Phillip Herald* merely predicted that 'it appears likely that the importation of labour from the New Hebrides' group, will in the course of a very short time amount to 1000 men a month'.[33]

Colonial society, however, was beginning to register its concern. Those islanders who remained as shepherds were far off by now, at Boyd's stations on the Edward and Murray rivers, but those at Twofold Bay, and far more those desperately searching for Lifu along the coast, were soon a matter of public disquiet. Some reached Sydney. In October a group of seven or eight entered a shop 'and, having closed the door, went round the counter, and began to make free with the bread and other eatables'.[34]

Genuine anxiety about their fate was also expressed. Paternalistic voices raised concerns about the ignorance of the islanders which made them like children, and like children unable to understand, or to be held to, any contract that they signed. The editor of the *Sydney Chronicle* asked why Boyd had deliberately chosen to recruit men from islands scarcely touched by European civilization, when there were many archipelagoes where traders and missionaries had begun to accustom their populations to the

7 *Labour Problems* 131

habits of the white man, and which would therefore have more understanding of the agreements they were entering into.[35]

Governor FitzRoy was slow to act but his officers were disquieted by Boyd's actions. In August the Legislative Council, at the instigation of Edward Deas Thomson, the Colonial Secretary, and J. H. Plunkett, the Attorney-General, agreed to an amendment (11 Vic, No. 9) to the Masters and Servants Act (9 Vic, No. 27), which made 'the Natives of any Savage or uncivilized tribe inhabiting any Island or Country in the Pacific Ocean or elsewhere' exempt from the provisions of the Act. When *Velocity* and *Portenia* arrived back in Sydney on 17 October with another fifty-four men and three women from the islands, Kirsopp found that the indentures they had marked were no longer valid. This left the new arrivals under no authority and no one's responsibility, for Boyd, once denied their labour, took no further interest in their plight.

Those employed as shepherds on Boyd's stations were also affected by the change. Suddenly freed from their indentures by the action of the Legislative Council, the islanders left in a body for Sydney to seek out their employer. Boyd's foreman tried to detain them, but the local magistrate had no power to intervene as they set out on their walk to Sydney. Their progress from the Riverina now became a source of bemused hilarity to journalists and country correspondents throughout New South Wales. Though it was admitted that they caused no harm to anyone during their long march across the colony, their alleged habit of rubbing their stomachs, while muttering 'Massa Boyd, Massa Boyd' and rolling their eyes, was described in glowing detail by the press. A well-organized campaign of not-very-genuine fear of their cannibalism, and of delighted prurience at their nudity, accompanied these reports, which played on the increasing dislike for Benjamin Boyd in respectable middle-class society.

For the newspapers, and for public opinion generally, the issue was seen in overtly racist terms. The editor of the *Australian* contemplated with horror 'a *monthly debarkation of 1000 ferocious homicides*, reeking with the blood of their fellows, with whose mangled flesh their unhallowed maws had most probably but recently been gorged'.[36]

Robert Lowe took up both the paternalist and the racist

threads of public opinion when he introduced the topic on the last sitting day of the Legislative Council. In a motion seconded by Charles Cowper, Lowe called for a government investigation of Boyd's operations, to see if they contravened British law. Both Lowe and Cowper had formerly been associates of Boyd in the heady days of the Pastoral Association, but by 1847 the old alliance of landed interests had broken up. Expedience versus morality was at issue, as it was in the concurrent debate about re-introducing convict labour. Both issues engaged the urban middle classes, who were opposed not only on moral, but also on economic, grounds to the introduction of cheap labour in any form.

Boyd himself drew comparisons between convicts and islanders in his letter to Sir William Denison:

> Hitherto, my island-labor experiment—denounced as it was, at first, by the interested and unthinking—has convinced me of its tendencies to good; and applying the principles which guided me in that experiment to wider and perhaps a less difficult field of action, I commend my plan for the removal of the unemployed holders of tickets-of-leave in Van Diemen's Land.[37]

This was an invidious comparison which did nothing to lessen the dislike in which he was held by colonists. By the end of 1847 Boyd had become a straw figure, a convenient target for any politician seeking popularity with liberal opinion, and both Lowe and Cowper were certainly courting public opinion by raising the issue of Boyd's kanakas.

Lowe's moral outrage was somewhat compromised by the fact, pointed out by Robinson, that he had waited until the last day of the session to raise the matter. In his speech he raised the spectre of slavery. There were parallels, he suggested, between Boyd's recruitment of Melanesians and the African slave trade only recently abandoned by Britain. In the first place, the trade was between a superior nation and an inferior one.[38] The Melanesians could have no understanding of the contract they had signed—'though neither a cannibal or a native of Tanna himself, he must say that he was utterly unacquainted with the meaning of a Kilmarnock cap himself'. Secondly, their recruitment had been accompanied by gifts to the chiefs, which might well, as in Africa, provide a further incentive for warfare, to provide prisoners for the trade. That Boyd considered his recruits as property was evidenced by his reference to them as a 'cargo of labour', as if they were the equivalent of 'a cargo of tea or sugar'.

Robinson's defence was weak. He argued that the policy was no more than an extension of their previous policy of employing Maoris in the whaling trade. He agreed that 'Asiatic or South Sea Island labour', which he deliberately linked together, was less desirable than European, but unless transportation or assisted immigration was re-introduced, capitalists must look elsewhere. There were 'hundreds and thousands' of islanders 'ready and anxious' to come.[39]

His main argument, however, was the worst kind of legal nicety: the recruitment of islanders could not be a slave trade because 'a clause in the Emancipation Act... provided that no slave trade could exist in any British colony whatsoever'. At one point in Robinson's speech, moreover, he is shown out in a lie. Lowe had criticized the cruelty of sending islanders from the tropics to the depths of a Monaro winter. Robinson responded that 'these natives were never intended for Maneroo'—but the previous January he had told his brother to prepare for the arrival of islanders at the Mafra station.

Lowe's speech was witty and cutting, but it gained little support. Moreover his confrontationist manner caused him, on two points, to lead where others would not follow. First, he criticized the government for its dilatory behaviour in not investigating Boyd's actions for a possible breach of the Slavery Acts; and second, he pursued a racist course in opposing *all* forms of coloured labour—and in 1847, many capitalists were considering importing indentured labour from the usual sources of such labour within the British Empire, China and India, as a solution to the colony's labour shortage. Robert Towns, for instance, had brought in coolies during 1846.

Both Lowe and Cowper could legitimately be accused of riding public opinion for their own reasons, and neither of them had spotless reputations in their own dealings with employees. Robinson drew attention to a case which Lowe's general servant had brought against him for an excessive workload, and Cowper had already been caught out, employing Van Diemen's Land ex-convicts supplied by Boyd and Robinson. Wentworth, who was Towns's brother-in-law, came to Robinson's defence. He reiterated the argument that because the slave trade was outlawed in the British colonies, Boyd's recruitment could not be a slave trade, and regretted that Lowe's allegations would have sunk the reputation of the colony 'yet lower amongst the sensitive old ladies of Exeter Hall'. Lowe and Cowper gained little support for their motion, which was eventually withdrawn.

Lowe's difficulty was that he had little evidence to back up his claims, for no one knew clearly what had occurred at Lifu, Tana and Aneityum. Ironically, by raising the spectre of slavery, which was illegal in a British colony, he made it much less likely that any participant in the recruitment would reveal what had occurred. However the questions raised by Lowe were also preoccupying FitzRoy's executive officers. During October 1847 Attorney-General Plunkett took affidavits from Boyd's employees: the captains, Edward Kirsopp of *Velocity* and George Lancaster of *Portenia*, the cabin boy, Henry Walpole, and a passenger on *Velocity*, William MacKenzie.

Plunkett did not take their statements on oath, and the affidavits showed, as might be expected, no evidence of wrong-doing. Little was made of the cabin boy's story that one man had jumped overboard, fourteen days out from Sydney:

> He appeared to be insane. He got into the Main chains with a large piece of wood in his hands ... I saw him after he got into the Water. He kept the piece of wood under his breast to keep him up—We could not lower a boat, it was blowing too hard and a heavy sea running—he was an old man I would say about 50.

The witnesses all insisted that the islanders had fully understood the agreements. 'I could not explain anything about money to them', Lancaster admitted, 'but I told them they would have muskets and gunpowder, Shirts and Trowsers and plenty to eat'. No one seemed to catch the irony of Kirsopp's subsequence statement that 'They believe anything told them by White people and their fears are easily excited'.[40]

Based on the witness of interested parties who had been reminded by Lowe's speech that slaving was a criminal offence, Plunkett's investigation could prove no wrongdoing. FitzRoy contented himself with noting that Boyd's speculation had been a financial failure, which was thus unlikely to be repeated, and the

7 *Labour Problems* 135

Colonial Office concurred: 'I cannot say that I regret the failure of Mr. Boyd's experiment... This will stop the Introduction of Savages from the South Seas'.[41]

But once raised, the questions would not go away. Disquieting rumours continued to spread about the methods used by Kirsopp to recruit his labourers. In 1847 Governor Grey of New Zealand, whose own record on native affairs was considered impeccable by the Colonial Office, reported these rumours to Whitehall and sent a copy of the report to FitzRoy in Sydney. Moreover, Wentworth's 'old ladies of Exeter Hall' also became involved. The Aborigines' Protection Society and the Anti-Slavery Association pressed the Colonial Office for an inquiry, and were able to substantiate their claims of misdeeds in the south seas with missionary letters.[42]

As a result of this pressure, a new investigation was conducted in Sydney in mid-1848, and details of a massacre during the second recruiting voyage began to emerge. Kirsopp's plan had been to use *Portenia*, the more unwieldy of the ships, as a base in which to hold those islanders already signed on, while *Velocity* sailed from island to island collecting further recruits who, from time to time, she trans-shipped to *Portenia*. This meant that the first islanders recruited remained on-board ship for a long time, during which, perhaps, they had time to question their initial decision. It also led to the close association of men from different islands, some of whom were traditional enemies. When *Velocity* arrived at the island of Rotumah, she already carried some dozens of islanders from Aneityum, Tana and Lifu. According to MacKenzie, these men were 'tampered with' by the chiefs at Rotumah, who intended to make them slaves. A number swam ashore and refused to return to the ship. Kirsopp and his crew landed and 'most imprudently' attempted to seize one of the chiefs of Rotumah as a hostage. In the subsequent skirmish, the second mate was killed, a seaman severely wounded and an unknown number of Rotumah islanders were shot.

It is a commentary on the colonial government's lack of concern that FitzRoy did not send the report on this affray to Britain until more than eight months later. In any case, Plunkett decided not to prosecute. As with so many cases of conflict in the Pacific islands, there was insufficient evidence for action under the Slavery Acts, and little else existed in the legal arsenal of the colonial government to control the actions of British subjects beyond Australasian shores. Governor Grey in New Zealand advocated the appointment of consular agents to monitor the activity of British subjects in the Pacific, and the Colonial Office sent the evidence, such as it was, to the Foreign Office in support of this recommendation.[43]

It was not legislative or diplomatic activity, however, but the experiment's financial failure which led Australian colonists to abandon the recruitment of Pacific islanders for another fifteen years. Even at the time, MacKenzie had had his doubts.

William MacKenzie was a passenger on *Velocity* whom Plunkett described as 'a gentleman of respectability and unconnected with Mr. Boyd', but this is certainly untrue. He was undoubtedly the anonymous correspondent of the *Port Phillip Gazette* who reported the voyage of *Velocity* for the newspaper. He had been given a free trip, he stated, 'my old schoolfellow, Mr. Boyd, having offered [it] as earnest of auld lang syne'. He certainly knew Archibald Boyd, who had runs in the same area, and had connections with Jardine, Matheson in Hong Kong, and he was also in debt to the Royal Bank.[44]

MacKenzie enjoyed his cruise, describing their travels around 'New Caledonia, the Isle of Pines, the New Hebrides, the Loyalty and Britannia Isles, etc.', but he was very dubious of the success of Boyd's proposition. 'It is yet a very problematical matter how far this description of labour will answer, both as to cost of its supply and qualification of the people as shepherds'. He estimated that the two ships each cost £10 per day to sail, so that 'those we have now on board cost already about 20 l. [£20] per head, a sum which will militate seriously against the cheapness'. He also doubted whether islanders could be recruited in sufficient numbers to justify the cost of the journey, an indication, perhaps, that recruitment was an uncertain process, less ruthless than outright kidnapping.

MacKenzie's doubt about recruitment costs supports the concerns of those, like Moutry and Brierly, who had to put the islanders to work. Boyd insisted that they were 'usefully and happily employed' until upset by trouble-making white men, but other reports suggest they did not easily slip into the habits of shepherds.[45] In any case, the legislative change which nullified Boyd's contracts turned his project into a financial disaster. In all his labour relations, Boyd depended heavily on enforcement of contracts under the Masters and Servants Act. Since in this case the attorney-general ruled that the contracts were invalid, Boyd's habitual reliance on legal sanctions let him down. He complained bitterly, and with some justification, that despite the lack of secrecy with which he had embarked on his scheme, the government had given no warning of its proposed legislative change, which was introduced after *Velocity* and *Portenia* sailed. If MacKenzie's estimate of the cost is accurate, Boyd must have lost several thousand pounds as a result of this three-month voyage.

Boyd's greatest loss, however, was not monetary, but the more ephemeral currency of public respect. His support for the reintroduction of convicts had won him few friends, but the importation of 'savages' made him a pariah amongst urban liberals, and embarrassed even his erstwhile associates.

A curious paradox emerged in the subsequent uproar. Boyd's importation of Melanesians, neither 'noble savages' nor ferocious cannibals but bewildered victims of their confrontation with white civilization, was cynical, ruthless and perhaps morally bankrupt. Despite Lowe's eloquence, his recruitment was not quite a slave trade, though it pointed the way towards the next generation of 'blackbirders'. But Boyd was less racist than his morally outraged accusers.

Robinson, in his defence of Boyd, insisted that 'Mr Boyd employed his servants, and chose them according to what they were worth, caring nothing whether they were Scotch, Irish, Negro, Coolie, or Chinese'.[46] He said no more than the truth. For Boyd and Robinson, the question of labour revolved around 'worth', because they saw labour in monetary terms, a variable parameter in the equation of profit and loss. Their workmen, as workmen, they saw scarcely at all. This attitude was reinforced by their lack of permanent commitment to the Australian colonies. The government and the liberals saw the islanders as a racial threat because they saw the long-term consequences of their arrival, but Boyd's singleminded concentration on the short-term left no room to consider, or be concerned by, these consequences. *All* labour was dispensable, to be hired as cheaply as possible, and discarded as economic circumstances dictated.

In the case of the islanders, their negligible wage of sixpence a week and a few clothes represented not their value, for no effort was made to assess it, but what they could be contracted for in ignorance of the state of the labour market in New South Wales. If white labour could have been hired at equally low rates of pay, there is no reason to suppose that Boyd would not have done so.

With the amendment of the Masters and Servants Act, Boyd's interest in his project ceased. Like any labour no longer bound by contract, the islanders were immediately discarded. It is impossible to know how many of these unfortunate men finally reached their homes again. Brierly buried the first of them at Twofold Bay in May, while at least two were reported to have died at the Woolshed run on the Edward River.[47] More apparently succumbed to the cold and new diseases on the Monaro stations, and yet more probably died during their winter trek of four hundred miles from the Riverina to Sydney.

At the end of October an inquest was held on the body of an unknown black man, found dead on the rocks off Fort Macquarie in Sydney. The coroner could not identify the man, but the jury suspected that he was one of Mr Boyd's savages, and recorded its criticism of his recruitment policy. Boyd denied any knowledge of the man, but added:

> I should not consider myself in any degree responsible, even if the unfortunate man alluded to had been one of the persons introduced by me, inasmuch as the wisdom of a late law, passed after they were engaged, placed them beyond my control or protection.[48]

Technically he was right. Morally most colonists disagreed. The remaining islanders remained around Sydney Harbour, begging for transport back to their islands. 'Many of them have come to Sydney', Boyd reported, '& we shall employ them in the Shipping where they are more useful than white hands'. Some took work with other employers in Sydney, and these dropped out of the record. Most of the rest finally gained passages to the islands, many on a French ship, *Arche d'Alliance*,[49] but it is doubtful whether many of them reached their own islands again, for Kirsopp had originally recruited them in small groups of fours and fives from a wide area of New Caledonia and New Hebrides.

Boyd's intention was to increase the supply of labour in New South Wales by any means, and in pursuit of that goal he had little concern for the social impact of that labour. He was, after all, only a sojourner, a point taken up by the *Australian*:

> To mere birds of passage—to the squatters of the day—men who look to Australia as but a temporary field for acquiring wealth to be lavished in Europe, it is, and no doubt will continue to be, a matter of utter indifference whether New South Wales shall rise in the social scale or grovel in [a] state of 'INTELLECTUAL BARRENNESS'.[50]

Boyd gave a personal interpretation of the events in a letter to John Sutherland:

> I mentioned in former letters that we had imported some South Sea Islanders for Shepherds they were sent to the Murray and were doing well, when the Government, aided by a few in Council passed a law (without precedent) to prevent the Master & Servants Act applying to them. This had no sooner been passed than the White laborers made the Interior most uncomfortable for them & by a well organised combination induced them to abandon their occupations, and when my Superintendents applied to the Magistrates, they were told that in consequence of the Masters & Servants Act they had no powers to interfere.
> ... The object of the Colonial Secretary was to keep the monopoly of Immigration in the hands of the Government, who are acting the part of the dog in the manger & neither import labor themselves nor allow any other person to do so. I think a personal feeling on the part of the Colonial Secretary towards me (for I am not on terms with him) had a good deal to do with the passing of this act, and as it is repugnant to the law of England I hope you will urge on Lord Grey to have it disallowed.[51]

This explanation carried little weight in England where Boyd received unfavourable publicity for his actions. With his skilled use of publicity, however, Boyd set out to manipulate this antipathy to his own ends. In his *Letter to Sir William Denison*, Boyd argued that he had been forced to recruit islanders because other forms of labour were unobtainable. Boyd's lobby in London also used a similar argument. A meeting of the Society for the Promotion of Colonization, held at Edward Lennox Boyd's home in late 1847, asked rhetorically why employers in Australia had been 'compelled to import barbarous tribes, whilst thousands and tens of thousands of their Christian brethren were starving in Great Britain and Ireland'?[52]

As in the case of land policy, Boyd sought a solution to his labour problems in Britain as well as in Australia: 'you & the other Banking Establishments', he told Sutherland, 'ought to sink all petty jealousies & mutually exert yourselves' to act as lobbyists, pressing the government to introduce labour into the Australian colonies. Otherwise, the future financial security of their investment would be at risk 'with yourselves & every similar institution connected with Australia simultaneously cooperating in forcing upon the Government an enlarged system of transportation & emigration depends the security of every penny which is invested here'.[53]

Boyd's attempts to change the pattern of labour relations were of limited success in New South Wales. In urging action on the directors of the Royal Bank, however, he touched a chord. Through the lobbying activities of his brother, Mark, and other associates, greater publicity was given to emigration to New South Wales. Eventually the lobby which formed around these associates of the Royal Bank took on a life of its own, moving beyond the immediate issues of land and labour to promote other projects such as steam communication with the colonies. For this and other reasons, it is necessary to look at events affecting the Royal Bank in the mother country.

8
The British Lobby

WHILE BENJAMIN BOYD embarked on ever wilder and more desperate schemes to reduce the costs of his enterprises in New South Wales, his associates in the Royal Bank of Australia in England were gradually being drawn towards financial calamity. The history of that trouble, viewed from the London end, is a necessary complement to the history of the Royal Bank in Australia. Boyd's extravagance both in financial and political matters was made possible by the lack of control exerted by the directors and employees of the bank in London. They failed to rein in his activities because for far too long they believed his promises, unrealistic though they now appear.

From the start, Boyd had insisted to Sutherland that the Royal Bank's activities should be discreetly managed, so that other companies would not copy his ideas. Later he feared government scrutiny. In early 1847 he wrote:

> I am particularly desirous that in any printed statement as little information as possible be given to the public, for it only gives a handle to the Government to oppose us in every way as they have already hinted that we are a combination becoming too strong for any Colonial administration.[1]

The habit of secrecy was thus entrenched. The board's tendency to resist the queries of their shareholders led it to resist self-criticism too. Besides, the financial security of the bank depended on its creditworthiness, and this could too easily be injured by

141

rumours of improbity. The first, tentative suggestions by board members that he should be replaced were successfully rebuffed by Boyd, and short of admitting their disquiet and replacing him there seemed little that the directors could do to control their over-mighty director from half-way around the world. Instead, they embarked on an ultimately disastrous course of concealing the real facts, such as they knew them, from shareholders and debenture holders alike.

The deed of settlement of the Royal Bank of Australia stated that the first annual general meeting of shareholders was to be held no later than mid-1845. Originally it had been intended that Boyd would return from the antipodes to conduct this meeting as chairman of the bank. By April 1845, however, neither Boyd himself nor any accounts had yet arrived from Sydney, and the level of anxiety began to rise: 'As we grow old time flies fast enough notwithstanding which I sincerely wish myself 6 months older to be on the other side of July', mused Wray.[2]

A letter to Sutherland finally arrived in time to be tabled at the meeting on 10 July but, while optimistic about the bank's future in the colony, Boyd spoke only in the most general terms of his investments. The inadequacy of this report was overcome, to some extent, by the presence of Samuel Browning, a Royal Bank employee who had returned from Australia the previous year. Extrapolating from Boyd's letter, Browning was able 'from his knowledge of the business in the Colonies [to supply] all that was necessary'.[3]

The directors explained to the thirty or forty shareholders present that Boyd and Robinson had decided 'to limit the transactions to the Bank to advances on collateral security of Live Stock, Produce, and other tangible property'. The profit, after expenses, was £26873 9s 8d. Liabilities included £116200, being the paid-up capital of £10 per share on 11620 shares, while assets included advances to the end of 1844 on 'sheep, cattle, horses, and stations for same, wool, Land, Horses, Wharves and discounts, &c.' of £341278 1s 4d. They recommended a dividend on shares of 5 per cent, and 5 per cent per annum continued to be paid, as it had been since October 1840, on the debentures of the bank. The shareholders, in their turn, moved thanks to Boyd and Robinson, re-elected the three directors who had, by rotation, stood down, and approved the dividend. There was, it seemed, general satisfaction.[4]

Behind this facade, however, the situation was becoming grave. Shareholders could be kept at bay, but other creditors were less easily appeased. In reality, the assets of the bank were far less accessible than the superficial statement to the general meeting had suggested. The Royal Bank held, as security, the properties of the Australian Wool Company, but the relationship between the two companies was unclear. Consignments of produce sent by Boyd and Robinson to London had been sent to Mark Boyd in his capacity as partner in the Australian Wool Company, rather than in his concurrent role as director of the Royal Bank; as a result, the bank received little in the way of remittances from the colonies. However, while Boyd and Robinson failed to send back accounts or remittances to the bank, they continued to send drafts. Boyd's personal debt to the bank finally totalled £336 295 9s 6d, with a further £79 485 5s 5d drawn to the account of the Australian Wool Company, while J. P. Robinson drew a total of £23 585 16s 10d.[5]

The Royal Bank could meet these drafts only by taking further loans from increasingly sceptical creditors. 'Our situation is now a truly painful one', Wray wrote to Robinson in March 1846,

> with liabilities for deposits due this year for £106 000—the payment of a dividend with about £15 000 p annum for Interest & for all of which we are utterly ignorant, as to how provision is to be made your letters being silent on this most important point... I much fear such measures will be adopted, as will create unpleasant feelings in all concerned; moreover I beg to prepare you for the return of our d[ra]fts unpaid, should many more appear.
>
> Trusting that this advice may be considered as a friendly warning.[6]

By now it was clear that Boyd would not be back for the next shareholders' meeting, scheduled for July 1846. 'I must candidly tell you that after having spent so long in a climate like this I do not think I could ever be a permanent resident in the mother country', he confessed to Sutherland,[7] but the pretext for his continued absence in New South Wales was the need to ensure a successful outcome of the squatting question. This gave an increased impetus to directors of the Royal Bank to maintain their pressure at the Colonial Office, since the return of the chairman of the bank seemed to depend on their success in changing government policy. The lobbying efforts of associates of the Royal Bank had already been important in bringing the squatting issue to public attention at home, and Mark Boyd and his friends worked hard to bring about changes in land policy which would increase the value of the Royal Bank's property in New South Wales. However, once brought together, the network of people with Australian interests co-ordinated by Mark Boyd to work against Gipps's 1844 regulations did not break up once this goal had been achieved. Instead the lobby turned its attention to other colonial concerns.

The areas involved were identified by Ben Boyd in his correspondence with the London directors, and reflected his preoccupations: the need for inter-continental steam communication, the inconveniences of the Navigation Acts and, above all, the need for labour for the Australian colonies. Eventually, however, the lobbying activities co-ordinated by Mark Boyd and the Hon. Francis Scott, the Parliamentary Agent for the New South Wales Legislative Council, took on a life of their own as they pressed the interests of a wider group of capitalists with investments in the Australian colonies.

The close co-ordination between Ben Boyd's activities in New South Wales and the efforts of his supporters in London is the more explicable because, during the 1840s, the world was beginning to shrink. Steam shipping had brought Bombay within four weeks of London and pressure was mounting, both in the colonies and in Britain, to extend this service further east to Singapore, China and the Australian colonies. By the end of 1845 a monthly steam service linked London and Hongkong, with a transit time of fifty-four days.[8]

While such transport relieved the tedium of inter-continental travel for the very wealthy, most passengers continued to rely on the slower, but cheaper, sailing ships. The main advantage of steam communication was that information of all kinds—commercial intelligence, personal letters and political information—could be transferred between London and her outlying ports much faster and more reliably than before. Steamships, though expensive to operate, were unaffected by the vagaries of wind and weather. Because the capital involved in establishing a line of steamships was vast, the viability of a steamship company often depended on its ability to secure a government mail contract. This conjunction of factors lies at the root of agitation to gain political patronage, which characterized the movement for steam communication during these years.

The association of the Royal Bank of Australia with the British shipping interest involved the Boyd network in another round of political activity. During the mid-1840s, Mark Boyd drew on the experience and connections he had acquired during his lobbying activities on behalf of the Australian squatting interest, and became a strong advocate of closer shipping links between Australia and Great Britain. He also had family and friends in the shipping trade. Edward Boyd senior had formerly been involved in maritime insurance, and some fragments of that network of associations seem to have survived. While it is not certain whether the Boyd family was personally involved with intercontinental steamships, their association with the St George Steam Packet Company is suggestive.

Mark Boyd's activities in Britain were supported by J. P. Robinson in New South Wales. The Robinson family had business interests on both sides of the Atlantic, and in shipping matters Robinson was always the dominant partner. As a former director of the St George Steam Packet Company, he had more experience with steam communication than any other shipowner in New South Wales. In the Legislative Council he consistently urged the need for better facilities for shipping in the colonies. Early in September 1845 he moved a humble address to be presented to Her Majesty, supporting the introduction of a mail route from Australia to Asia.[9]

The following April a meeting was called in London to propose the extension of the London to Bombay shipping route to Australia. Lieutenant Waghorn was the star attraction. Since 1827, when he had first proposed the establishment of steam communication to India by way of Egypt and Suez, Waghorn had become the leading advocate of the 'overland route' to the East. He now proposed the extension of steamships from India to Singapore, China and the Australian colonies. According to the *Colonial Gazette*, which may be responsible for the disconcerting lack of geographical knowledge, he proposed a route 'from

Singapore to a port in Java, thence to Port Essington in Batavia, thence to Wednesday Islands [Thursday Island] in Australia, and thence to Port Jackson'. Sir George Larpent, Chairman of the Peninsular and Orient Steam Navigation Company, was elected chairman, and other supporters included the Hon. Francis Scott, and a number of businessmen associated with the colonies, such as Robert Brooks, a major wool importer, and Mark Boyd.[10]

In his speech to the meeting, Mark Boyd stressed the importance of the link between English business and the Australian colonies, quoting extensively from Robinson's speeches in the Legislative Council to show the volume of business that already existed between Britain and her Australian colonies. He argued forcefully that such a communication would

> facilitate the investment of capital for the gradual development of the boundless resources of Australia and New Zealand. It would establish much greater confidence in all mercantile transactions connected with the colony... [and] lead to a large emigration of a highly respectable class of capitalists, with their wives and families, who are at present deterred undertaking the voyage from its tediousness. [He added somewhat obscurely that it] would accelerate the introduction of numerous necessary reforms in the local governments of the Australian colonies, and permit public opinion in England to exert its salutary influence on the acts of the colonial executives, and aid in preventing the colonies suffering grievous wrongs to which they are at present constantly subjected.

With suspicious precision he predicted that the new steam service would reduce the distance to fifty-six days and eight hours between London and Sydney.[11]

A 'Sub-Committee of the Association of Merchants, Bankers, Traders and others, of the city of London' was established to lobby the government on behalf of Waghorn's scheme. Further meetings were held, and on 19 October Sir George Larpent told the Colonial Office that the London merchants would support the establishment of a route through Singapore and Java if the government would furnish an annual grant of £100 000.

On 10 February 1847 Waghorn wrote to Earl Grey to support this proposal. He drew heavily on his association with the Boyds, quoting at length from Mark Boyd's speech of 17 April:

> The speaker I allude to was Mr. Mark Boyd, of the eminent firm of Boyd Brothers and Co... brother to Mr. Benjamin Boyd, Chairman of the Pastoral Association of New South Wales, member of the Legislative Council, &c.; and a gentleman who is not more esteemed for those private virtues which add lustre to his well-acquired opulence, than for the public spirit in which he so worthily exercises his great energies and intellectual accomplishments.

Browning, Sutherland and Scott also came in for their share of praise in Waghorn's account. A subsequent deputation to Earl Grey on 16 February comprised Larpent, Waghorn, and three men from the Royal Bank, Mark Boyd, John Sutherland and Samuel Browning. The meeting, however, was unsatisfactory. The government was 'anxious for Steam, but owing to the events of Ireland, [was] not likely at present to make any advance towards this important object'. Sixty-eight corporations and individuals representing the Australian interest in the London mercantile community subsequently signed a petition to the Queen on the same subject.[12]

Meanwhile the subject received close attention in New South Wales where J. P. Robinson had first raised the issue. A Select Committee of the Legislative Council was appointed in October 1846 to investigate the viability of different routes. It recommended a subsidy of £500 per month towards the cost of the proposal. A series of meetings was called in Sydney to discuss the prospects of steam communication, a committee was formed, details of the extent of trade and postal services between England and Australia were collected, and two companies, the Pacific [Peninsular] and Orient[al], and Screw-propeller Company, were approached for further information. Benjamin Boyd appears to have played no part in these activities, but Adam Bogue, one of Boyd's associates, published an open letter on the subject to Earl Grey in which he advocated the Singapore-Java route proposed by Waghorn and his associates.[13]

In London, the India and Australia Steam Packet Company was incorporated by royal charter on 20 May 1846 to raise one million pounds sterling in £20 shares. The original advocates of steam communication from the London Tavern meeting, Sir George Larpent, Lieutenant Waghorn, the Hon. Francis Scott and Mark Boyd, were amongst those who initially petitioned the Queen for a charter. They were supported by 'many of the leading mercantile men in London', particularly those with Australian connections such as Robert Brooks, John Gore and Co., Jacob Montefiore and P. W. Flower. In addition to Mark Boyd, the Royal Bank of Australia was represented by Adam Duff and Samuel Browning. Larpent subsequently became chairman, but in the later prospectus for the company no member of the Royal Bank is mentioned.[14]

At this point, however, conflict began to emerge amongst the various parties contending for government support. The 'fearful commercial crisis' during 1847 intervened, and the India and Australia Steam Packet Company was unable to begin operations as intended. During August 1848 rumours circulated in the London newspapers that the India and Peninsular Steam Company (apparently the India and Australia Steam Company) had been granted a government mail contract, and Mark Boyd, Francis Scott and Charles D. Logan, now back in England, approached the Treasury for clarification. Nothing further seems to have occurred until 27 June 1849 when, with the worst of the financial crisis over, another meeting was called to try to breathe new life into the project. Scott and Mark Boyd were both there, the latter regretting 'that this question had been unfairly and most injudiciously kept in abeyance during the last three years and a half'.[15]

It seems that the proposals of the various companies were plagued by conflict over the most appropriate route, an argument in which the Australian colonists enthusiastically joined, for the chosen route determined where the terminus of the line would be. A line through Torres Strait, favoured by Waghorn's party, would favour Sydney and offer benefits to inter-colonial shippers, such as Ben Boyd, who could then forward mail to the southern ports. A route via the Cape of Good Hope, on the other hand, would land mail at other Australian ports before reaching Sydney, whereas the first port of call for a line across the Pacific would be Auckland. Such debate may well have retarded a government decision. Perhaps, too, government subsidies were not yet sufficient to guarantee a profit on this route. After more procrastination, in 1851 a Select Committee of the House of Lords again investigated the prospects of steam communication to the colonies; but it was not until 1853, after the discovery of gold had greatly increased the passenger traffic to Australia, that P & O began a regular steam service to Australia, and a mail contract was finally negotiated with the company in 1858.[16]

Despite the keen interest he showed in the question and his long involvement with the shipping lobby, Mark Boyd insisted that 'he individually was in no way connected with the Peninsular and Oriental Company, but being extensively connected with New South Wales, he was deeply anxious to see a steam communication with those extensive colonies set on foot with all despatch'.[17] His involvement with the India and Australia Steam Packet Company also seems to have lapsed, for he was not mentioned in the prospectus of the company published in August 1847. By then the Royal Bank was facing its own financial crisis, and Mark Boyd and his colleagues apparently decided that discretion was the wiser path. However, urged on by Ben Boyd, the Royal Bank network continued to take a lively interest in public shipping policy in Britain.

The growing importance of steam communication in the 1840s coincided with a reassessment of the practicality of protection in the shipping industry. Many shipping lines were successful despite the pressure of competition. Thus although government support in such areas as mail contracts was keenly sought, many shipowners were becoming confident of their ability to survive in a free-trade empire. Government regulations associated with the operation of the Navigation Acts were viewed as interference, and resented by shipowners both in Britain and the colonies. Pressure was rising during the 1840s for an end to the Navigation Acts; Benjamin Boyd and his associates shared in this agitation.

The origin of the Navigation Acts goes back to Cromwell's day, when British shipping was threatened by competition from the Dutch. The Acts required that all cargoes between British possessions must be carried in British-registered ships, employing British crews. Trade between British and foreign ports was restricted either to British ships, or to ships of that foreign power. The impact on the Australian colonies was seen by colonial shipowners as an inconvenience and a barrier, leading to several particular problems of local concern. For instance, under the Navigation Acts, colonial trade in the Pacific could be conducted only in British or British colonial ships, but by the 1840s large numbers of American ships were trading in the islands. Australian shipowners complained that foreign ships were cheaper than the British product, thus out-competing them in the Pacific trade.

There was also a problem with the employment of non-British labour on colonial ships, forbidden under the terms of the Navigation Acts, but an extremely common practice in the Pacific islands. Boyd was only one of many shipowners who employed South Sea islanders in his whaling fleet. The annexation of New Zealand in 1840 offered a ruse for Australian ships; henceforth the term 'New Zealander' seems to have stood for all Pacific islanders, since Maoris alone amongst the islanders were British citizens.[18]

One local problem had certainly not been envisaged by the Navigation Acts. The large numbers of ships operating in the Pacific region meant that ships were sometimes wrecked in the islands or along the Australian coastline, sold in this condition, and patched up sufficiently to be employed in the local trade. But they could not be registered or insured if they did not appear in the Lloyd's Register. The only way that the colonial purchaser could recover his purchase price was to take the ship, uninsured, to Manila, where the local authorities could be bribed to provide Spanish registration, or to the Persian Gulf, where there were buyers who did not care about registration. Either option was inconvenient and risky.

Most of Boyd's ships were bought locally, and his eagerness to expand his fleet led him to buy ships of doubtful registration. On one occasion he bought a French whaler, *Bourbon*, which had been wrecked on the coast of Van Diemen's Land:

> after purchasing that vessel, [he] would have repaired her in Sydney and sent her to sea as a British whaler; but in consequence of being prevented by the Navigation Laws, and not willing to risk the sending the vessel up the Persian Gulf to Muscat or Cochin China, he turned her into a coal hulk, and she was in fact of little use, merely lying off his own town of 'Boyd', Twofold Bay.[19]

8 *The British Lobby* 151

Associated with the Navigation Acts in the minds of colonists was the Vice-Admiralty Court, which implemented the Acts, regulated the relations between shipowner and crew, and supervized safety regulations. Such apparently benign activities, coupled with the restrictions of the Navigation Acts, aroused the ire of colonial shipowners. Because of the very great capital investment that a ship represented to its owner, the court's power to delay a ship and its cargo in port while legal matters were resolved was costly, and deeply resented by the shipowners.

Agitation against the actions of the court was growing. On 28 February 1846 a meeting was held at the Royal Hotel in Sydney to consider ways of overcoming these grievances. Boyd and Co. subscribed £2. Subsequently a deputation of merchants and masters of vessels presented the governor with a petition outlining their complaints. The governor referred the matter to the Legislative Council.[20]

The following month the whaler *Margaret* returned to Sydney after a season in the whaling fields with 185 tuns of sperm oil. Like most whaling crews, the men aboard *Margaret* were bound by the articles of agreement under which they signed on for the whaling voyage, and for the subsequent voyage to London where they would each be paid a specific share, or 'lay', of the catch. However, the articles did not state the length of that contract, and by mid-1846, some of the crew were getting restless. Before the ship could leave for home, the cook deserted, found himself a sympathetic lawyer, and brought a claim of £100 against the ship for non-payment of wages. The marshall of the Vice-Admiralty Court then arrested the ship while the case proceeded. Eventually the captain agreed to pay out the cook, as well as a number of sailors who followed him, irrespective of the legality of the proceedings, as the most expeditious means of getting the ship released. *Margaret* was registered in the name of B. Boyd; her agent was Boyd's associate, Stuart A. Donaldson.[21]

Subsequently, 'Mr. B. Boyd undertook the duty of calling the attention of his London friends, not only to the particular case in question, but to the pernicious bearing of the whole of the Navigation Laws upon the maritime and trading interests of New South Wales'. On 11 July he wrote to his brother in London. News of the repeal of the corn laws had just reached Australia— good news to Boyd who, together with other colonial merchants, had already petitioned the Queen and houses of parliament to allow the import of Australian wheat and flour into England without duty.[22]

This news had wider implications. 'I am exceedingly happy to see that Sir Robert Peel has carried the corn question', he wrote; 'it is all in favour of Australian wool, and it is my opinion that in the general system of free trade which must inevitably follow, the Navigation Laws will go by the board'. Boyd then went on to complain bitterly about the current operation of 'our vexatious and partial Admiralty laws', which had led to such incidents as that involving *Margaret*, where a ship might be placed 'at the mercy of a refractory crew... abetted by designing long-shore attorneys'. This was a difficulty which foreign competitors were able to avoid.

Boyd's criticisms arrived in London at a time when the Navigation Acts were already under consideration. In January 1847 Mark sent his brother's letter to one of the chief advocates of free trade, Joseph Hume, MP, to use in any way that might advance his cause. Hume had a long-established interest in New South Wales as a former director of the Australian Agricultural Company, and he responded sympathetically. A Select Committee of the House of Commons was being set up to inquire into the Navigation Acts, and Hume invited Mark Boyd 'to find in the city some well-informed men to collect information, and... to expose the abuses and burdens of the present system'. He also advised Ben Boyd, 'and all who think like him', to organize public meetings and petitions in the colonies on behalf of the same issue.[23]

Mark Boyd responded by bringing Samuel Browning to Hume's attention. Browning had risen from a comparatively lowly position as Ben Boyd's clerk to become a trusted servant of the Royal Bank. In 1847 he was forty-five years old, and his evidence to the select committee testifies to how eventful life could be in the mid-Victorian age. He had lived, he told the committee, in France, Holland, Germany, Portugal, 'and likewise almost every part of the United States' during the 1830s, working as a merchant for some part of this time in St. Louis. Coming to New South Wales in 1841 as an employee of the Royal Bank, he had since visited, on Boyd's business, 'all the Australian colonies' including Port Essington. During 1843 he visited 'Chusan, Amoy and almost every China port; in fact, the Five Ports, the Philippine Islands... the Indian Archipelago, Java, Singapore, Hong Kong and Macao &c.'. The following year he returned to Britain.

As a result of this wide experience, Browning was able to speak with considerable authority on mercantile and maritime matters. He gave evidence over three days, from 16 to 23 March 1847, and he answered 679 questions. Moreover his performance was carefully rehearsed, for he and Mark Boyd had spent 'some hours a day, twice or thrice a week' with Hume before the committee met, developing their case.

He argued strongly, as might be expected, in favour of the freeing of restrictions on British and British colonial shipping. He spoke favorably of colonial shipbuilding: 'The copper has to be imported, and that is dear... and labour is dear; but the timber is very cheap. I think you could build a very good ship in Sydney, and rig her, for 12 l. [£12] a ton'. However, German ships bringing immigrants from Hamburg to Adelaide could not, under the present restrictions, carry copper ore from South Australia to Sydney where it was needed for shipbuilding, 'but must go elsewhere and seek a freight'. Colonial whalers, he thought, were disadvantaged in a variety of ways by competition from the Americans, who not only had cheaper ships, but could employ Pacific island labour, and augment their whaling activities by trade amongst the islands. Shipowners were further disadvantaged because they were forbidden to purchase or operate foreign ships. Browning had no doubt that if colonial shipowners were freed to compete on equal terms with American whalers, and 'permitted to procure their ships where ever they chose, they would beat the Americans out of the Pacific whale trade'.[24]

Browning's advocacy did not go undisputed. He laid great stress on the difficulties entailed in purchasing foreign wrecks, a problem which the committee rightly regarded as trivial in its impact—though not, perhaps, to the luckless purchaser, Ben Boyd. Robert Brooks, another witness to the committee, took a much more sanguine view of the operation of the Navigation Acts, as the following exchange illustrates:

1163. In the course of your Transactions have you experienced

any Injury or Inconvenience from the practical Application of the Navigation Laws?
Not the slightest in any way.
. . .
1194. Do you understand the Operation of the Navigation Laws?
No, I do not thoroughly. Very few Men do, I think.
1195. Are you aware of any Inconvenience in the Colonial Trade, arising from the Operation of the Navigation Laws?
I do not know of any whatever.
1196. Do you know of any Dissatisfaction or Complaint having been expressed till recently in the Colonies from the Navigation Laws?
I never heard of any, not even recently.[25]

Neither Browning's enthusiastic advocacy nor Brooks's laconic responses are likely to have swayed the members of the committee, for, like most such bodies, it was less interested in new arguments than in the vindication of a decision already implicit in its selection of witnesses. The trend in British government policy was strongly in the direction of free trade; Browning's evidence confirmed, but did not influence, this decision.

Why, though, did the Royal Bank party so strongly wish for an end to the Navigation Acts? From New South Wales, Boyd urged an end to government interference, and it is certain that particular incidents, such as the seizure of *Margaret* and the prodigal waste of *Bourbon*, rankled. However he was not the only shipowner who chafed at the restrictions of the Navigation Acts. 'The sooner our Navigation Laws are abrogated the better', commented Robert Towns; 'let us build and repair our ships at the cheapest market, I am not afraid of any nation'.[26]

It was in keeping with Boyd's *laissez-faire* philosophy that he saw all government interference as a hindrance in his quest for profit. He had already opposed government attempts to curtail his claims to land; he would soon be embroiled in a controversy over government opposition to his freedom to find labour in the cheapest market. Government control over British shipping, through the operations of the Navigation Acts and the Vice-Admiralty Courts, was likewise an obstacle to be overcome.

The shrillness of the argument arose from the knowledge that Boyd and Co. was not as profitable as he had hoped. Colonial whalers believed they were losing the edge to the Americans, and it was easy to blame this on government interference hamstringing British shipowners in their attempt to compete with foreigners. In fact, falling profits resulted from the fall in whale numbers in the deep-sea killing fields, a result of over-fishing for several decades.

Boyd, however, remained optimistic about the future of the colonial whaling industry. Because colonial ships were closer to the killing grounds they were away from port for a much shorter period than the three years or more necessary for a British or American ship. Hence there were fewer problems with a restless crew, and the cost of equipping the ship was far less. In early 1847 Boyd outlined his plan to Sutherland: 'If I had twenty small Brigs varying from 150 to 200 Tons... which... ought to be got for £2,500 each I would almost engage with cheap provisions supplied from Twofold Bay & one half manned by South Sea Islanders, to send home after paying all expenses including freight of Oil, £50,000 a year'.[27]

As usual, Boyd's boundless optimism seems to have been conveyed to his London friends. The *Economist* reported in late 1848 that a meeting had been held at No. 1, New Bank Buildings, to establish a new company 'to prosecute the southern whale fisheries',[28] and while the names of the participants are not mentioned, the address, only three doors from Mark Boyd's offices at No. 4, is suggestive.

In 1847 Adam Bogue reported that Boyd was about to launch a new project to harvest *bêche de mer* in northern Australia to export to markets in China.[29] Boyd still had the capacity to envisage new schemes, but with hindsight one might ask why, five years after his first arrival in New South Wales, he had gone no further than anticipating such projects? Boyd's enthusiasm was limited to the planning of such projects; their execution required persistence and patience, and he was too easily distracted from commercial activity to the possible political implications of his plans. Ironically, the great advocate of *laissez-faire*, who opposed government interference at every turn, depended on his influence with successive British governments through the lobbying activities of his brother and friends, as a shortcut to the financial success which he was too impatient to achieve by more orthodox commercial means.

The new governor, Sir Charles FitzRoy, half-brother of New Zealand's governor, Robert FitzRoy, arrived in Sydney on 2 August 1846. His ship was towed in through the heads of Sydney Harbour by *Cornubia*; in his first description of FitzRoy, it is clear that Boyd hoped the new governor would be as easily led; 'Sir Charles Fitzroy... has arrived & has been well received', he reported on 3 September, '& I hope we shall have a new order of things. he seems as far as we can judge disposed to adopt a conciliatory policy. all we now want', he added, foreshadowing the next battle for his banking friends, 'is a large immigration for the increase of our stock'.[30]

Certainly FitzRoy was disposed to be more accommodating towards the squatting interest. In the memorable phrase of J. M. Ward, he 'stood for no inconvenient principles', and the resolution of the land question early in 1846, news of which preceded him to Sydney, relieved him from much of the antagonism that had faced Gipps. FitzRoy was certainly aware of the sentiments of the London capitalists who represented the squatting and commercial interest in England. On 3 March a deputation 'of gentlemen interested in New South Wales' had met him to put their views on colonial policy before he left for Sydney. The gentlemen concerned were the four key figures of the Boyd lobby, the Hon. Francis Scott, Mark Boyd, J. W. Sutherland and Samuel Browning. Just before his departure he was presented with an address 'from persons interested in the colony', which covered those issues closest to the hearts of the squatters: land policy and emigration.[31]

It was emigration, rather than land policy, that concentrated the minds of the London lobbyists. Many of those involved in lobbying for steam communication were also the men involved in pressing the government for greater emigration to the colonies, for it had become a truism to British investors that profits in the antipodes depended on reducing the cost of labour. Besides, the emigrants would travel in their ships, and increase their profits.

Labour, its shortage in the colonies, and the consequent high wages it commanded, was a constant theme in Boyd's letters home. If only he could get labour more cheaply, he could make his wool-growing enterprises profitable. He enthusiastically supported moves in England to reintroduce transportation, and 'to empty her Prisons & Workhouses by sending the inmates of both to this country'. In 1847 he expanded on this theme:

> I cannot understand how the British Government can be so blind as to expend Millions in temporary releif [sic] in Scotland and Ireland when the same money expended in Emigration would send the paupers here where they would cease to be a burden on the Parishes & would become large consumers of your manufactures. All we want is an influx of population to set this colony ahead.[32]

Once again co-ordinated action between Boyd and Robinson in New South Wales and the Royal Bank lobby in London was used to bring the issue of labour to public attention. Boyd put the labour issue most explicitly to Sutherland in March 1848, by which time the financial difficulties of the Royal Bank were acute. Having outlined the problems they faced as a result of the economic crisis in Britain that year, he went on:

> You may very naturally ask what is to be done under such circumstances... I unhesitatingly say that with yourselves & every similar institution connected with Australia simultaneously cooperating in forcing upon the Government an enlarged system of transportation & emigration depends the security of every penny which is invested here.
> ...This is a point upon which you & the other Banking Establishments ought to sink all petty jealousies & mutually exert yourself to carry. For however little the London Boards of some of those institutions may consider they are implicated in the question of Wages, I can inform them that there is not a Bill which they hold in this colony... but in reality is dependent on this very question.[33]

Boyd was ungrateful. His constant reiteration of the board's duty to push the cause of emigration was unnecessary, for Mark Boyd and his friends were already doing their utmost to promote the cause.

On 16 December 1847 a meeting was held at the home of Edward Lennox Boyd, the next brother after Ben and Mark, with a view to the consideration of Australian interests. Forty-three men were present. The Boyd clan was represented by Mark and Edward Lennox Boyd, their cousins Archibald and his brother William Sprott Boyd of London, Archibald Boyd of New South Wales, and John Boyd, MP, a more distant cousin from Ulster. The Royal Bank was further represented by J. W. Sutherland and John Connell, the Secretary G. H. Wray, Samuel Browning, and Ben Boyd's former employee in Port Phillip, William Westgarth. Of the remaining thirty-two, some, such as the Hon. Francis Scott, Sir Thomas Mitchell and John Yates, Secretary of the India and Australia Steam Packet Company, can be closely identified with the same interest group, while some, such as Captain Chisholm and Samuel Sidney were already associated with emigration, and others, such as Jacob Montefiore, had business links with Australia. Out of this meeting was formed the Society for the Promotion of Colonization.[34]

The society's aims were broad and occasionally conflicting, for it attracted a membership too wide to have a single philosophy. It had links, for instance, with the Colonial Reformers, and Sir William Molesworth, the chairman of the select committee which ended transportation to New South Wales, became a member. To the extent that any one idea came to dominate the society, however, it was the enthusiastic espousal of private emigration, subsidized by wealthy sponsors, to the Australian colonies. While the benefits for Australia of a large immigration of workers was clearly foremost in the minds of its members, the atmosphere of financial crisis in Britain at this time allowed the society to promote emigration as a solution, too, to the problems of the mother country. In the words of one editorialist: 'with mouths wanting food in one country, and food wanting mouths in another, we must send the mouths to the food, that the one may be satisfied, and the other may be consumed'.[35]

The most indefatigable advocates of private emigration were Mark Boyd, the Hon. Francis Scott and Charles D. Logan, sometime Secretary of the Pastoral Association. Accompanied from time to time by other members, and supported by local dignitaries in each district, these three men travelled widely throughout Britain, speaking to meetings which were called to promote emigration to the colonies. The first meeting was in London in July 1848. Then they turned their attention to the provinces.

In August they addressed a meeting in Brighton, chaired by the High Constable at the Town Hall. It was already midnight when Mark Boyd got up to speak, but, despite efforts to disrupt the speeches by 'some persons who cloaked their folly and obstruction under the designation of chartism', he spoke at length, emphasizing the safety of the passage, the morality of sleeping arrangements aboard the ships, and the opportunities awaiting those who dared break their ties to a homeland which had failed to feed them:

> If you have no difficulty on the Saturday night to provide what everybody in Australia has provided for him—viz., 10 lbs. of butcher meat, 10 lbs. of flour, 2 lbs. of sugar, and a quarter of a pound of tea—if this occasions you no difficulty—if you can lay your heads on your pillows, and say to yourselves 'Well, if death overtakes me I leave my wife and children, if not in affluence, at least independent—no poorhouse staring them in the face,'—if this be your position, working men of Brighton, I shall not ask you to emigrate against your will.[36]

The pattern was to be repeated elsewhere. In September they were at Southampton, in October they were invited to Swindon by the directors of the Great Western Railway, whose workmen were being laid off. In November they went to Leeds, and in December to Birmingham and Stafford. At each town, the speeches were fine-tuned to meet the particular interests of the local populace. In Brighton, for instance, Mark Boyd emphasized that the Australian fisheries would welcome the 'honest-looking, hardy, blue-jackets' of the Sussex coast; at Swindon, addressing railway workers in the Mechanics Institute, he stressed 'matters connected with machinery, working in iron, metals, steam-engines, tool-making, etc.'.

In their eagerness to encourage labourers to emigrate, the speakers painted an excessively rosy picture of life in Australia. Mark Boyd told his Southampton audience that servants in New South Wales were paid more than £50 a year, with food, clothing and accommodation—at the same time Ben Boyd was complaining that wages had risen to £30.[37] Though Ben Boyd had admitted in his open letter to Governor Denison that he avoided recruiting men with families, Mark Boyd stressed the opportunities available in Australia to single women and families:

> in Australia a poor man found his wife and children a source of substantial profit to him... There no man's home was ever rendered wretched through want of the necessaries of life, and his wife, sons, and daughters, enlarged, instead of encroached upon, his means... In Australia... of all assistance there is none so greatly needed as that of females, in the capacity of domestics, governesses, and wives.

Such rhetoric was carefully calculated to appeal to his audience, but the experience of female emigration in the 1840s shows how far it was from the truth. Nor can Ben Boyd's sentiments have been unknown to his brother. The 'chartists' in Brighton were right to object. Behind the promises conveyed with almost revivalist fervour by Mark Boyd and Francis Scott lay a cruel deception; the first priority of the Society for the Promotion of Colonization was to keep faith with the needs of Australian capitalists, not with the English working people to whom they appealed.

Such a discrepancy between English expectations and Australian reality was, however, very common. Mark Boyd may have embroidered evidence he knew to be exaggerated, but his rhetorical flourishes were the common currency of the period. Imperial patriotism also played its part. In a year when California was offering workingmen an alternative prospect of riches beyond the dreams of avarice, it was a matter of pride to stress to British workingmen the opportunities available to them in British colonies.

It is equally difficult to distinguish between altruism and self-interest in the case of Ben Boyd's friend and fellow director of the Union Bank of London, Sir Peter Laurie. In 1846 he published a pamphlet entitled *Killing no Murder; or, the effects of separate confinement on the bodily and mental condition of Prisoners in the Government Prisons and other gaols in Great Britain and America*. In it he argued strenuously against the new system of penitentiaries which was beginning to replace the older system of punishment: transportation of convicts to the Australian colonies. Laurie opposed the new prisons as both cruel and costly;

while his argument was sound, it also coincided with moves to reintroduce transportation to New South Wales. Wray's comment on Boyd's evidence to the Select Committee on Transportation implies some such connection: 'Your evidence... may I trust be in time to prevent Lord Grey passing his Bill—your Friend Sir P. L. is highly delighted with it, & has had an interview with Lord Brougham who had applied to him for advice on this important business previous to giving his opinion in the House'.[38]

The disadvantage for the directors of the Royal Bank of Australia of this preoccupation with labour supply, even more than of the similar, earlier emphasis on land policy, was that it offered a long-term solution to an immediate problem. A company increasingly embarrassed to meet its creditors could not afford to dissipate its efforts in an area where any benefits would be indirect. Boyd believed that if the labour problem was solved, the colonial economy would recover, and his property would then increase in value irrespective of any direct benefit to himself as an employer of labour. Perhaps—but time was running out.

The first annual general meeting of the Royal Bank in 1845 passed off successfully. At the meeting in July 1846 the shareholders were given an equally favourable impression of the bank, and their dividend was increased to 6 per cent. Yet only two days later, Wray wrote to Robinson to inform him of their 'serious dilemma'. The first debentures, sold in large numbers during the euphoric months of 1841, were beginning to fall due. Debenture notes with a face value of £26 000 fell due on 1 August, another £30 000 on 16 August, another 24 000 in November, and 26 000 in February 1847. Without remittances from Australia, Wray warned, 'the result will be not only the immediate winding up of the Establishment... but we shall also be open to the severe attacks of those, who will naturally accuse us of having misled them'. Just so—and only two days earlier, too![39]

To cover their immediate crisis, the directors were forced to borrow funds. On 29 July 1846, the very day of the shareholders' meeting, the bank borrowed £25 000 for four months at 5 per cent from the United Kingdom Insurance Company, whose resident director was Edward Lennox Boyd, Ben and Mark's younger brother, and the holder of ten shares in the Royal Bank of Australia. Soon more money had to be borrowed at 6½ per cent, at 7 per cent, and eventually at 8 per cent. Constant negotiations were also required to persuade debenture holders, mainly large Scottish banks and insurance companies, to renew their notes as they reached maturity.[40]

Despite Wray's persistent jeremiads to Boyd and Robinson, warning of the impending doom faced by the bank, no remittances of any size arrived in London. Large amounts of produce had, in fact, been sent from Sydney during 1843, 1844 and 1845, but they were sent to Boyd Bros. and Co., and the proceeds never reached the Royal Bank.[41]

The expenses of Boyd's enterprises, however, had to be met by the bank. During 1845, Ben Boyd drew advances amounting to £44027 on the Royal Bank to meet the costs of wool-growing and shipping, and his private expenses. Next year, perhaps in response to the urgings of the London management, his advances dropped to £14765 in the first half-year, and £7398 in the second. Robinson, on the other hand, continued to spend. Between 31 December 1846 and 7 July 1847, for instance, drafts in his name, payable on the Royal Bank in London, totalled £27850.[42] Their different pattern of borrowing probably reflects the different roles the partners played in the operation. Boyd was the instigator of new ideas, and by 1846 he had begun to be more cautious about expanding his establishment. Robinson, on the other hand, was responsible for the day-to-day running of the business, and these recurrent costs, met by drafts on the Royal Bank, were less easily reduced.

On 14 October 1846 the board of directors finally acted, writing to Boyd and Robinson to order a full accounting of the assets of the Royal Bank in Australia, a list of its employees, and its annual expenses. Further, they asked them to explain 'what Interest we have in the Township of Boyd, & of the Vessels employed, & also to what extent we are concerned in the Australian Wool Company', evidence enough of just how little control the London directors had exerted over Boyd and Robinson's activities to this time. They also instructed Boyd and Robinson to begin divesting the bank of its stock and stations.[43]

Even now, however, the power which Boyd, by sheer personality, had exerted over his associates was evident. In an accompanying letter to Boyd, Wray bewailed the pain that he had suffered because he was obliged to remonstrate with him, though 'in truth you must allow that we have not complained without reason'. As an employee of the bank, he had no choice but to write 'in terms not the most courteous', and 'to this cause I attribute my *never* receiving a reply from Mr. Robinson, but for your silence I know your objection to letter writing'. Such an abject apology was apparently treated with the contempt it deserved, for Boyd continued to ignore Wray's appeals.[44]

Little change occurred as a result of the board's ultimatum. Robinson's drafts continued throughout 1847, though by September, those for salaries were written in the names of the bank's employees rather than in his own name. This precaution ensured that, if the bank would or could not meet the drafts, the employees rather than Robinson would suffer.[45]

Boyd remained adamant that the property he had accumulated should not be sold. By 'the latter end of 1851', he promised Sutherland, sufficient funds would be remitted to 'pay off every Deposit Note which has been issued'. However he refused to touch even the increase of his flocks until 1848: 'were I to value every weaned Lamb & other young Stock at the prices in the Market I could swell up an income perhaps the most extraordinary which had ever been exhibited', but he would not sell, 'For if the least idea got abroad that I wished to realize it would have the immediate effect of knocking down the price of Stock... In fact it would create a perfect panic in the Stock market'. Soon, he promised, he would begin to send money at the rate of £40 000 per annum, but in the meantime—nothing.[46]

The effect of this classic psychological strategy of alternate promises and postponement was to intensify the frustrations of the directors. At the same time, paradoxically, it reassured them that the assets of the bank were such as to justify their borrowing further against the profits which, though temporarily unavailable, would eventually begin to flow.

During 1847, however, this illusion was wearing thin. The year began badly, with a famine winter in Ireland. Credit tightened, as the trade cycle bottomed out, and interest rates rose. This made the Royal Bank's task of borrowing money more difficult, and debenture holders were unenthusiastic about rolling over their paper on the promise of 5 per cent dividends, particularly as the company's credit was growing ever more suspect.

A trickle of remittances arrived from Sydney, in the form of wool, tallow and oil, but wool prices were low, and the proceeds were offset by the steadier flow of drafts on the bank. Other produce was sold by Boyd in Sydney; the proceeds were ploughed straight back into his enterprises, not transferred to the board in Britain.

On 11 August 1847 the third annual general meeting of shareholders was held. Sutherland opened the meeting by describing the very satisfactory settlement of the land question, and stressing the need for a large supply of labour, and for steam communication. Profit, however, had fallen, he told the shareholders, because of the high price of labour and falling interest rates in the colonies. According to the minutes, the meeting passed without incident, thanks were expressed to the board members, and all the directors, including Ben Boyd, who by rotation stood down, were re-elected. The actual scene, as described by Wray, was very different, with 'all the Directors... suffering much mental anxiety... which is visibly telling on some of them in undermining their health'.[47]

The bank was, by now, kept afloat only by its close alliances with other organizations: the Union Bank of London, in which Sir Peter Laurie and Ben Boyd were directors; the United Kingdom Insurance Company, with Edward Lennox Boyd as Resident Director; the North British Insurance Company, of which Ben and Mark Boyd were resident directors. These firms were so closely linked, as creditors, to the Royal Bank of Australia, that their boards hesitated to deliver the *coup de grâce* which would inevitably topple their ailing associate. The kinship network had first determined that the Royal Bank would borrow money from particular institutions, but there were financial, as well as personal, reasons why this weakest link should now be sustained.

Nonetheless something had to be done. When further drafts, amounting to £4600, arrived in October 1847, Wray told Boyd that they 'indicate on your part a determination to bring us down and in which I am fearful you have succeeded'. On 1 November the board announced a call of £5 per share. Times were hard, and they had little expectation that many shareholders would respond, but they were pressed to make the call by their creditors. A conflict between the large institutional creditors, who held debentures in the bank, and shareholders, mostly small investors who as proprietors in the company were liable for its debts, had begun to emerge. Under pressure from the institutional creditors, the board also agreed to send William Sprott Boyd to New South Wales to wind up, 'quietly', the affairs of the Royal Bank.[48]

9
Retrenchment

WILLIAM SPROTT BOYD arrived in Sydney to take over control of the Royal Bank's activities in Australia on 13 March 1848, only to find his cousin markedly changed by his years in New South Wales. The ebullient, charismatic figure who had arrived in a blaze of publicity had become, within six years, an unpopular figure not only to the working class he had exploited, but also amongst his own peers. Given his labour policies, Boyd's unpopularity with the working class is understandable; the growing antipathy towards him from his own class is a more problematic matter.

Boyd's prestige in New South Wales reached its peak by mid-1844. He was an acknowledged power-broker, as chairman of the Pastoral Association and through his superior contacts in Britain. Throughout 1844, Boyd identified himself closely with the squatting interest; as the popularity of the squatters waned in subsequent years, so Boyd's popularity faded too.

One indication of dwindling support for the Boyds came with the return of Archibald Boyd to Australia in December 1844. The *Atlas* worked hard to promote a sense of obligation towards Archibald Boyd amongst squatters, and public meetings were held around the colony to 'express...thanks...for his patriotic, energetic, and able exertions with the Colonial Minister during his recent visit to England to establish a Fixity of Tenure, &c'.[1] But the meetings were, in fact, indifferently attended, and held only in near-Sydney areas rather than in the unsettled districts.

9 Retrenchment 167

Late in 1845 a by-election was held for the Legislative Council seat of Port Phillip. Archibald Boyd stood, but he was defeated by Captain Maurice O'Connell. It was, noted Gipps with pleasure and relief, 'a result wholly unexpected, and the more important, because it was accompanied by a pretty intelligible demonstration on the part of the people of Port Phillip, that they would no longer support the Council in their extreme measures of opposition to Her Majesty's Government'.[2]

In mid-1846 the changes in land policy were announced by the British government. These changes re-established Boyd's credibility as a power-broker, for it was widely believed in the colony that it was the Boyd interest which was responsible for negotiating the new order—a belief carefully nurtured by sympathetic newspaper reports, notably in the *Atlas*, of the Royal Bank lobby at work. By then, however, the squatting interest was no longer, if it had ever been, a single united front. Factions developed over two issues: the price of land; and the advisability of importing cheap labour, whether convict, coloured or indentured. Boyd's position on these two issues placed him at odds with many of his erstwhile associates. As Boyd's apparently constitutional stand against Gipps became revealed for what it was, he found himself at odds with more principled opponents of the governor's regulations. In September 1846 Robert Lowe moved that the Council declare its support for a minimum price for Crown Land. In doing so, he precipitated a clash with the cormorant squatters. His move brought into the open the self-interest of the squatters, for if the price of land was lowered, men holding licences to Crown Land could expect to see their runs gradually sold off for freehold. Robinson declared that a lower price would mean 'utter ruin for every squatter in the colony', but Lowe gained support from the more moderate members to win his motion, ten votes to eight.[3]

Robinson and Lowe had worked closely together on a number of issues, including support for a national system of education, where Robinson's Quaker principles and Lowe's antipathy to an established church found common cause. Robinson retained a healthy respect for Lowe's capacities; 'by the bye [he] is a dangerous man to correspond with', he warned Sam Browning in 1847, 'as he is sure to publish any letters he may receive but he is a person it is just as well to keep in with'.[4] But this was not always possible, and on the issue of the price of land the demarcation was clear. Robert Lowe's growing hostility to Boyd was reflected in the pages of the *Atlas*; the paper continued to berate him even after Lowe ceased to write for the journal.

As always, the land question had constitutional implications, and as the colonists grew more experienced in political affairs, constitutional issues began to assume more importance in the public debate. Like others of his class, Boyd feared the growth of a democratic spirit. He saw the squatters as a bulwark against such a development, the natural leaders of society with whom the government must eventually form an alliance, by harnessing their anarchic energies:

> their habits... of unrestricted freedom... defending themselves not only from the incursions of the Blacks but the encroachments of their neighbours... almost always armed ... if misgovernment were once to induce them to get committed the Mother Country would find that no amount of troops that she could afford to send would ever restore good feeling... under proper Government would not only themselves remain attached to the Institutions of home but would lay the foundation of Monarchical Institutions which might last for centuries—on the other hand goad them a little further and the seeds of a Republic are sown at once.[5]

These sentiments were not unusual. They formed part of the common stock of rhetoric by which the colonists hoped to assert themselves against a doctrinaire British position. Yet the squatters failed to fulfil that role of natural leaders that Boyd claimed for them. They seemed to other colonists to lack the civic virtues, they were too interested in increasing their own wealth without concern for the social costs of their labour and land policies. Boyd, the arch-squatter, represented all that was worst in 'the haughty, gentlemanly, selfish class'.[6]

The anti-transportation movement became the occasion for the emergence of an articulate urban middle class. In the absence of a more socially responsible leadership within the propertied classes, Lowe and Cowper, both elitist in their sympathies by birth and education, eventually shifted their allegiances to claim the leadership of the urban radicals. Their objectives were liberal, moderate and respectable. Boyd's reputation as a 'cormorant'

9 Retrenchment

squatter, as a harsh employer, and as an advocate of all forms of cheap labour had made him a bogey in the eyes of the immigrant working class. Even employers questioned the wisdom of his labour policy when it began to threaten the racial and social composition of society. So unpopular was he that Cowper and Lowe were able to gain political advantage from their public opposition to Boyd within the anti-transportation movement.

By 1847 Boyd's ability to sway public opinion was declining. The end of the depression gave him less leverage over those who might once have been in his debt, while, ironically, better economic conditions failed to arrest his own financial decline. His capacity to influence events had been based on two advantages over other colonists, both of which were failing him. The first was his access to seemingly unlimited funds; the second the strong backing he received from his London network.

By the end of 1847 his funds were seriously depleted. He did not respond conscientiously to the London board's pleas for retrenchment, but some effort was made, and his personal drafts on the bank fell during 1846 and 1847. With fewer funds for patronage and display, Boyd was seriously restricted in his customary forms of influence, though he still managed, in a variety of ways, to continue his habit of gaudy display. He subscribed money to the Homebush Races and raced his own horses there. He donated a set of bells to the Presbyterian Church, and spent £100 buying fossils collected from the Condamine River, to send to England. He became a member of the Society for the Promotion of the Fine Arts in Australia (subscription one guinea), and appeared at all the fancy dress balls in his highland costume. And he still sailed and entertained stylishly aboard *Wanderer*.[7]

Perhaps Boyd's reputation for lavish patronage, particularly of the gentlemanly sports, continued to work for him, for he seems to have been on reasonable terms with the new governor. Unlike the workaholic Gipps, Sir Charles FitzRoy and his sons were sportsmen who took an exhuberant view of life more compatible with Boyd's own style. A common interest in horse-racing seems to have given Ben and his brother Curwen some influence with the FitzRoys.

But this display was increasingly threadbare, and behind it lay the prospect of ruin. Boyd's letters to Sutherland during 1846 and 1847 continued to exhibit unremitting optimism, but panic may have been one cause of Boyd's increasingly desperate gambles, and hazardous schemes could backfire. The costs of his importation of kanaka labour in particular, in lost reputation and public disapproval, far exceeded any benefits he might hope to gain.

The second source of Boyd's power was the steady support of his London lobby. As the previous chapter shows, his network continued to work on his behalf throughout his remaining years in New South Wales, pressing for changes in land policy, recruiting labour, urging the advantages of steam communication. However, as the activities of Mark Boyd, the Hon. Francis Scott and their associates gradually moved into more general areas of colonial policy making—especially with the formation of the Colonization Society—the direct link between Ben Boyd in Australia and his friends and relations in England was broken, at least in the public perception. As their lobbying activities took on a life of their own, Boyd himself became increasingly irrelevant to the activities of his London associates.

Boyd's position in colonial society was thus already under siege when, on 13 March 1848, William Sprott Boyd arrived, armed with a power-of-attorney to take over from Ben as manager of the Royal Bank of Australia in the Australian colonies.

William Sprott Boyd was Benjamin Boyd's cousin. After some years in Canton and Macao working for Jardine, Matheson and Co., he returned to Britain in the early 1840s 'on the look out for some safe employment of my time'. At one stage, he seems to have contemplated a parliamentary career but this came to nothing. Instead he invested his savings in a variety of speculations in the China trade. He also bought shares in the Royal Bank of Australia, and sent £5000 to Ben Boyd to invest in New South Wales.[8]

In November 1847 the directors of the Royal Bank of Australia appointed him to replace Ben Boyd as manager of the bank in New South Wales for two years at an annual salary of £1000. His appointment was a rare stroke of genius by the bank's directors.

9 Retrenchment

Boyd had so far resisted direction from London by arguing that he would respond only to someone of equal rank—an effective bluff, since none of the directors had the least desire to visit Australia. In chosing Boyd's cousin, this bluff was called.[9]

However W. S. Boyd was a large shareholder in the Royal Bank, and this coloured his decision to accept the appointment. 'The mismanagement of some matters in New South Wales in which I am interested', he told a friend, 'has induced me to take a run to that country'. He later confirmed that he had agreed to the appointment only because of his personal interest in retrieving the moneys he had invested through Boyd and the Royal Bank in New South Wales. He left a power-of-attorney with his brother Archibald, a lawyer who also worked as an agent for Jardine, Matheson and Co. in Leith and London. His intention was to stay in Sydney for at least two years; he brought his wife and children with him, and even asked a friend in Hongkong to find and send him a good Chinese cook! 'I like this colony very well—at least what I have seen of it', he wrote within a week of his arrival, 'and I daresay I shall be able to make it out for a year or two'. He was known, 'from his wealth & snow white hair in China... by the Sobriquet of the Silver Lion'.[10]

W. S. Boyd's instructions were to retrench, gradually selling off the assets of the bank so that its mounting debts in Britain could finally be paid. Now at least the directors would receive regular information from Sydney. W. S. Boyd's previous experience as an agent in a mercantile firm extending widely through east Asia meant that he knew the importance of regular correspondence. Unlike Ben Boyd, he had acquired the habit of writing letters. On the other hand, his first reports from Australia on the Royal Bank's investments differed only in their frequency from those of his cousin.

W. S. Boyd arrived to find Ben ill in bed, suffering from 'a very serious attack of inflamation of the lungs', perhaps a bad cold, possibly pneumonia. It is tempting to suspect that he was malingering, for his meeting with his cousin must have been an awkward one. Pneumonia in pre-antibiotic days was a killer, and Robinson's death later the same year from scarlet fever should warn us not to underestimate the hazards of even minor illnesses—but the reason he gave for his illness, 'brought on by too great attention to business, when suffering from cold, and by anxiety of mind', seems unlikely.[11]

The meeting between the cousins was surprisingly amicable. Ben admitted that his reports had not been 'so complete' as they might have been, but explained that he feared that 'such information being published in England might have been used to the prejudice of his endeavours to obtain leases' of his squatting runs. He insisted that his activities had been sanctioned by the directors, and that his plans were based on the assumption that the bank's capital would not be called up before 1852. Since most of this capital was in the form of debentures, sold between 1840 and 1843 at five years maturity, this assumption was wildly unrealistic. But W. S. Boyd made no comment, accepting instead Ben's own reason for the failure of his enterprises, the high price of labour: 'The labourers become in fact the masters and dictate not only the pay they are to receive, but the work they are to do'.

Nor was he more than mildly critical of Ben's direction of the bank's activities, though 'You will no doubt be as surprised as I was to find that there are no mortgages of any kind', except large loans to Boyd and Robinson themselves, to Boyd's cousins Archibald and Wilson Maitland Boyd, and smaller amounts to three other men.[12] He was also surprised that there was little stock on the runs. Because he could not afford to pay for good superintendents at the present high rate of wages, Ben explained, the increase of the flocks had been lost. Whaling was declining in profitability, and there seemed little prospect of selling *Juno*.

The inconsistencies in W. S. Boyd's report become more evident when set beside Boyd's enclosed report. This consisted of a reiteration of many of his arguments in justification of his original decision to eschew legitimate banking business in favour of the colony's 'only real wealth... its pastoral resources' and whaling. Predictably he blamed his failures on the high cost of labour, but he insisted that by 1852, 'every engagement of the Royal Bank will be finally paid off by the annual revenue alone'— but, he added, labour must drop to £15 per annum. His promises were supported with a detailed breakdown, for the next four years, of the income to be expected from his enterprises.[13]

His estimates were dubious. They assumed stable high prices for wool, sheep, cattle and whale oil; an annual increase in the wool clip of 15 per cent; a rise in the price of sheep for boiling down purposes from 5s to 6s during 1849; no decline in the whale catch; and a steady £5000 a year income from *Juno*. He estimated the income from Boydtown at £1000 in 1848 and subsequent years, and even this, it soon became clear, was optimistic. Few of these assumptions were valid, for Boyd could only guess at the prices of labour and produce in the next few years. He assumed that the stock from which this income derived would continue to increase. By 1852, despite the boiling down of sheep and cattle and a growing export of horses, his stock would, he promised, amount to half a million sheep, 55 000 cattle and 2200 horses. Yet in 1848, drought had affected both fertility rates and the fat content (for tallow) of his livestock, and his southern stations were suffering from scab. Whaling was risky at best, and whale numbers were widely admitted to be falling. The *Juno*, which Boyd claimed earned £5000 per year, was in fact chartered only on a short contract, and W. S. Boyd soon discovered that she was operating without insurance cover.

The bank's most valuable asset was land. Boyd estimated that his squatting land amounted to three million acres, and would increase in value, 'having now got it secured by Crown leases. The bulk of it for grazing purposes is as secure as if it was held in fee simple'. The size of this property, however, carried its own problems for, as Boyd had pointed out on previous occasions, his possessions formed such a substantial portion of the land and livestock of New South Wales that, if they were all put up for sale together, they would inevitably lead to the collapse of local prices. Ben Boyd warned, and W. S. Boyd agreed, that 'the only effect of such an attempt will be to knock down the value of all Stock in the Colony without being able to realize anything'.

In fact the arrival of W. S. Boyd in New South Wales had already weakened Boyd's credit in the colony. The rumours of possible collapse spread widely, and resulted in the equivalent of a 'run' on the bank. Boyd, like other employers in country districts, paid his workforce not in cash but with tokens. These tokens usually remained in circulation for several months but, in a few days at the beginning of July 1848, as the rumours of impending bankruptcy spread, about £3000 in tokens were presented for payment.[14]

Despite the promise of future riches, in the present reality the Boyd cousins needed to borrow money immediately to keep the operation afloat. Even before W. S. Boyd's arrival, Ben had begun to borrow money locally to cover his immediate expenses. One of his whalers, *William*, was mortgaged for £3000, while another £5000 had been borrowed from Captain George C. Forbes on the security of *Portenia* and *Velocity* against an expected profit from the sale of livestock in New Zealand.[15]

Meanwhile, the most recent drafts on the Royal Bank by Boyd and Robinson were refused in London and returned to New South Wales, further publicizing their predicament. The directors' message was inescapable. W. S. Boyd could expect no help from home; on the contrary, he must make the colonial properties pay their way, *and* remit money to meet the bank's commitments in Britain, or the whole financial pack of cards from which the enterprise was built would collapse.

Retrenchment began, though not on the scale intended by the bank's directors. Although W. S. Boyd decided not to put the bank's property up for sale, he tried to reduce the costs of the enterprise. The agencies in Van Diemen's Land, Melbourne and Adelaide were closed, the lease on Boyd's business premises at Church Hill was not renewed, and some of the salaried employees were retrenched.[16]

W. S. Boyd was faced with two problems. The immediate one was the need to find money to keep the establishment running. 'Till the Wool Crop comes in I cannot see my way towards making any remittance at all', he admitted to the directors:

> money cannot be drawn by any means from hence to meet your engagements of 1847 and 1848 nor even a quarter of them...
> Mr. Boyd has not the means of carrying on from day to day without borrowing from his neighbours; and all his property if now brought to the hammer would not fetch £100,000... If you cannot persuade the Union Bank and the other creditors to wait, there is no haven for our Ship—we must be wrecked.

Nonetheless, despite this calamitous assessment, W. S. Boyd

insisted: 'I do not blame Mr. Boyd, he has been beaten by circumstances and I fear has worn himself out in the strife'. He allowed himself to be persuaded by Boyd that it was wiser to wait until the rise in prices that his cousin, Micawber-like, promised would come.[17]

Any serious reorganization, however, also depended on arranging some compromise with Ben Boyd, for it seems from his letters that W. S. Boyd was being threatened with litigation if he asserted his control over the property, and was unsure of his legal position. 'I am fully persuaded the Deed of Settlement does not authorize my holding the property for the Bank unless Mr. Boyd & Mr. Robinson be declared Bankrupt by legal process', he told the directors, although in fact the deed of settlement stated no such thing. The real difficulty lay in determining where ownership lay, for Boyd's estimated three million acres were licensed in the names of individuals, not in the name of the bank. W. S. Boyd therefore had to move circumspectly if he was to reclaim the legal title to this property for the shareholders of the Royal Bank. There was also the threat that Boyd could declare himself bankrupt, in which case the Royal Bank would lose the £100 000 it had lent Boyd in the name of the Australian Wool Company, and have to fight with other creditors for a share of the property registered in Boyd's name. Moreover, since the bank was not a chartered company, it had no corporate standing, therefore 'no one [would] lend sixpence to [it] because... no action could be raised against it without citing each Shareholder'.[18]

W. S. Boyd's solution was tendencious, but perhaps it was the best he could do, not only in his own interest, but in the interests of the shareholders as well. He arranged for the transfer of 'the whole property' of the bank to his own name, and in early July he announced that his lawyer had begun work on the division. It was not an easy or, one imagines, a pleasant task, for the problem lay in determining what property belonged to the bank, and what to Boyd personally or through other companies or partnerships. Boyd insisted, for instance, that the whalers were his own, while other property such as *Terror*, and Boydtown itself, were mortgaged, and the money credited to him.

These tangled claims were still being teased apart by lawyers when, on 13 August, J. P. Robinson died. He was only thirty-three, and his death from scarlet fever, normally considered a disease of childhood, was a profound shock to those around him. 'Quaker Robinson of the Royal Bank ... closed his accounts with this World, and retired to his narrow freehold in the Burying Ground'.[19] It was a sad end to all his ambitions. Robinson had been the backbone of the Royal Bank, handling the daily business with an efficiency never matched by his partner. He was also a quiet but effective politician. He chaired several select committees where he showed his administrative skills, though he lacked the flair or oratory of more powerful personalities such as Wentworth or Lowe. At times, his position on the land question sat oddly with the social issues he espoused, and upon which his Quaker principles were firm: a broad-based secular education system, the abolition of capital punishment, the end of the military establishment. He was an important figure in the political and financial life of New South Wales, yet he remained almost unknown beyond his public image.

His death placed W. S. Boyd's careful negotiations at risk, for his properties—squatting stations at Shannon Vale and Yarrowich in the New England District, Canal Creek in the Darling Downs, and Laidley Plains and Beaudesert in Moreton Bay—had not yet been transferred to the bank at the time of his death. W. S. Boyd apologized to the directors for his remissness. He explained that he had obtained a power-of-attorney from Robinson, enabling him to sell some of the property immediately, and his solicitor had been in the process of preparing a mortgage on the remainder when Robinson was taken ill. Robinson 'was not then in a fit state to sign it', for he became ill on the eighth, 'continued delirious till the fever had completely subdued his strength on the 12th Inst' and died the next evening.

But W. S. Boyd failed to inform the directors that, on 20 June, he had transferred Robinson's properties to his own name. Aware by now that the bank was close to bankruptcy, he had decided to ensure that he was not personally hurt by the impending collapse.[20]

The price of silence in this unsavoury little affair seems to have been collusion with his cousin, for in the same letter that announced the death of J. P. Robinson, W. S. Boyd also announced that he had struck a deal with Ben Boyd. The deal was considerably more generous than the division of property he had proposed some weeks earlier. That scheme had been abandoned, 'for many reasons which it is unnecessary to enumerate'. Instead, W. S. Boyd now agreed to take Ben's property in return for giving him a discharge from all claims of the bank except for the calls on shares. The bank thus got title to the squatting runs, together with their stock of cattle, sheep and horses; the land at Eden and Boydtown with its buildings; Boyd's land in Sydney at Kissing Point and on the Parramatta Road; and the ships *Terror, Rebecca* and *Portenia*, as well as the steamers *Juno* and *Sea Horse*.[21]

Ben Boyd retained considerable assets: the whalers *Fame, Margaret, Lucy Ann, Juno* and *Edward*; approximately 800 acres of land in the county of Auckland; everything relating to his whaling activities both at Boydtown and at Duke's Wharf, Sydney; and his personal effects, amongst which he included the yacht *Wanderer*. W. S. Boyd estimated the total value of these assets at £4000—a low estimate, for six months later Boyd sold the whalers alone for £5000.

Somehow Ben Boyd had managed, by fraud or collusion or sheer good luck, to retain those portions of his business which he believed to be most capable of generating an income. Five whalers, the whaling boats and other equipment at Boydtown, 'the stores and slops at Duke's Wharf appertaining to the Ships & Whalers'—together these could form the nucleus of a successful whaling enterprise, and Boyd still had faith in the future of the whaling industry.

Much of the property that went to the bank, on the other hand, was heavily encumbered. Part of Boyd's land in Sydney was mortgaged for £2000 to Samuel Lyons. Boydtown was mortgaged to George C. Forbes. Boyd had tacitly acknowledged that the town was a failure when he estimated its income at a mere £1000 per annum. Stripped of its whaling facilities, it was a liability, as were *Juno* and *Sea Horse*.

W. S. Boyd was also confronted with evidence of Ben's incompetence in little things. Boyd had not supplied his stores in recent months, 'owing he says to much having been stolen and the impossibility of getting honest people to look after them'. His experiment in breeding horses had not prospered. After importing six stallions at considerable expense, Boyd had not paid attention thereafter: 'No care appears to have been taken to preserve the breed, the mares running with the Young Horses & so degenerated till all the young stock are small & of little value'. The sheep were dying of catarrh on the Monaro stations, and because of the drought the cattle had wandered off into the mountains in search of food.[22]

And so on. There is little advantage in cataloguing, item by item, the evidence of Boyd's failures. By the end of August, W. S. Boyd was already lamenting that 'In the whole field of Mr. Boyd's operations there is not one bright spot nothing that has or is paying a profit, so you may imagine what a sickening business it is to take charge of'. By October he was outlining bitterly the 'fallacy of Mr. Boyd's letter of 20th April' in its optimistic expectations.[23]

Potentially the most important assets to come to the bank were Boyd's squatting runs, but only a few properties, such as the horse stud at Capertee, on the headwaters of the Hawkesbury River, had as yet been transferred to leasehold under the new provisions of the Waste Lands Act. W. S. Boyd now set in train the legal processes which would convert the others. Although it was now too late for Ben Boyd, the security of tenure for which he had campaigned would ultimately increase the value of these runs, but in the short term there were problems either in selling the land or in generating an income from it. The properties were unmanageably large and unsurveyed, and they were difficult to sell. 'I now find there will be much difficulty in getting even a fair price as things go for the Murray Station', reported W. S. Boyd. 'They are too large for the generality of purchaser & Government will not sanction a division of the runs which will therefore be sold at a great disadvantage, probably at a half what could be got if the Station could be divided'.[24]

The uncertain nature of squatting property meanwhile caused problems. Boyd controlled many river frontages, and in a year of drought other squatters from the back blocks drove their flocks through in search of water. Such action was theoretically trespass, but during 1847 Boyd discovered that juries were unsympathetic—when he brought a suit of trespass against a neighbour, and demanded £1000 damages for infecting his sheep with scab.

The jury found in Boyd's favour on the second charge, but noted that the boundaries were unclear, and awarded him only one farthing, without costs. 'Disputes respecting boundaries are interminable', complained W. S. Boyd.[25]

Gossipy Sydney society gloated over the fall of one of its tallest poppies:

> The Establishment in Church Hill has gone to the Dogs... a large shareholder Sprott Boyd... sailed into the Harbour one Sunny Morning with the powers from the 'Royal Bank Directors' to 'look up' Big Ben—which he did most rigorously and unscrupulously—he displaced 'The Ben'—The Quaker Robinson died under the Harrow—& Benjamin Boyd, who is really a good hearted Man as I know him in private was hurled from his pinnacle by his Cousin Sprott the Silver Lion.[26]

Such amused condescension amongst his own class was a widespread response to Boyd's woes, an indication of how little he had been accepted or befriended by his peers. The 1848 election for the Legislative Council became the occasion for a considerable display of hostility against the Boyd faction, now so divided against itself that it could offer little defence.

Boyd's erstwhile associates, Lowe and Cowper, took a high profile as anti-transportation candidates. Cowper stood for Cumberland, by now an outer metropolitan seat which was strongly influenced by the convict debate. On the hustings at Parramatta, Cowper charged Boyd with uttering a *'wilful untruth'*. Boyd demanded an apology. Cowper consented to withdraw only the word 'wilful', insisting that Boyd 'had *uttered what was untrue*'. Precisely what Boyd was accused of is unclear, for no newspaper was prepared to face Boyd's wrath by repeating anything but the most veiled innuendo.[27] As a result of this insult, Boyd travelled out to Parramatta to demand satisfaction of Cowper, but 'Slippery Charlie' wisely declined to fight—though the *Atlas* noted that the odds favoured him, since he would have had a target twice his own size. Boyd was left to suffer the humiliation of public disdain.

Duelling had a long history in the Australian colonies, but by 1848 society was unsympathetic. The aristocratic conceit of the 'affair of honour' was anachronistic in a community already toying with ideas of democracy. The *Atlas*, after a careful consideration of the questions of honour involved on both sides, concluded that 'a *leaden bullet* is equally appropriate as a *souvenir* for the *leaden head* of a man of honor'.[28]

The election was equally unpropitious for other members of the Boyd clan. Archibald Boyd was defeated in his attempt to win the northern seat of Gloucester, Macquarie and Stanley, while W. S. Boyd toyed with the idea of standing for the Legislative Council for the electorate of Port Phillip, but ran into opposition from the separationists who resented their continued representation by carpetbaggers from the north. The local squatter and politician Edward Curr rallied opposition to the Boyds:

> We are on the eve of a general election. Our candidates will be Robinson, Mr. Sprott Boyd, Foster—and who else? ... I have serious thoughts of proposing *my Horse*. You remember him at the public meetings, and he certainly has many qualifications for the office, and is well known as his master and much more popular.[29]

In the event, to Curr's outrage the contenders included W. S. Boyd, Archibald Boyd, J. P. Robinson, and Adam Bogue, Boyd's former overseer and a shipping associate. In his opinion such a combination threatened to make Port Phillip a 'borough for the Boyds':

> William Sprott Boyd, Archibald Boyd, Robinson *Boyd*, and Adam Bogue *Boyd*. How well those names would have read following each other invariably upon the same side of the question! ... In taking the sense of the House, *Sprott Boyd* and his tail would always have counted four votes.[30]

The returning officer formally called for nominations for the Port Phillip electorate at the Melbourne Courthouse on 28 July. The separationists, under the leadership of Curr and John Fawkner, were present in strength; the Boyds were far away. The separationists prevented *any* candidates from coming forward, and at the end of an hour the returning officer was left with one nominated candidate—Earl Grey, the Secretary of State for the Colonies, who was duly elected member for Port Phillip in the New South Wales Legislative Council.

The Boyd faction had been overtaken by events. The political debate was now too complex for any family to attempt to create a rotten borough. Curr and Fawkner were making a point: if Port Phillip could not be represented by a local figure, it might as well be in the hands of someone ten thousand miles away. But, once more, the widespread hostility towards the Boyds was a useful lever with which to mobilize public opinion.

Earl Grey was not obliged to take his seat in Sydney. New writs were issued for the election, and the return of nominations was moved from tumultuous Melbourne to placid Geelong. But the Boyds avoided further humiliation and did not nominate. Perhaps it was chagrin, perhaps genuine cynicism which later caused W. S. Boyd to explain to the directors that his reason for seeking election had been to save money by franking letters: 'Postages. These are dreadfully heavy. When Mr. Robinson was in the Council, the greater part was saved, and partly on this account I stood for Port Philip, the result of which you are no doubt aware of'.[31]

Meanwhile, the other family politician, Archibald Boyd, had also felt the cold wind of retrenchment. On his arrival in New South Wales, W. S. Boyd had expressed his amazement that the only bank loans of any size were to Boyd's friends and relations. His own family feeling being less expansive, he called the loans in, thus precipitating Archibald Boyd's bankruptcy. In January 1849, he left the colony hurriedly, 'obliged... it is said to evade the suit of creditors [by] embark[ing] on a Sunday morning outside, or between Sydney Heads'. In this way he was able to escape his Sydney creditors, but his Scottish estate was subsequently sold up to meet his debts and he spent the remainder of his life earning a living by writing novels.[32]

There were other sufferers too. Boyd had been one of the largest employers in New South Wales, and his labour force at all levels was caught up in the failure of his empire. During October 1848 William Moutry, the manager at Boydtown, sued Boyd 'and others' for outstanding wages and compensation amounting to £2500. The immediate result of Moutry's suit was Boyd's arrest for the debt, and he spent several days in Darlinghurst gaol until bail could be found. Boyd's imprisonment finally made public to any remaining innocents the plight of his empire. W. S. Boyd was in Port Phillip at the time, and he treated his cousin's plight with little sympathy, seeing it, rightly or wrongly, as an attempt by

Moutry and Boyd in collusion to embarrass him into accepting responsibility for the debt.

> Mr. B. Boyd called at my office to-day—the first time for many months, to say that Moutry had told him he did not wish to trouble him, but hoped thro' him to get at the Bank, & giving him to understand that if he assisted in this he would not be troubled—This Mr. Boyd said he had refused to do, but his object in coming to me was clearly to tell me that if I would not assist in settling with Moutry, he would assist him in making it appear that the Bank was responsible. A very gentlemanly proceeding considering all things, but I am not surprised at anything Mr. Boyd may now do.[33]

Moutry was determined to see that the Royal Bank, rather than Boyd individually, was made responsible for the debt. He was wise to make the attempt, for Boyd responded to threat by divesting himself of his assets. He sold his whalers to T. W. Campbell for £5000 and leased *Wanderer* to him at the nominal rate of £10 per annum, for three years. He transferred his remaining land at Twofold Bay to his sisters.[34]

Perhaps the most shabbily treated of Boyd's victims were the passengers of *Bermondsey*. After years of pressure from the Legislative Council for immigrant ships to disembark their passengers at destinations other than Sydney or Melbourne, the emigration commissioners in London agreed in 1848 to send shiploads of assisted emigrants to the secondary ports. One ship was sent to Moreton Bay, where they were readily employed. The other, *Bermondsey*, went to Twofold Bay, much to the anger of the *Atlas*: 'Mr. Boyd and Mr. Boyd's agents have good bold faces, and are deeply interested in Boyd Town. The Emigration Commissioners are not such ungracious gentlemen as not to indulge them with a couple of cargoes of human beings to stock their township'.[35]

Bermondsey left Gravesend on 29 August 1848, carrying 111 adult labourers and their families. She arrived at Twofold Bay on 7 December to find that much of the Boydtown establishment had been dismantled: 'very great disappointment has been felt by many', reported the Immigration Board,

> in consequence of the place answering so little in reality to the accounts that have been published of it at home . . . landed in a

barren and peculiarly uninviting spot that possesses in appearance none of the advantages they have been led to expect, it is hardly a matter of surprise that they should consider themselves at least *partially* deceived.[36]

The long period of false promotion of Boyd's activities took time to end. In 1848 William Wells published *A Geographical Dictionary or Gazetteer of the Australian Colonies*, devoting seventeen pages to 'flourishing' Boydtown; and as late as February 1850 the London *Morning Chronicle* referred to the 'efforts of Mr. Benjamin Boyd' as 'an important chapter in some future history of our Australian colonies, as from his determined energy an impulse has been given to emigration which no future official supineness can eradicate'.[37]

Meanwhile the immigrants on *Bermondsey* were left to their own devices. Some found work locally, though not with Boyd, as shepherds, sawyers or hutkeepers; others, mostly those with families, were forced to make their way as best they could back to more populous areas of the colony. By early 1849 the Boyd experiment at Twofold Bay had been virtually abandoned.

By now Boyd and his cousin had fallen out entirely. W. S. Boyd complained that Ben was making unreasonable trouble for him in his efforts to sell up and appeared 'half deranged'. 'It is of no use growling now', he wrote, 'but I often think how surprising it is that a large body of people should have put themselves in the power of such a schemer as B. B. without the least knowledge of business in its commonest principles. He is certainly well calculated to originate a scheme but wants the energy & perseverance to carry it out'.[38] From W. S. Boyd's investigations, it now emerged that Ben had sent cargoes to England which were assigned to Mark Boyd, and treated as the property of Boyd Brothers, although it was the produce of whalers and sheep stations purchased with the funds of the Royal Bank.

W. S. Boyd's disillusion with the Royal Bank's future, and his fear for his own financial future, ultimately led to a breach of faith with the directors which followed the same pattern as the earlier fraud. Late in 1848 the oil from the Boyd whalers was sent back to Britain aboard *Lady Margaret*, in the name of Benjamin Boyd, endorsed by W. S. Boyd, and directed to the hands of W. S. Boyd's brother Archibald, a merchant and lawyer of Leith and London.

Archibald was well aware of the bank's parlous financial condition. Not only had he received private letters from his brother, but he was a trustee of the marriage settlement of his cousin Archibald, of Broadmeadows in the New England District of New South Wales. Mrs Archibald Boyd's settlement included Royal Bank debentures, and in December 1848 he wrote to Sutherland to complain that the bank had fallen behind in its payments. He also knew, since he held his brother's power-of-attorney, that the bank had fallen behind in paying William's salary of £1000. Meanwhile over ten thousand casks of whale oil had been sent to Archibald's hands, and he refused to release it until his family's debts were paid. The directors took legal action to get control of the cargo but Archibald, a lawyer, managed to stall the transfer throughout 1849. On 5 December 1849 he finally paid a mere £193 to the bank, the 'net proceeds' of the sale, having first extracted the money his brother claimed he was owed.[39]

Such action was undoubtedly illegal, for neither W. S. Boyd nor Mrs Archibald Boyd was a secured creditor. Together with the directors' discovery of W. S. Boyd's double-dealing in relation to J. P. Robinson's property, it sealed Sprott Boyd's fate. He had not succeeded in raising any money for the Royal Bank's British creditors; he had, probably illegally, reached a generous independent agreement with Ben Boyd to divide the bank's property; he had shown a disturbing family resemblance by refusing to follow direction from the board.

The directors were also under increased pressure from their creditors, in particular the Union Bank of London. Two further calls on shares were made, for £5 per share on 13 March and £2 10s per share on 15 May, but the response, in the midst of depression and uncertainty about the future of the bank, was poor.[40] Consequently, in April 1849 the directors chose a new manager for their affairs in New South Wales, Boyd's former clerk, Samuel Browning.

Browning was appointed at £1000 per year and given £250 for the travel costs of himself and his family, a far cry from the £200 per annum he had earned as a bank employee a decade earlier. He left Plymouth in May and arrived in New South Wales on 2 September 1849. W. S. Boyd had left the colony exactly two weeks earlier, on 19 August, a matter of both suspicion and amusement to the citizens of Sydney:

> He had a fine House at Woolloomoolah, entertained well, a pleasing wife of tender years he had, but suddenly in less than a week, Furniture Carriages, Horses & wines went to the Hammer, & he & his Wife went away.—This was a town's talk, especially as he was so anxious & determined to sail that at his *own* expense he had a steamer to tow him out:—
> People marvelled—but in a week or ten days after 'The Lion' left who should arrive from the 'Royal Bank' but Sam: Browning to pounce upon 'The Lion'—but the Lion was as nimble & cunning as a monkey—He sacked, sold off, collected in every farthing he could get & bolted.[41]

Ben Boyd remained, 'taking his Shilling dinner at Entwistles'. To avoid Moutry's litigation, he had divested himself of most of the property which his cousin had left to him, and there was little else left. He still pinned his faith on whaling. The 1848 shipment, after all, had amounted to ten thousand casks. Another successful season might yet restore Boyd's personal fortune, even though his reputation as a businessman was in tatters. But whaling entailed grave risks. In July 1849,

> One of [his] whaling barques, the Fame ... returned to Sydney after a most unsuccessful voyage of thirteen months. The disastrous result preyed so heavily upon the mind of the master, Captain Kean, that he destroyed himself. Placing himself on the floor of his bed-room, with a bason [*sic*] and looking-glass before him, he cut his throat, and was found with his head in the bason.[42]

At such an impasse, many men would have despaired. Boyd's imagination took wing. He was, and had always been, a gambler; now the last throw must be made. On 26 October 1849 he sailed from Sydney in *Wanderer*. Thrown on his wits once more by ill-fortune, Ben Boyd's outrageous, intemperate and ultimately disastrous years in New South Wales were over. He left a debt of £415 780 in New South Wales.

From Jervis Bay, he wrote a last letter to 'My dear Sam'. Over several pages, he described the yacht's progress down the coast of New South Wales, the anchor they lost, the southerly buster encountered, and their problems with the rudder. Nowhere did he make any attempt to explain, to justify or to apologize for his actions. Arrogantly he left instructions to his former clerk, and without a shadow of irony he concluded: 'I do not wish any person to suppose that I have left one penny unpaid. Now my good fellow attend to this at once'.[43]

He was on his way to California.

10
The Wanderer

When man, hard up, can no more borrow,
And finds, when press'd, he cannot pay;
When heartless bailiffs, on the morrow,
Are safe to come, (if not to-day).

The only way his debts to settle,
To wipe off all longstanding scores,
Is bolting like a 'lad of metal'
For CALIFORNIA's golden shores.

NEWS OF THE GOLD discoveries reached Sydney just before Christmas 1848 and provoked immediate interest in debt-ridden New South Wales. Not all these goldseekers were escaping the law, but 'bolting' to California with unpaid debts became notorious enough to be celebrated in poems. In all, more than two thousand passengers sailed from Sydney for San Francisco during 1849 in forty-eight ships, and smaller numbers sailed from other ports in Australia and New Zealand.[1]

California was also a new market for the colonies. William Sprott Boyd considered the possibility of sending *Juno* to California for sale, and on 20 July the *Sydney Morning Herald* contained an advertisement calling for passengers for such a trip. Passengers were to pay £35 cabin, £15 steerage for the privilege of travelling with speed and comfort. However *Juno* did not sail. Few goldseekers could afford such luxury, for many of them had chosen California as a solution to unemployment or bankruptcy.[2]

Boyd joined the 'bolters' on 26 October 1849, when he sailed out of Sydney Harbour and, 'according to Royal Yacht privilege, waived [sic] his hand at the Customs House'. The special privileges of the Royal Yacht Squadron finally served to protect him from the possibility of prosecution. Leaving the harbour, he encountered a brig just arriving from the goldfields whose 'black crew was sufficiently indicative that there were inducements for the White folks to remain in California'.[3]

San Francisco was Boyd's destination, but characteristically he took a tourist's route to get there. After brief visits to Auckland and Tahiti during December, he arrived at Hawaii on 26 February 1850. Hawaii was a Polynesian kingdom in which power was shared between the chiefs, headed by King Kamehameha III, and a white executive. The Minister of Foreign Relations was Boyd's old friend Robert C. Wyllie, who came from the same south-west corner of Scotland from which so many of Boyd's associates were drawn. Wyllie had been a businessman in the City of London during the 1830s, before going to Mexico, and eventually to Hawaii.[4]

Wyllie became deeply enmeshed in the politics of the Hawaiian kingdom, promoting Hawaiian expansionism throughout the Pacific, and keen to develop a close relationship with the Australian colonies. The example of this miniature, but determinedly independent, Pacific state appealed to Boyd, already interested in the prospects of an island kingdom. As a result of his visit, Wyllie wrote to FitzRoy to suggest that a Hawaiian consulate should be established in Australia, and nominated Thomas W. Campbell as Consul-General for the Australian colonies.[5]

Wanderer's brief sojourn at Honolulu provoked the sort of adulation which had accompanied Boyd's first weeks in Australia. He invited the press aboard, and played host to King Kamehameha III, the Premier, the Minister for Foreign Relations and the British Consul-General. 'As we left the *Wanderer* we could not help admiring the good taste of the owner in arranging everything so tastefully for his comfort, and we hope often to welcome the members of the yacht squadron to our harbour', reported the local newspaper. To Boyd's gratification, the King-in-Council ordered that no port charges should be levied on *Wanderer* 'or any other yacht navigating for purposes of pleasure or service'.[6]

From Hawaii, Boyd and *Wanderer* sailed on to San Francisco. California was the goal for many Australians, and Boyd's arrival on 29 March cannot have gone unnoticed amongst the 'Sydney Ducks' who had established 'Sydney Town', a rackety area of town later known as 'The Barbary Coast'. Australians had a bad reputation in San Francisco. The local population assumed they were all ex-convicts, and undoubtedly there were unsavory elements amongst them. Most, however, were men seeking relief from their debts, and from unemployment in the colonies, through the lottery of a goldrush, in which brawn was more valuable than brains or birth, and luck most important of all. Their backgrounds were very different from Benjamin Boyd's, and the arrival of such a colonial celebrity in their midst must have been disconcerting. For non-Australians, however, his arrival was just one amongst thousands. The *Alta California* reported *Wanderer*'s arrival in the shipping columns, and republished from the Hawaiian newspapers the report of Boyd's rescue of a native craft off Honolulu, but beyond that California ignored Ben Boyd.[7]

San Francisco was in a state approaching anarchy, for the Spanish authorities had been unable to control the huge immigration or to maintain law and order. Boyd's particular talents were of little value in such a society. He was not prepared to soil his hands like other diggers in the democratic search for a golden lode. Early in 1851 Charles Nicholson reported the gossip from Sydney: 'The last heard of "*little* Benjamin", was that he was seen with a pick and a pannikin, washing the auriferous sand in California'. The reality was quite different. Boyd did travel inland to the goldfields, but he took seven or eight Pacific islanders—the crew from *Wanderer*—with him, and it was they who did the digging.[8]

Boyd and his workers were unsuccessful. He stayed on in California for nearly a year, but apparently without success. Meanwhile the atmosphere became menacing. At the beginning of May a fire destroyed much of the town and, in the looting and riot that followed, the townsfolk identified Australians as the major culprits. On 8 June meetings were held, and a Committee of Vigilance was established. Three days later a Sydney man was caught stealing a safe, and lynched by the vigilantes. Other Australians were hanged during the following weeks.[9]

On 3 June 1851 *Wanderer* left once more for the Pacific. According to John Webster, who wrote the only full account of this voyage, *Wanderer* left San Francisco 'After some weeks of preparation and delay', but other evidence suggests that Boyd's decision to leave was taken abruptly. Amongst his associates in California was an Australian sea captain, Frank Aaron. According to his son, Aaron accompanied Boyd and his crew to the diggings, and Boyd agreed to appoint him as his sailing master to 'bring the "*Wanderer*" back to Sydney'. At the last moment, however, Boyd engaged an American captain instead, 'only . . . a day or two before the Yacht sailed'.[10]

If this is so, why did Boyd take such precipitate action? Was his apparent change of plan premeditated? Did he really intend to return to Australia, where Browning was still attempting to unravel the tangled thread he had left? Was his departure influenced by the vigilantes who were both anti-Australian and anti-British?

Wanderer sailed undermanned, perhaps because sailors were reluctant to leave the golden shores of California on a voyage of unknown destination. Apart from the remnants of his original islander crew, Boyd took with him Aaron's replacement, the American sailing captain William Ottiwell. George Crawford, mate, and Gillwell Barnes, seem to have been Australians, but also joined Boyd in San Francisco. The travelling companion about whom we know most was John Webster, whose account, *The Last Cruise of the Wanderer*, provides the only substantial record of their voyage. Webster, yet another lowland Scot, had a sawmill and trading business at Hokianga in New Zealand, and trading links with both John Logan Campbell of New Zealand and Robert Towns of Sydney. He arrived in California as supercargo on a ship bringing flour and potatoes from New Zealand. Boyd appointed him captain of *Ariel*, which left San Francisco as *Wanderer*'s tender. Instead of sailing on *Ariel*, however, he joined Boyd and the others on *Wanderer*, leaving *Ariel* in the hands of its master, Bradley, and a native crew. Webster was familiar with Maori culture and language; he was therefore a considerable asset to Boyd in his explorations in Polynesia, where the language was sufficiently similar to allow some communication.[11]

Wanderer's first landfall was Hawaii. They sighted the snow-capped summit of Mauna Kea on 25 June and arrived three days later in Hilo Bay on the island of Hawaii. Hilo was a quiet port, whose small trade was with whalers avoiding the higher prices of the larger centre of Honolulu on Oahu Island. The travellers stayed on the island of Hawaii for nearly a fortnight. The highlight of their stay was a visit to the volcanic crater of Kilauea, the legendary home of the goddess Pele. Accompanied by native guides, they walked for two days to reach the volcano; their descent into the crater took a further day. As Webster recounted, the descent was fraught with danger:

> As we descended, the whole cone shook and trembled to its foundations, and several fissures opened in the sides, from which flowed liquid lava. Over one of them we had to leap. I got over first, and perceiving Mr. Boyd hesitating, I cried, 'Leap for your life!' a piece of advice he immediately followed, when we together beat a retreat under a shower of stones and ash.[12]

On their return to the surface, the men found their shoes burnt beyond repair, and had to return the two days march to Hilo Bay barefooted. Boyd was now about fifty, older than his companions and notoriously overweight. His spirit was as willing as ever for such daredevilry, but he must have felt his years on such excursions.

Webster, like Boyd, was impressed by the Hawaiians' 'model government' and their 'rapid strides in civilization under their King Kamehameha III'. Nevertheless they were offended by their only confrontation with the authority of the Hawaiian state. The novelty of life aboard *Wanderer*, with her Polynesian crew, apparently attracted some of the local lads, and eight came aboard with the intention of joining the crew. They were welcomed by Boyd, for the yacht was so undermanned that the white men had been obliged to help sail her from California. However Hawaii strictly controlled the employment of its indigenes beyond its territorial waters, and it was illegal for Boyd to recruit Hawaiians in this way. When a native constable came aboard to arrest the youths for absconding from their homes, 'Mr. Boyd ordered the fellow off, as he was rather presuming'. The white men's respect for this model state stopped short of willing obedience to its laws. Eventually, through the mediation of Wyllie, Boyd was obliged to post a bond of $500 against the young men's safe return within three years.[13]

Wanderer left Hilo on the evening of 10 July, bound southwest for the Kingsmill group of islands. Despite Boyd's friendship with Wyllie he did not return to Honolulu. Three days out, they passed a schooner from Sydney and heard for the first time that gold had been discovered in Australia.

The irony was apparently lost on Boyd: gold had been in Australia all the time, while he had travelled across an ocean to seek it in California. But he was not to be diverted from his new objective by a metal which had proved elusive once already. Despite the self-indulgence of his style of travel, his voyage had a definite end in view: 'to establish a Papuan Republic or Confederation, to lay a foundation of some sort of social and political organization, on which the simple machinery of an independent state might be afterwards erected'. This object was about to be attempted.[14]

Boyd's plan had had a long gestation period. In the months leading up to his initial departure for Australia, he had approached the British government to enquire what would be their attitude to the establishment of a settlement in the south seas. 'It is... my intention to visit the Islands in the Pacific Ocean and should I find the resources of any of them sufficiently inviting ... I propose to make arrangements with the Natives to form Settlements upon one or more of them.' On this occasion Lord John Russell had replied with customary prevarication that he '[did] not feel, that he [could] enter into any engagement on behalf of H.M.Government at present'.[15]

Now, after a decade in which he had pursued other ambitions, Boyd set out to fulfil that dream of a private empire. In the intervening years 'Rajah' Brooke, a fellow member of the Royal Yacht Squadron, had won his kingdom, and become a national hero. Boyd had already been attracted by the island patriarchy of Tristan da Cunha, and his visits to Hawaii may have confirmed his belief that small island states could be both viable and profitable, if their governments were directed by white advisors such as Wyllie.

Much of the Pacific was a no-man's-land, for the islands lay outside the recognition of the European powers. Daring Europeans could settle without legal constraints, taking land on whatever terms they could negotiate with the islands' indigenous owners. However any claim to land that Boyd might make, by occupation or by purchase, would only be secured in international law if he could confirm his claim through an internationally recognized government. Of all the island groups of the Pacific, Hawaii was the only one whose status as a nation was generally recognized by treaties with European powers. By arranging for the appointment of T. W. Campbell as Hawaiian Consul in Sydney, Boyd helped to strengthen that independent status, while setting up the precondition for his own future land claims to be recognized by a sympathetic Hawaiian official. Boyd's experience of inadequate tenure over his squatting runs had apparently made him cautious about acquiring more land to which he could secure no legal title.

Stripped of its rhetoric, *Wanderer's* company was embarked on a land grab. Boyd was searching for suitable land outside the control of the great powers. The growing trans-Pacific trade between the two golden lands of California and Australia, as well as the expanding trade within the Pacific itself, had increased the potential value of islands as trading posts and shipping ports. Avoiding European contact, Boyd steered a course for some of the most isolated and least known islands in the Pacific Ocean.

On 5 August they arrived in the Kingsmill Islands. This group, later to form a part of the British protectorate of Gilbert and Ellice (Kiribati), lies across the equator in a wide scatter of sparsely populated coral islands through which *Wanderer* and her company sailed during the early days of August. Amongst the crew was a man from Ocean Island, Timmararare, who acted as interpreter; with his help they were able to visit villages, barter goods, and gain a superficial understanding of local customs.

They were at once tourists and potential invaders, eager to enjoy exotic native hospitality in return for trade goods, but increasingly nervous now that they had strayed beyond the relative security of more frequented islands. They sighted land first on 5 August and were in their turn sighted. A fleet of canoes, estimated by Webster at more than one hundred, bore down on

Wanderer. In response they 'unleashed the deck guns, and ran them out to be in readiness should the natives prove hostile'. They were reassured, however, by the presence of women and children amongst the boats. As the yacht and canoes came together, the islanders crowded aboard, until 'compelled at last to use force to drive them from the deck [with] the flat sides of our cutlasses we pushed the men over the side'. Unabashed, the two groups then engaged in barter, exchanging tobacco for coconuts and fish.[16]

Similar encounters were repeated throughout the island groups, the Europeans anxious and edgy but not as yet resorting to arms, the islanders eager to get their hands on prized European goods, in particular tobacco and iron. With their growing sense of isolation, the white men's nervousness increased. At Drummond Island there was a minor altercation when an islander boarded *Wanderer* and refused to return to shore. His father was paid off by Boyd with tobacco and an iron file, while the son joined *Wanderer*'s crew. The tender, *Ariel*, had already left, 'being under the impression that treachery was intended on the part of the natives; she being manned only by a native crew, with the exception of the sailing-master, Bradley'.[17]

Boyd and Webster went ashore at several islands, visiting a number of villages which they found clean and well ordered. However they found nowhere suitable for Boyd's 'republic'. The islands were difficult to approach, even in the whale boat, for they were surrounded by coral reefs. There was no natural harbour to form the basis of a port, and the soil was shallow, growing little besides coconuts. Most unsatisfactory of all as a possible refreshment station for European shipping, there was no water. The islanders depended on coconut milk, and fresh water for *Wanderer* was found only with difficulty in deep caves in the coral where rainwater collected.

On 12 August they left the Kingsmills, following *Ariel* on to Ocean Island where they left their interpreter, Timmararare, with 'a large box full of wealth, in the shape of figs of tobacco, knives, and files'. They spent a week there, then headed further south to Stewarts Island, which they sighted on 28 August. They were now without an interpreter, but Webster and Barnes went ashore to visit the village and meet the chief: 'The old man holds a mild patriarchal sway over his people, and they all live in peace and plenty', reported Webster.[18]

Eight years later, on 25 August 1859, John Webster set out in a sworn affidavit that 'on the First day of September 1851... Benjamin Boyd obtained an absolute cession by purchase and Treaty of Stewarts Islands or Sikyana'. Webster subsequently presented the affidavit to the Hawaiian Consul in Sydney (no longer T. W. Campbell) in an unsuccessful attempt to convey these 'possessions', which he claimed to have inherited from Boyd, to the Kingdom of Hawaii, thereby gaining a secure title. In proof he appended the following agreement:

> Be it known unto all Men that I [Blank] King and Sole Proprietor of the islands in the South Pacific Ocean known as Stewarts' Islands... by these Presents, do grant, bargain, sell, assign and convey unto Benjamin Boyd the aforesaid islands... for certain valuable consideration by him to me in hand paid at the time of the execution thereof to wit the sum of one thousand dollars ($1000) in merchandise... And further that the aforesaid Benjamin Boyd, his heirs, administrators or assigns...shall have full power and control over all the inhabitants of the aforesaid islands, introducing or expelling all and every such persons as he or they shall deem requisite.[19]

There is no reference to this truly remarkable document, or the negotiations which must have preceded it, in John Webster's published account.

Having laid in a fresh supply of coconuts, for water was short, they set sail for the Solomons and arrived at San Christoval on 6 September. *Wanderer* had now crossed the racial boundary from Polynesia into Melanesia, and neither the Europeans nor their Polynesian crew were impressed with the inhabitants. 'They were not prepossessing in their appearance, neither were they confiding in their manners, and positively refused to come on board the yacht', Webster complained.

Their caution was understandable, for these people had had few encounters with white men, and those often unhappy ones. While they were eager to barter for iron implements—files, knives, nails and tomahawks—the islanders had no interest in, or apparent knowledge of, tobacco. Eventually, through the careful use of gifts, some of the islanders were persuaded aboard. One, called Isitado or Lisitado, carried a paper in a bag around his neck. At Boyd's request, Isitado willingly gave him the paper to read. It was a note from the captain of a French corvette, *Ariadne*, informing visiting Europeans that the mountain tribes on San Christoval had killed three French missionaries in April 1847, and that he had punished this massacre the following March, when his crew had burned two villages, killing and wounding several men. Three years later the islanders still treated foreigners with understandable trepidation.

Their anxiety was shared by the men aboard *Wanderer*. Boyd and his companions set a watch at night, but tension mounted as the islanders gradually became more venturesome and began to steal. They would paddle silently out to the yacht under cover of darkness, until one night Boyd, seeing one 'stealing under the bow', fired one of the swivel guns and sank a canoe.

Yet if the islanders were less hospitable than the Polynesians of the Kingsmills, the islands themselves were far superior for what Boyd had in mind. After about a week, during which they gradually gained more confidence ashore, the white men began to explore, attended always by Solomon islanders pleased at the profligacy with which the visitors shot pigeons and parrots for sport and the cooking pots.

On 10 September Boyd went ashore 'to kill a mess of birds for breakfast', but in general he was the most cautious of the four, preferring to explore by boat. As a result of one such exploration in the whale boat, they discovered Makira Bay, a 'very beautiful harbour ... an inner bay, forming an extensive sheet of water, entirely land-locked', and with draught to thirty fathoms within a stone's throw of the shore. Such a harbour undoubtedly answered the purpose of the trading station Boyd had in mind, but the islanders of the district remained 'very equivocal'.[20]

One day Crawford and Webster went exploring towards the mountains, taking with them two crew members and two locals as guides. They reached a particular track with fresh footprints, where the islanders became angry and refused to go further. The two white men persisted with their exploration alone. Chasing a flock of parrots, Webster found himself separated from Crawford:

When preparing to fire, I felt an indescribable feeling of uneasiness—an undefined sense of danger. Casting my eyes around, I saw at a few yards distance the dark form of a native rise slowing from a crouching posture, as if he had been in ambush. He had in his hand a formidable spear. I placed my back to the trunk of a tree. We surveyed each other in silence for some minutes. Whatever his intentions might at first have been, he now assumed a friendly aspect. Throwing his spear on the ground, he came forward, and pointing to the tree above, said '*Manu, manu!*' (bird), and expressed, by signs, his desire that I should fire at the parrots; but, under the circumstances, I thought it advisable to retain the charge in my gun.[21]

He rejoined Crawford, who said that he, too, had imagined a form in the undergrowth. Webster was wise not to fire in such circumstances. Although the Europeans' weapons gave them an advantage under favourable conditions, spears or bows and arrows were formidable weapons. In a tropical climate, rain or surf could wet the gunpowder, making firing unreliable, and a skilled warrior could easily throw a spear while his opponent was still reloading.

Their sense of vulnerability to native weapons increased their apprehensiveness. Isitado was the only chief with whom a relationship of trust seemed to develop. On 17 September Boyd and his friends left their first anchorage at 'Wanderer's Bay', and sailed into Makira Bay, where Isitado's village was located. During the journey, they were caught in a severe gale which blew away *Wanderer*'s foreyard and topsail, and they entered the bay in some disarray. Because of the yacht's condition, they now had to remain at Makira Bay for some time while Crawford set out to replace the spar from a tree which they felled on the beach. This enforced rest gave them more time to explore, but also increased the possibility of conflict with the islanders. Crawford suffered the repeated theft of his tools, while the Europeans, in their unbounded curiosity, gave offence by intruding into the private and sacred places of the villagers.

Early in October (probably 3rd or 4th), matters between the two groups came to a head when Crawford, who was still working on the spar, discovered an axe missing. He and Ottiwell entered the village, where they discovered the thief and retrieved the axe in a struggle during which some spears were thrown. The two men got back to *Wanderer*, which was then moved until she lay directly 'opposite the village, so close in shore that her bowspit hung over the land'.

With their guns in position, the white men 'entered into a treaty of compensation' with the villagers through Isitado, demanding five pigs and a hundred yams, 'which were marked down on paper by Mr Boyd. On this original document appeared the figure of a pig, with five marks below it, and also a figure representing a yam, with one hundred marks underneath'. Isitado, 'who appeared to understand the thing perfectly', delivered the first instalment of pigs and yams that evening, whereupon Boyd agreed to waive the compensation, returned the pigs, and paid for the yams. The negotiations ended, according to Webster, with singing and dancing on the shore, and a response performed by *Wanderer*'s crew. It was against the background of this threatened show of force that Boyd negotiated another of his 'treaties' with the 'principal chiefs' of Makira Bay.

In his published account, Webster wrote:

> Mr Boyd thought so highly of this splendid harbour, that he determined, at an early opportunity, entering into a treaty with the principal natives of the locality, for the purpose of acquiring and holding a tract of land, including Makira, for future commercial purposes. The only drawback would be the hostile disposition of many of the other native tribes.[22]

According to Webster's later affidavit, the 'purchase or treaty' took place on 5 October 1851:

> At a meeting of the Principal chiefs of the island of San Christoval...held at the bay of 'Makira'...We the undersigned chiefs of said island were desirous that it should be occupied by white people and request Benjamin Boyd Esquire...to be our chief and to introduce the said people amongst us, and whereas the said Benjamin Boyd having agreed to take upon himself...such authority, We the aforesaid chiefs have this day granted to the aforesaid Benjamin Boyd his heirs and assignees all our right, title and interest both collectively and singularly in the said island, for him and

them... the said Benjamin Boyd giving... to us the aforesaid chiefs goods to the value of two thousand dollars ($2000) which we by these presents acknowledge to have received.[23]

The next morning, 6 October, *Wanderer* left San Christoval. Before leaving Makira Bay Boyd followed the example of the French captain of *Ariadne* by leaving a note for future visitors:

> We found the Natives quiet and obliging supplying us with all necessaries of the Vegetable kind... We found excellent Wood for a foreyard which we made on Shore and the Natives offered all assistance in their power—still they are apt to pilfer the tools if left about—This I give to the Chief Lisitado whom we found a very respectable person.[24]

Like the French, he left the note, together with a playing card (the Ace of Hearts), in the bag which Isitado carried around his neck. They were discovered there three years later by Captain Denham of HMS *Herald*.

Wanderer reached Guadalcanal on 11 October, but it was not until three days later that Boyd and Ottiwell, exploring in the whale boat, were able to find a secure anchorage for the yacht. Webster recollected the great beauty of the place, with tree-clad hills casting their shadows over a beautiful sheltered cove, and the exhilaration of the travellers: 'Mr. Boyd never appeared in better spirits; walking up and down the deck, exclaiming "Is this not delightful!"' But the 'wild natives shouting and yelling... whether as a welcome or otherwise, it was impossible to say', cast a shadow over their safe anchorage. Delayed by the broken spar at Makira Bay, *Wanderer* had missed her rendezvous with *Ariel*, and they were quite alone at Guadalcanal, an island even more remote than San Christoval from European experience. It was a fact of which they were all very much aware as they 'gazed upon a country seldom seen, and, perhaps, never trodden by civilized man'.[25]

After several nights becalmed between San Christoval and Guadalcanal, *Wanderer* was short of water and firewood. They were also short of meat. Webster and Boyd therefore planned to go ashore in the morning to shoot birds, and Webster cleaned his gun and filled his shot belt and powder flask, leaving his equipment on a table in readiness for the morning's 'sport'.

As a precaution, they took it in turns to keep a watch throughout the night—and Webster slept in. He woke shortly after 6 o'clock to find that Boyd had already started for the shore in the dinghy, taking with him one crew member, a Ponapan called Kapentaria. He had also taken Webster's gun and powder flask, and left his calling card on the table. He called out to Webster to expect him back for breakfast, and the dinghy disappeared into the small creek running into the bay.[26]

During the next hour the men aboard *Wanderer* heard several shots from the shore, but took no notice. They began to register concern, however, when numbers of Melanesians began to gather on the shoreline, trying unsuccessfully to entice the Europeans ashore with promises of birds and women. Then the islanders came out in canoes towards *Wanderer*, and managed to board the yacht by means of the bow spit. Her crew was issued with pikes, while the white men hastily loaded their small arms under a hail of spears, arrows and stones. At first, Webster says, they held their fire: '"Keep from firing," I said, "remember Mr. Boyd"'. Such caution could not last long, and they discharged their guns 'with murderous effect'. Two crew members were badly injured in the skirmish, and an unknown number of islanders were killed or wounded. The Polynesian crew fought fiercely, killing the wounded as they lay on the deck and throwing the bodies overboard, while Webster and his companions finally managed to load *Wanderer*'s guns and fired directly into the canoes. Defeated, the islanders retreated to the shore. 'We gave three cheers', said Webster, 'and our native crew danced and sang their songs of triumph'.

In the following hours, this primitive blood lust was demonstrated by the actions of both Europeans and Polynesians. *Wanderer*'s company believed that Boyd and Kapentaria were already dead, especially after they saw a man running along the beach wearing Boyd's hat. Their response was savage. While Crawford and the two injured Polynesians remained on board, Webster, Ottiwell and Barnes, with the remaining eight crew members, came ashore to search for Boyd's body. About 150 yards upstream from the bay, they found his dinghy, and followed his tracks into the woods, until they came to a place where there were signs of a skirmish:

in front of his last footsteps there lay in the sand the wadding of his double-barrelled gun. From the position of these waddings, it appeared he must have fired both barrels at the same instant, and as far as we could judge they must have been fired close to the surface of the ground, from the regular manner in which the waddings lay. Around, the spot was thickly indented with the naked foot-prints of the savages. I noticed the marks made by one in particular. He must have been in the attitude of throwing a spear. I ascertained this by placing my feet in the marks, which were also directly in front of Mr. Boyd's last tracks, and in the line of his last shot.[27]

After this detective work, the party was bent on retribution. They found Boyd's belt with some cartridges in one of the canoes, then unsuccessfully searched the village before setting it on fire. *Wanderer*'s crew joined in the revenge, and Webster was disconcerted, on returning to the beach, to find that they

> had literally hewn the dead native in pieces, and were dancing like fiends, signifying their intention to cook the mutilated members of the defunct savage, in order to gratify to the uttermost their desire for revenge. It was with some difficulty we could prevail upon them to relinquish their horrible intentions.

On the other hand he saw no need to restrain their own thirst for vengeance. The next day they searched a second village, then burned it, destroyed a taro plantation, smashed two more canoes, and cut down some banana trees: 'in that way a handful of men in presence of hundreds of foes, were ... enabled to inflict a merited punishment on the latter'.

In a third village, they found a skull. It was still fresh, and from the long black hairs attached to the scalp, they decided it belonged to Kapentaria. 'It appeared to have been baked', Webster recorded with distaste, though it is hard to imagine when, in the chaos of the previous day, anyone in the area could have found time to cook a human body. They destroyed that village too. But by now a storm was brewing, and the party returned with some difficulty to the ship. The next morning, they put to sea before the gale, and were soon far away from the destruction they had wrought on Guadalcanal.[28]

A slightly different report of Boyd's death and its aftermath was published in the *Illustrated London News* the following April, based, it was said, on the log of *Wanderer*, and signed by William Stiwell (*sic*), master, George C. Crawford, mate, John Webster and Gillbank Barnes. While the chronology is slightly different from that given in Webster's account, the same concern with retribution, and with the vindication of their actions, is strong. According to this account, no destruction took place until the day after Boyd's death, when the first of two villages was demolished. 'We then returned to the ship, and having consulted together, it was unanimously considered our duty to run every risk in search for the remains of the late Mr. Boyd'.[29] This pact, like Webster's call to 'Keep from firing; remember Mr. Boyd', rings a little hollow. It would not be surprising if, in the heat of battle and the subsequent orgy of destruction, they had little time to consider Boyd's possible recovery, dead or alive.

The third account of Boyd's death come from a very different source, that of the Solomon islanders themselves. According to the oral tradition, recounted to a district officer by 'an old chief who was born less than 20 years after the event', Boyd

> went exploring up the small river near the village, watched with trepidation by the natives since this river led to a hill regarded as sacred.
> There was an urgent meeting of the villagers, and it was decided that the risk was too great of the party violating the taboo, with dire results to the people, the warriors were therefore instructed to wipe out the party and it was speared to death.

Another version, recounted in old age by the son of one of the participants, is as follows:

> My father told me that when he was about eleven years old, a ship which his people called NGAUNGAU (ie. 'ship belonging to the devil') came into Wanderer Bay and anchored.
> Gaoliu, the chief of the villages of Koraga, Avisi and Ravu, sent his 'malagai' (warriors) in canoes out to the ship, and they tried to tow it ashore with ropes. The Europeans on board laughed at their vain efforts and discharged some musket shots in their direction, probably in fun. The canoes scattered and everyone went off in fear.

Next morning these people came back and lay in hiding in the jungle around the shore by Sugu. They saw a dingy come ashore. Its crew went to the south side of the Sugu creek, and one man, who was the Captain of the big ship, took his gun and went into the jungle on the north side of the stream. He was a very big, stout man.

While he was looking for pigeons to shoot, the captain came into the spot where all the warriors were lying in wait. They surrounded him and tried to take hold of him. He shook them off with no difficulty, as he was very strong. They then fell on him with their 'Raundama' (wooden swords) and killed him. They cut off his head and took it to Gaoliu at Koraga. He washed it and immersed it in salt water and then exposed it to the sun, and when only the skull was left, placed it in his 'kusu' (a collection of shells and skulls in a rock niche.)

The body of Captain Boyd lay where he was killed, and the crew never recovered it. Reprisals were made by the crew and one man, Posena, was killed.

At a later date other ships came to Sugu to punish the people for killing Captain Boyd, and the villages round *Wanderer* Bay were bombarded. To this day a depression is visible in a rock by the shore at Koraga, where a cannon ball, fired at the village, struck and dislodged some stone.[30]

As if in sympathy with the stormy events of these days, the weather now turned against *Wanderer*. The yacht left Guadalcanal in a tropical squall which lasted for some days. She was showing wear and tear, as the loss of her foreyard off San Christoval had already demonstrated. Tropical seas had particular problems, and she may have been invaded by sea worms. Boyd had loved the little yacht, and had sailed her across three oceans, but she was now in the hands of four fearful men whose only immediate ambition was to get back to civilization in safety. *Wanderer* was no more than the means to this end.

Because of their abrupt departure from the Solomon Islands, they were short of water and firewood. In an emergency, fresh water could be distilled from seawater, but for this they needed fuel. In their need, they began to cannibalize the ship itself.[31] They burned all the spare spars first, then eventually one of the whale boats as well, so that by the time they sighted land on 7 November, somewhere near Cape Moreton on the east coast of

Australia, *Wanderer* was in a sorry and dilapidated state, unable to withstand further gales.

They sailed south from Cape Moreton, hoping for a break in the weather, until at Port Macquarie they anchored opposite the bar, 'under the lee of a rocky point in 7 fathoms... We were unable to stand to sea', recollected Webster, 'on account of our disabled spars, both masts being sprung'. On 13 November they fired their guns for assistance. A pilot came out and, somewhat reluctantly because of the tide and the state of the yacht, agreed to conduct them over the bar. Although they had thrown away the ballast to lighten the ship, she struck the bar as she was coming in on a falling tide. Out of control, she hit the rocks, water broke through the decks, and *Wanderer* was wrecked. Because they were relatively close to shore, the crew was able to rescue most of the yacht's contents. In a locked cabinet in Boyd's bedroom, they found a portrait of Boyd's supposed love, Emma Green.

> Thus fraught with disaster, terminated a voyage in its commencement all sunshine and joy. As the graceful yacht glided from one bright Island to another, our little company of 'Wanderers' dreamt not of the dark future which awaited them. From the moment that our gallant commander fell so suddenly and so unexpectedly, amidst the ruthless savages of Guadalcanar, it seemed as though an evil fortune brooded over the yacht; and, in one short month after the death of him whose pride she had been, her torn fragments lay scattered on the beach, and the wanderings of the 'Wanderer' were at an end![32]

In 1899, the *Galloway Gazette* published a curious story. About 1838 Ben Boyd had presented a bell to the church at Penninghame, the parish in Wigtonshire in which Boyd's grandfather had been minister. One day, some fifty years later, an elderly, white-haired stranger appeared at the church and asked to see the bell and its inscription. No one in Penninghame knew who the stranger was, though the *Galloway Gazette* suggested that he might have been the original bellmaker. The curate took him up to the belfry, and there, as the two men looked down at the bell, the old man told a strange story. Ben Boyd had come to watch while his bell was being cast, and had then thrown 'some heathen metal gods' into the molten metal, which were still, presumably, fused with this Christian ritual object.[33]

What can be said about this strange tale? Who was the old man, and can his story be believed? What led Boyd to incorporate heathen idols in his bell? And why did the *Galloway Gazette* assume, nearly fifty years after Boyd's death, that its readers would be interested in this probably apocryphal story of Benjamin Boyd?

Boyd drew to himself many myths. Some, like this one, are frankly puzzling. Some are the remnants of old mysteries, deliberately suppressed. On 28 March 1843, for instance, an advertisement appeared in the *Sydney Morning Herald* signed by Francis Robinson of 1 Macquarie Place, Sydney:

ROYAL BANK OF AUSTRALIA. The undersigned being about to proceed to London for the purpose of instituting an enquiry into the affairs of this Establishment, will be happy to attend to the interests of any Shareholders resident in Sydney.

Boyd's lawyer, G. Cooper Turner, responded the following day with a second advertisement, telling the *Herald*'s readers that he had 'received instructions from Messrs. Boyd and J. Phelps Robinson to take the necessary proceedings to put that individual (he being insane) under proper restraint, and to add that they have been compelled to resort to this course in consequence of threats of a dangerous tendency having been made use of by Francis Robinson towards them and others'.[34]

Can Turner's suave explanation be accepted? There is, as far as I have been able to discover, no further reference to Francis Robinson, either in England or Australia. He had no appointment in the Royal Bank of Australia, and is not mentioned in J. P. Robinson's will, amongst his other relatives. Who was he?

Some of the tales associated with Boyd can be traced to an explicable source. The persistent rumour, for instance, that Boyd had entertained royalty aboard *Wanderer* may recall his days in the Royal Yacht Squadron, for Victoria and Albert were frequent visitors at Cowes. However it is more likely this is a confused memory of Kamehameha III's visit to *Wanderer* while she was in Honolulu harbour in early 1850.

Other legends seem to have grown disproportionately from an

original seed of fact. Mark Boyd relates that his brother wheedled an invitation to Queen Victoria's coronation from the master of ceremonies; by 1936, an amateur historian in New Zealand reported that Boyd was High Steward of Scotland at the coronation.[35]

Some stories developed from a misreading of the record. Boyd sent banknotes and coin for the Royal Bank of Australia in his ships during 1841 and 1842; aboard *Wanderer* he took £1000, in the form of eight hundred sovereigns and four hundred half-sovereigns. By 1956 this had been transmuted to the splendid claim that 'they had sovereigns for Ballast'.[36]

The first, and most persistent, of all the myths that surrounded Boyd was the rumour that he was still alive, marooned or held prisoner on Guadalcanal. There were precedents for such a belief. White men and women such as William Buckley in Port Phillip or Eliza Fraser on Fraser Island had indeed been found living with Aboriginal groups, though the pillage of Boyd's companions following his disappearance made it unlikely that Boyd could have survived their departure for long. An alternative suggestion was that Boyd had left Guadalcanal in some way—for what had become of *Ariel*? The final possibility, which for obvious reasons could not be explicitly stated, was that Boyd had been killed in different circumstances, perhaps at the hands of his companions. There were, after all, no witnesses to his death, and only four Europeans, most of them strangers, could report on the events surrounding his disappearance.[37]

Within weeks of Boyd's death, the first suggestions surfaced in the press that his death did not take place in the way stated by the survivors, 'and that communications have been made to the authorities... particularly with regard to the movements of the "Wanderer" since the death of Mr. Boyd, that have led to the issue of warrants for the apprehension of a part of the crew'. Although these suspicions were not followed up, the behaviour of the survivors immediately after their arrival at Port Macquarie was curious. They did not seem to mourn their dead companion, nor even respect his personal privacy. The wreck of *Wanderer* was stripped of its furnishings, and Boyd's most personal possessions were put on display at Port Macquarie. These included his highland costume (said to be worth £500), his Bible, a gift from his mother, and his jewellery. Other possessions were taken by

Webster, who refused to part with them until a bill of £121 was met by the Royal Bank.[38]

Meanwhile the survivors accepted the hospitality of Captain Innes, the Police Magistrate at Port Macquarie, and, at least in the recollection of the young women of the household, recovered from the tragedy with remarkable speed: 'How much I wish you were here to help us to entertain "The Wanderers"', wrote Annabella Boswell to a friend, 'and take them to the garden to get figs and peaches... Maria has been staying with us... and... enjoys a little flirtation'.[39]

Boyd's death seemed to lie but lightly on the consciousness of Webster, Crawford, Barnes and Ottiwell. It was a different matter for the shareholders, debenture holders and directors of the Royal Bank of Australia, by now deeply involved in litigation in the Court of Chancery in London. Boyd's death further confused an already confused issue. Mark Boyd was most seriously affected, for he could not inherit his brother's entailed Scottish estate until Benjamin's death was proved. In the absence of such proof, Scottish law stated that a legatee could not inherit until one hundred years after the birth of the missing testator. As a result of the Royal Bank's difficulties, Mark Boyd faced bankruptcy, so he had a strong financial motive, in addition to more personal ones, to solve the mystery of his brother's disappearance.[40]

Other motives for encouraging further investigation may have been more tortuous. On 30 April 1852 the *Chef du Cabinet* of the French government wrote to Edward Lennox Boyd expressing the sympathy of the Prince President at the fate of his old friend Ben Boyd. He added that Louis Napoleon was 'extremely desirous of aiding in the search to be undertaken by your countrymen. He has... desired the Minister of Marine to draw up pressing instructions for the Naval Station of the Pacific'.[41] Louis Napoleon had known Boyd while in exile in England, and his concern might be purely friendly, but the Solomon Islands were of interest to the French government, and the search for Boyd served as a useful excuse for further French naval activity in the area.

Interest in Boyd's fate revived when in October 1854, *Oberon*, a small island trading vessel, returned from the Solomons with a hearsay report that the crew of an American whaler had seen trees at Guadalcanal on which the name 'Benjamin Boyd' had been carved, and had heard reports from the islanders of a white man living on the island. This news caused the merchants of Sydney, led by Boyd's old rival Robert Towns, to charter *Oberon*, which returned to Guadalcanal to investigate the report. The crew questioned the islanders, who showed them a skull which they claimed was Boyd's, and which they sold to *Oberon*'s captain for twenty tomahawks. However the experts in Sydney decided that the skull was Melanesian. This was the heyday of phrenology, and the experts' decision was accepted, much to the chagrin of Boyd's heirs, who were reputed to have offered £1000 for the genuine article.[42]

Despite the alacrity with which the search was mounted, other voices in Sydney continued to imply that more was known of Boyd's certain fate. The radical *People's Advocate* hinted as much in its editorial:

> As the dark side of this humane and spirited conduct, it is rumoured that the probability of Mr. Boyd being alive was communicated a month ago to some party or parties in Sydney who act as agents in the unfortunate gentleman's affairs, but it was treated by them with the coolest indifference instead of lighting up the warmest feelings of hopeful excitement.[43]

Towns's group of merchants had approached FitzRoy to send an official expedition following the first reports from *Oberon*, and a second, quasi-official search of the Solomons was conducted by Captain Denham, RN in HMS *Herald*, between 24 November 1854 and 9 January 1855. Denham was a logical choice to lead the search, since the *Herald* was available on the Australia Station, but he also had a personal involvement. He was a relative by marriage of Mark Boyd and he had been a director of the ill-fated India and Australia Steam Packet Company.[44]

Like the French, the British also had interests in the Solomon Islands, and Denham explored both San Christoval and Guadalcanal with more than Boyd's death in mind. His investigation of Boyd's fate was thorough, if somewhat bizarre. He took with him from Sydney a full-length oil painting of Ben Boyd. On his arrival at Guadalcanal, he invited the three local chiefs on board to receive presents. It was a formal occasion, the ship bedecked with flags, the officers in full uniform, and Boyd's portrait so placed 'to meet the eyes of the Chiefs on entering [Denham's] cabin'. When the chiefs arrived, the first and second identified 'the Great man who so & so killed', while the third, thus accused, turned and ran—and was shot dead.[45]

As a commentary on the anthropological beliefs of nineteenth-century British sea-captains, this is a splendid story, but it is most unlikely that the chiefs concerned would have recognized Boyd's features from any such portrait painted in a European style. However the tale was a useful corroboration of the truth of Boyd's death, which Denham concluded had taken place almost immediately after he set foot on Guadalcanal. His report of the proceedings of HMS *Herald* subsequently formed an important part of the evidence tendered by Mark Boyd in his effort to prove his brother's death—though a skull would have been more conclusive. The issue dragged on until the 1860s, long after his bankruptcy in 1856.

Mark Boyd's bankruptcy was only one of many personal tragedies which resulted from the failure of the Royal Bank of Australia. The litigation between shareholders, debenture holders and directors continued throughout much of the 1860s.[46]

Boyd's life, his disappearance and the probable manner of his death, were the very stuff of legend. His death became a *cause célèbre*. He was not, of course, the first white man to die in the Pacific. The crew of his own ship, *British Sovereign*, had died in the New Hebrides in 1847, without eliciting much more than routine sympathy in New South Wales and none at all in England. But Boyd had been a prominent figure in colonial society for a decade, and was well known to London society as well. Louis Napoleon certainly expressed regret at Boyd's fate, and Queen Victoria is said, on somewhat dubious evidence, to have been saddened by Boyd's death, and to have invited John Webster to show her his paintings of *Wanderer* during his visit to Britain in the late 1850s.[47]

The irony that the man who first brought Melanesian labour to New South Wales should finally be killed by those same islanders did not escape the colonists, and the image has remained potent since. 'Poor gentleman, he has paid dearly for his trafficking with the Cannibal islands', was the general view. They 'ate "Massa Boyd"', wrote Manning Clark, and made Boyd's fate a symbol of the demise of a whole way of life, as the 'mighty men of renown' of the 1840s gave way to the new social élites of gold and self-government. Australia's penchant for cutting down tall poppies was never more dramatically gratified, and because of the almost universal dislike for Boyd in New South Wales, regret at his fate was singularly muted. The assumption that he had been eaten merely added titillation to a good story.[48]

Late in 1853, the Walker family, Boyd's neighbours and rivals in the Twofold Bay area, sold their land to the Twofold Bay Pastoral Association for £75 000. They could have expected only £20 000 for the same property a few years earlier, estimated a relative, 'such is the effect of gold discovery on pastoral property'.[49] It was the final irony of Boyd's ironic life. Post-humously, his claim that his lands could make a fortune for the Royal Bank of Australia if only he could keep control of his holdings until 1852 proved correct. But it was gold that changed the value of land, that provided labour for the pastoralists, that brought steam communication to the colonies and that made men rich. And no one could predict a gold rush. It was also gold that spelled the demise of Boyd's type—'the haughty, gentlemanly, selfish' class he represented.

In the following decades speculators and carpetbaggers continued to arrive from Britain seeking easy wealth in the colonies. The bitterness of Boyd's labour relations was repeated—and exceeded—with the reintroduction of indentured Pacific island labour in the 1860s. But self-government soon brought democracy, and with it the moderation, though not the elimination, of the influence of large employers in the political process. Above all, self-government put an end to the most blatant aspects of the lobby system. Henceforth, policy on colonial issues would be debated openly, and was usually decided in the colony itself. Access to power through such a lobby as that manipulated by the Boyd family would never again be possible.

When Benjamin Boyd founded the Royal Bank of Australia in London in February 1840, he already had an anachronistic view of the place of the merchant adventurer in white settler societies. His view was based on the personalized and privateering exploitation of the outposts of empire. These elements of imperialism did not vanish overnight from colonial relations with Britain. Merchant adventurers may have become less relevant in the more bureaucratic age of imperialism, but older traditions lingered, particularly when supported by such networks of influence as Boyd could manipulate.

For nearly a decade, Boyd used privilege, patronage and publicity in his own interest, but the potency of these weapons gradually waned and became ineffective when confronted with antipathetic public opinion and his own financial incompetence. Finally he retreated from New South Wales and his insoluble problems to join a long line of Europeans for whom the Pacific Islands became a refuge from the hard world of mid-Victorian economic reality.[50] By the time he disappeared in the Solomon Islands, Boyd's style of merchant adventurism was on the same road to extinction as the wood pigeons he shot along the way.

Appendix

SUMMARY OF THE AFFAIRS of the ROYAL BANK OF AUSTRALIA,

TOTAL RECEIPTS

	£	s.	d.
Cash received by the directors for calls	82,632	14	2
Profits made as shown by the books	4,215	17	4
Interest charged to the directors	37,507	6	6
Cash borrowed on debentures unpaid (not including interest) £282,600 0 0			
Other debts 74,562 5 8			
Carried down to debit of "winding up account"	357,162	5	8
	£481,518	3	8

"WINDING-UP" ACCOUNT,

	£	s.	d.
To debts unpaid, as above, brought down	£357,162	5	8
To amount applicable to pay costs of claimants, &c., should the call produce the amount estimated per contra ...	10,952	15	9
	£368,115	1	5

Reproduced from the Wryghte Report, 1854.

212

from 19th February, 1840, to the 1st July, 1854.

TOTAL DISBURSEMENTS

	£	s.	d.	£	s.	d.
Paid expenses of London office	36,121	15	10			
" dividends	40,601	16	6			
" interest	106,463	15	3	183,187	7	7
Bad debts in London	10,137	8	6			
Loss on Consols	129	6	2	10,266	14	8
Advanced to the Sydney branch (exclusive of interest)				287,895	3	10
Cash				168	17	7
				£481,518	3	8

1st JULY, 1854.

By property remaining in Australia in discharge of £287,895 3s 10d. advanced to the Sydney Branch as above, estimated to produce	£154,672	0	0
By cash and exchequer bills, collected by the official manager since the "winding up" order.—Balance	29,243	1	5
By the master's call on the contributories of £100 per share—Computed to produce	184,200	0	0
	£368,115	1	5

MEM.—The proceeds of the produce now in England unsold, and on the way from the colony, will, it is expected, be sufficient for the maintenance of the stations and the contingent charges of winding up.

W. CHARLES WRYGHTE, Official Manager,
4, Shamcrook Court, Basinghall Street,
1st July, 1854,

Abbreviations

AAC	Australian Agricultural Company
ADB	*Australian Dictionary of Biography*
AJCP	Australian Joint Copying Project
ANU	Australian National University
AONSW	Archives Office of New South Wales
CO	Colonial Office
Col. Sec.	Colonial Secretary
FO	Foreign Office
GG	*Government Gazette*
HRA	*Historical Records of Australia*
ML	Mitchell Library (Sydney)
NLA	National Library of Australia
NSW LC *V&P*	New South Wales, Legislative Council, *Votes and Proceedings*
PRO	Public Record Office (London)
RBA	Royal Bank of Australia
SMH	*Sydney Morning Herald*

Notes

Introduction

[1] Webster, *The Last Cruise of the Wanderer*, p. ii.
[2] Guildhall, July 1846, *In the Queen's Bench. Boyd v. The Corporation of the Royal Exchange Assurance*.

1 Early Life of a Merchant Adventurer

[1] Anthony Slaven, *The Development of the West of Scotland: 1750-1960* (London: Routledge & Kegan Paul, 1975), p. 136; Summons... William Paul against Edward Boyd etc. (Scottish Record Office).
[2] By 1837 the income from the property was so insignificant that a cousin, Wilson Maitland Boyd, complained that it had failed to provide an annuity of £20 per year, promised under the terms of his grandfather's will.
[3] Mark Boyd, *Reminiscences*, p. 95.
[4] Anon (June 1836), 'Parish of Cadder, Presbytery of Glasgow, Synod of Glasgow and Ayr', pp. 402, 408.
[5] Cf. Naomi R. Lamoreaux, 'Banks, Kinship, and Economic Development: The New England Case' in *Journal of Economic History*, vol. 46, 1986.
[6] *The Times*, 15 May 1833—Sir Peter Laurie was chairman of the same appeal. My thanks to Dr Barrie Dyster for this reference.
[7] *SMH*, 23 August 1844.
[8] Mark Boyd, *Reminiscences*, p. 102; *Wigton Free Press*, 9 December 1794.
[9] Mark Boyd, *Reminiscences*, pp. 19, 93, 129.
[10] Ibid., pp. 349ff.

215

216 Notes (Chapters 1-2)

[11] Ibid., p. 291.
[12] *Wigton Free Press*, 25 May 1824; Richardson, 'The Parish of Penninghame' p. 186; Summons...William Paul against Edward Boyd etc. (Scottish Record Office).
[13] *Dumfries Weekly Journal*, 8 August 1826; *Wigton Free Press*, 14 November 1826.
[14] Register of Stockbrokers' applications (Guildhall, City of London).
[15] North British and Mercantile Insurance Company, *Centenary, 1809-1909*, pp. 6, 37; e.g. Robert Cockburn (Chairman) to Edinburgh Board of Directors, 20 July 1836, in North British Insurance Company, Minute Books (Edinburgh), No. 5. 1833-1840.
[16] *Dumfries and Galloway Courier*, 21 August 1833.
[17] Peter Laurie, Diary; *Dumfries and Galloway Courier*, 16 May 1835.
[18] P.G. Laurie, *Sir Peter Laurie, a Family Memoir*, pp. 180-1; Peter Laurie, Diary, 9 January 1839.
[19] Will of Joseph Phelps Robinson, PRO/J90/1349/3.
[20] Summons...William Paul against Edward Boyd (Scottish Record Office).
[21] Mark Boyd, *Reminiscences*, pp. 94, 250, 302-4; Morquard, Chef du Cabinet, to Edward Lennox Boyd, 3 April 1852, quoted in *SMH*, 11 August 1852.
[22] *ADB*, vol. 1 (Melbourne: Melbourne University Press, 1966); *SMH*, 26, 30 July 1843; Paul de Serville, *Port Phillip Gentlemen and Good Society in Melbourne before the Gold Rushes* (Melbourne: Oxford University Press, 1980), p. 206.
[23] Robert Brooks to Ranulph Dacre, 14 June 1841, Robert Brooks and Company Papers.
[24] *Morning Chronicle* (London), 12 March 1842; Margaret Steven, *Merchant Campbell, 1769-1846: A Study of Colonial Trade* (Melbourne: Oxford University Press, 1965).

2 Establishment of the Royal Bank of Australia

[1] S.J. Butlin, *Foundations of the Australian Monetary System 1788-1851* (Sydney: Sydney University Press, 1953), p. 619; see also F.G. Clarke, *The Land of Contrarieties: British Attitudes to the Australian Colonies 1828-1855* (Melbourne: Melbourne University Press, 1977), p. 136.
[2] Indenture of the Royal Bank of Australia, 3 August 1840.
[3] B. Boyd to J.W. Sutherland, Plymouth, 9 November 1841 (Private), PRO/J90/1446.
[4] The Royal Bank of Australia and Winding-up Acts, 1848 and 1849—

ex parte Walker and others, Vice-Chancellor's Courts, 22 April 1854 before Vice-Chancellor Sir J. Stuart, Judgment, *Bankers' Magazine*, vol. 14, 1854, p. 516; Wryghte Report.
5 Roxburgh's evidence, appearing for the Official Receiver in Royal Bank of Australia—in re M. Boyd, Court of Bankruptcy, 14 April 1855, *Bankers' Magazine*, vol. 15, 1855, p. 324.
6 *London Post Office Directory*, 1837, p. 755; *Gentleman's Magazine*, obit. June 1865, pp. 796-7; *Croydon and Sutton Advertiser and East and Mid-Surrey Reporter*, 19 August 1871.
7 In *Reminiscences*..., Mark Boyd's book of recollections and gossip, he mentions amongst his early associates Robert Coates, otherwise known as 'Romeo' or 'Diamond' Coates, the fabulously wealthy son of an Antiguan planter who became notorious for his collection of diamonds, his amateur theatricals, and his friendship with the Prince Regent. On 6 September 1823 Coates, who was then fifty-one, married a much younger woman of fortune, Emma Anne Robinson, daughter of Lieutenant William McDowell Robinson, RN. (Robinson, *The Life of Robert Coates*, p. 203). Coates eventually ran through his fortune, and was forced to retire to Boulogne, but his wife's settlement seems to have remained intact. His biographers are coy, but at some time his marriage failed, and by the early 1840s the name of Mrs Coates was regularly linked with that of Mark Boyd (e.g. W. P. Craufurd to G. H. Wray, 23 October 1844, PRO/J90/1346/4: 'my sister has written to Mark & also to Mrs. Coates'). Coates finally died, aged seventy-six, in February 1848, and Mark Boyd married his widow the following December. Mrs Coates was almost certainly related to J. P. Robinson. She certainly belonged to a shipping family, for two of her brothers, Edward and Charles, became admirals.
8 Will of Joseph Phelps Robinson, PRO/J90/1349/3.
9 *London Post Office Directory*, 1837, pp. 778, 785.
10 Wryghte's Report speaks of 'Mr. Smith of Liverpool'; Frank J. A. Broeze, 'Private Enterprise and the Peopling of Australia, 1831-50' in *Economic History Review* (2nd series, vol. 35, 1982), pp. 242ff; Minute Book, RBA, 25 November 1840, PRO/J90/1332.
11 Minutes, 26 August 1841, North British Insurance Company, Minute Books (Edinburgh); Wryghte Report.
12 Benjamin Boyd to Lords of Her Majesty's Privy Council for Trade and Plantations, 24 October 1840; Draft, Colonial Office to Benjamin Boyd, 19 November 1840. Both in HRA, series 1, vol. 21, pp. 54-6.
13 Draft, Russell to Boyd, 19 November 1840, PRO/CO201/302.
14 *Bell's Life in London*, 31 March 1839, 1 March 1840.
15 The legend probably refers to Boyd's hospitality to the King of Hawaii

in 1849, but it is just possible he may have entertained the Queen.
[16] Minutes, 30 January 1849, North British Insurance Company, Minute Books (Edinburgh).
[17] Yarborough to Normandy, 9 December 1839, PRO/CO323/226; Gipps to Russell, no. 97, Executive, n.d., PRO/CO323/226; 'J.S.', 5 January 1841, on ibid.
[18] 27 November 1841, quoted in *SMH*, 19 April 1842.
[19] Minute Book, RBA, 25, 26 August, 9 September 1840, PRO/J90/1332.
[20] *Bankers' Magazine*, vol. 14, 1854, p. 516—this estimate does not include the costs of the ships already sent out.
[21] Portrait of Miss Emma Green, 7 Hanover Ter., London. Later Mrs David Brittan of the Orient Line Founders, Alan Lennox-Boyd Papers.
[22] James Struthers to Huggins, 26 April 1843, PRO/J90/1348/3.

3 First Speculations

[1] 22 December 1840; 19 April 1842.
[2] Wray to Boyd, 22 March 1842, PRO/J90/1422.
[3] W.S. Boyd to Directors of the RBA, 24 May 1848, PRO/J90/1419/B91; *SMH*, 28 July 1841.
[4] 'Garryowen' (*Chronicles of Early Melbourne*, p. 337) thought that Robert Fennell was Joseph Phelps Robinson's cousin; James Graham, on the other hand, believed he was a relative of Boyd's. James Graham to Stuart Donaldson, 20 March 1846, quoted in Sally Graham (ed.), *Pioneer Merchant: The Letters of James Graham 1839-54* (Melbourne: Hyland House, 1985) p. 135. Their salaries were as follows: Edward Rennie, £250; Richard Webb, £300; David McCan Laurie, £250; Samuel Browning, £200; Thomas Craufurd, £250; Robert Fennell, £200; George Robinson, £100 (draft of the letter of acceptance of RBA employees, in Minute Book, RBA, 25 August 1840, PRO/J90/1332).
[5] Brierly, Journal of the Wanderer.
[6] *Athenaeum*, 25 June 1842. The letter is in the third person, but Wray to B. Boyd, 4 July 1842, PRO/J90/1422, suggests that Boyd was the author (Brierly, Journal of the Wanderer).
[7] Brierly, 2 April 1842, Journal of the Wanderer.
[8] Westgarth, *Personal Recollections*, p. 38; 'Garryowen', *Chronicles of Early Melbourne*, p. 572; Hugh McCrae (ed.), *Georgiana's Journal. Melbourne, 1841-65* (2nd ed., Sydney and Brisbane: Brookes, 1966) pp. 66-71.
[9] Westgarth, *Personal Recollections*, p. 38; Alan Barnard, 'Augustus

Notes (Chapter 3) 219

Morris', *ADB*, vol. 4 (Melbourne: Melbourne University Press, 1972); G. L. Buxton, *The Riverina 1861-1891: An Australian Regional Study* (Melbourne: Melbourne University Press, 1967) p. 117.
[10] Wray to Craufurd, 16 November 1842; Wray to Boyd, 21 December 1842, PRO/J90/1422.
[11] *SMH*, 19 July 1842.
[12] John Logan Campbell told a sad tale of a 'youth who had been boasting of what *his* letter of introduction to the governor would do for him ... that exalted personage, holding up the letter between himself and the window, peered keenly through the missive and asked, "Do they lithograph these things now?"' (John Logan Campbell, *Poenamo. Sketches of the Early Days of New Zealand*, London: William and Northgate, 1881, p. 38).
[13] Westgarth, *Australia Felix*, p. 184.
[14] *SMH*, 21 July, 12 August 1842.
[15] Gipps to Stanley, no. 116, Financial, 8 July 1842, PRO/CO201/321.
[16] 16 August 1842.
[17] *SMH*, 10 September 1842.
[18] *SMH*, 14 October 1842.
[19] B. Boyd to J. W. Sutherland, 17 August 1842, Minute Book, RBA, PRO/J90/1332.
[20] Wryghte Report; *Bankers' Magazine*, 1856, p. 498.
[21] B. Boyd to Sutherland, 17 August 1842, PRO/J90/1332; B. Boyd to W. S. Boyd, 20 April 1848, enclosure in W. S. Boyd to the directors of the RBA, 26 April 1848, PRO/J90/1419/B91.
[22] Westgarth, *Personal Recollections*, p. 38.
[23] Wryghte Report.
[24] James Brooke to Mrs Johnson, 3 May 1844, in Templer (ed.), *The Private Letters of Sir James Brooke*; Wray to Webb, 14 September 1843, PRO/J90/1422.
[25] Crauford to [Wray?], 23 April [1843], PRO/J90/1346/4.
[26] Rusden, *History of New Zealand*, p. 277.
[27] *Sydney Herald*, 28 August 1840; *Southern Cross*, 22 February 1845.
[28] Rusden, *History of New Zealand*, p. 277.
[29] Shortland to Cooper, 24 August 1842, in Col. Sec. Dept, Internal Affairs, I, (New Zealand Archives).
[30] Shepherd [*sic*] to Boyd and Robinson, 27 January 1843, in ibid.
[31] Griffiths to Boyd and Robinson, 8 April 1843, in ibid.
[32] Boyd and Robinson to Griffiths, 8 April 1843, in ibid.
[33] Minute, George Gipps, 18 April 1843, 43/2942 in Col. Sec. Dept, AONSW.
[34] *Southern Cross*, 20 May 1843.

[35] Boyd to Sutherland, 17 August 1842, PRO/J90/1332.
[36] Boyd and Robinson to Shortland, 20 April 1843, Col. Sec. Dept, Internal Affairs, I, (New Zealand Archives).
[37] Boyd and Robinson to Shortland, 7 August 1843, in ibid.
[38] Trevelyan (Treasury) to G. H. Wray, 3 April 1843, enclosure, in ibid.
[39] Boyd to FitzRoy, 7 December 1843, in ibid.; Wray to Ben Boyd, 20 March 1843, PRO/J90/1422.
[40] Boyd to FitzRoy, 7 December 1843, in Col. Sec. Dept, Internal Affairs, I (New Zealand Archives).
[41] Wray to Webb, 22 April 1844, PRO/J90/1422; *The Times*, 19 April 1844. For a more detailed examination of this whole incident, see Marion Diamond, '"Most Injudicious... Most Injurious": The Royal Bank of Australia's Loan to the New Zealand Government, 1842' in *New Zealand Journal of History*, vol. 20, 1986, pp. 64-72.
[42] 23 September 1846.

4 A Lust for Land

[1] Probably a relative of the RBA's director, William Petre Craufurd. Westgarth, *Personal Reminiscences*, pp. 42-3; R. Spreadborough and H. Anderson (comps), *Victorian Squatters* (Melbourne: Red Rooster Press, 1983) p. 99.
[2] Westgarth, *Personal Reminiscences*, pp. 45-7.
[3] Ibid., p. 49; Mitchell to 'my dear Livy' [his son], 'in my tent near Harvey's Range', 18 December 1845, Sir Thomas Mitchell Papers, vol. 7, Misc.
[4] NSW LC V&P, 1844, p. 586.
[5] Commissioners of Crown Lands and Emigration, 30 September 1844, 44/1212,1213, enclosure in Stanley to Gipps, no. 12, 30 January 1845.
[6] S.J. Butlin, *Foundations of the Australian Monetary System, 1788-1850* (Sydney: Sydney University Press, 1953) pp. 340-5.
[7] See Marion Diamond, Ideas of Landed Property in New South Wales in the 1840s, unpublished paper presented to Law and History Conference, La Trobe University, Melbourne, May 1987.
[8] Excerpt in *SMH*, 16 February 1843.
[9] William Wilmington to Stanley, 31 October 1844, enclosure in Gipps to Stanley, no.162, Executive, 23 September 1845, PRO/CO201/354.
[10] Gipps to Stanley, no. 107, Executive, 17 May 1844, *HRA*, vol. 23, Series 1, p. 602.
[11] Mark Boyd to G. W. Hope, MP, 31 May 1845, PRO/CO201/363; Gipps to Stanley, no. 36, Executive, 12 February 1846, *HRA*, vol. 24, Series 1, p. 767; B. Boyd, 3 June 1844, Minutes of Evidence taken before the

Select Committee on the Crown Land Grievances, NSW LC V&P, 1844, p. 152.
[12] F. G. Clarke, *The Land of Contrarieties* (Melbourne: Melbourne University Press, 1977) p. 138.
[13] Richardson, 'Parish of Penninghame', p. 182; Gipps to Stanley, no. 36, Executive, 12 February 1846, *HRA*, vol. 24, Series 1, p. 767; Westgarth, *Personal Recollections*, p. 38.
[14] The region covered by 'Maneroo District' was larger than the area currently known as 'Monaro', for it included the coastal strip east of the high country. The spelling varied at different times; W.K. Hancock identifies at least six further variants. To differentiate between the larger squatting district and the present landlocked region, I have used the obsolete term 'Maneroo', which was, in any case, the spelling of choice for Ben Boyd. See W.K. Hancock, *Discovering Monaro: A Study of Man's Impact on his Environment* (Cambridge: Cambridge University Press, 1972) p. 3.
[15] The information for the previous three paragraphs comes from a variety of sources. I am grateful first of all to Mr Gerry Langevad, a post-graduate student at the University of Queensland, who has compiled a computerized data base of all squatting runs published in the New South Wales *Government Gazette* during the 1840s. Further clues to the location of runs come from Wells, *Gazetteer*; G.L. Buxton, *The Riverina, 1861-1891* (Melbourne: Melbourne University Press, 1967); W.K. Hancock, *Discovering Monaro*, op. cit.; D. Waterson, *Squatter, Selector and Storekeeper: A History of the Darling Downs 1859-93* (Sydney: Sydney University Press, 1968); R. Walker, *Old New England: A History of the Northern Tablelands of New South Wales, 1818-1900* (Sydney: Sydney University Press, 1966); R. Spreadborough and H. Anderson (comps), *Victorian Squatters* (Melbourne: Red Rooster Press, 1983).
[16] *Arden's Sydney Magazine*, October 1843.
[17] Henry Lawson, 'The Men Who Made Australia', in R. Ward (comp.), *The Penguin Book of Australian Ballads* (Melbourne: Penguin Books, 1964) p. 155.
[18] S Mourot, *This Was Sydney: A Pictorial History from 1788 to the Present Time* (Sydney: Ure Smith, 1969) p. 142.
[19] *Weekly Register*, 30 March 1844.
[20] *Weekly Register*, 7 September, 21 December 1844, 30 August 1845.
[21] *SMH*, 27 January 1844.
[22] Wray to B. Boyd, 20 March [1843], PRO/J90/1422.
[23] Wray to Webb, 11 April [1843], 14 September 1843, PRO/J90/1422.
[24] B. Boyd to J.W. Sutherland, 7 October 1843, PRO/J90/1446.
[25] B. Boyd to J.W. Sutherland, 3 January 1844, PRO/J90/1446/B147.

5 The Squatting Interest

[1] Letter to the editor, *SMH*, 22 May 1844. Edward William Terrick Hamilton later became governor of the Australian Agricultural Company. See article by J.R. Robertson in *ADB*, vol. 4 (Melbourne: Melbourne University Press, 1972).

[2] Stephen Roberts, *The Squatting Age in Australia, 1835-1847* (Melbourne: 1935, reprinted 1964) refers to Gipps's 'occupation' and 'homestead' regulations, and these terms have become generally current. They were not given these titles at the time; Gipps to Stanley, no. 84, Executive, 16 April 1844, *HRA*, vol. 23, p. 547.

[3] James Stephen, Minute, 12 September, on Gipps to Stanley, no. 84, Executive, 16 April 1844, PRO/CO201/345.

[4] Gipps to Stanley, no. 4, Executive, 10 January 1846, *HRA*, vol. 24, Series 1, pp. 685ff. In Boyd's home parish of Penninghame, some leases were for life, while others were for periods of nineteen, twelve or nine years duration, and they were hedged about with provisos regarding crop rotation and other improvements (Richardson, 'Parish of Penninghame', pp. 184-5).

[5] W. Wilmington to Gipps, 30 August 1844, enclosure in Gipps to Stanley, no. 206, Executive, 16 September 1844, PRO/CO201/349.

[6] C. Rolleston to Colonial Secretary, 30 March 1844, NSW LC *V&P*, 1844, quoted in K. Buckley, 'Gipps and the Graziers of New South Wales, 1841-6', Part 2, *Historical Studies*, 1956, p. 181; ibid., p. 187.

[7] *SMH*, 5 April 1844; Gipps to Stanley, no. 84, 16 April 1844, *HRA*, vol. 23, p. 545.

[8] *HRA*, vol. 23, Series 1, note 56, p. 856.

[9] *Sydney Chronicle*, 16 January 1847; Gipps to Stanley, no. 107, Executive, 17 May 1844, *HRA*, vol. 23, Series 1, p. 602.

[10] Gipps to Stanley, ibid; Buckley, op. cit., Part 2, p. 179.

[11] *SMH*, 22 May 1844.

[12] *Weekly Register*, 13 April 1844; Stanley to Gipps, no. 12, 30 January 1845, *HRA*, vol. 24, Series 1, p. 219.

[13] Gipps to Stanley, no. 75, 3 April 1844, *HRA*, vol. 23, Series 1, p. 511.

[14] *SMH*, 22 May 1844.

[15] B. Boyd, 3 June 1844, Minutes of Evidence taken before the Select Committee on the Crown Land Grievances, NSW LC *V&P*, 1844.

[16] See, e.g., J.M. Ward, *James Macarthur: Colonial Conservative, 1798-1867* (Sydney: Sydney University Press, 1981) pp. 100-3.

[17] B. Boyd to Stanley, 16 April 1844, enclosure in Gipps to Stanley, no. 85, 17 April 1844, *HRA*, vol. 23, Series 1, p. 549. Boyd wrote the letter in triplicate, and he told the colonial secretary in a covering letter, 20 April 1844, that he was sending a copy separately from the Governor's

Notes (Chapter 5) 223

Despatches—thereby implying some doubt that Gipps would forward the letter. In this, he misjudged the governor's integrity.
[18] On 26 April 1844 he married Elizabeth Dreddingstone in London (*SMH*, 15 August 1844).
[19] *SMH*, 23 December 1844. Scott and Archibald Boyd had been at Cambridge together. My thanks to Assoc. Prof. T.H. Irving for this information.
[20] Wray to B. Boyd, [28?] May 1844, PRO/J90/1422.
[21] Mackinnon to Archibald Boyd, 10 July 1844, in *SMH*, 23 December 1844.
[22] Archibald Boyd to B. Boyd, 18 July 1844, in *SMH*, 23 December 1844.
[23] *SMH*, 24 December 1844; *Atlas*, 14, 21, 28 December 1844.
[24] See Correspondence with Parliamentary Agent, printed 20 December 1844, in NSW LC *V&P*, 1844.
[25] A.D. Stewart (Perth, Scotland) to Wray, 28 October 1844, PRO/J90/1348/3.
[26] Mackillop to Manager of the RBA [Wray], 24 June 1844, PRO/J90/1347; Buckley, op. cit., Part 2, p. 190; *Weekly Register*, 2 August 1845.
[27] Mark Boyd, *Reminiscences*, pp. 70-3; Mark Boyd to G.W. Hope, MP, 31 May 1845, PRO/CO201/363.
[28] This probably indicates that he was a trustee under Boyd's marriage settlement. Policy no. 2221 (signed London): Archibald Boyd, The Honble Francis Scott, Mr John Connell & William Sprott Boyd on the life of Archibald Boyd Stockholder New South Wales. (North British Insurance Company, Minute Book, Edinburgh, 8 August 1844).
[29] Ruth Knight, *Illiberal Liberal: Robert Lowe in New South Wales 1842-1850* (Melbourne: Melbourne University Press, 1966) p. 108. It was an open secret that Lowe was the editor of the *Atlas*. In her correspondence, his wife frequently referred to his editorial activities, although he constantly denied his involvement.
[30] 30 November 1844.
[31] 5 April 1845.
[32] *Weekly Register*, 31 May 1845.
[33] Stathan and Forster to James Macarthur, 1 November 1844, Macarthur Papers, vol. 31.
[34] E.H. Stathan, pro Stathan and Forster to James Macarthur, 28 December 1844, in ibid.
[35] Gipps to Gladstone, Separate, 28 May 1846, *HRA*, vol. 25, p. 73.
[36] *SMH*, advertisement, 10 September 1844; *Atlas*, 14 June 1845.
[37] 'Jack Squaresail's Address to the Port Phillip Electors', *Weekly Register*, 14 September 1844.
[38] *Port Phillip Herald*, 15 October 1844.

224   Notes (Chapters 5-6)

[39] Correspondence relating to Vacant Seat, ordered to be printed 10 October 1844, NSW LC V&P, 1844.
[40] NSW LC V&P, 27, 28 August 1845.
[41] B. Boyd to the Electors of the District of Port Phillip, 23 August 1845, printed in *Atlas*, 30 August 1845.
[42] Gipps to Stanley, no. 205, Executive, 23 November 1845, *HRA*, vol. 24, p. 641; Stuart Donaldson to James Graham, 27 March 1846, in S. Graham, *Pioneer Merchant: The Letters of James Graham, 1839-54* (Melbourne: Hyland House, 1985), p. 139.
[43] B. Boyd to J.W. Sutherland, 31 June 1846, PRO/J90/1446.
[44] B. Boyd to J.W. Sutherland, 19 September 1845, PRO/J90/1446.
[45] B. Boyd to J.W. Sutherland, 31 January 1846, PRO/J90/1446.
[46] B. Boyd to J.W. Sutherland, 9 September 1845, PRO/J90/1446; see Peter Burroughs, *Britain and Australia 1831-1855: A Study in Imperial Relations and Crown Lands Administration* (Oxford: Clarendon Press, 1967) pp. 296-330; see also T.H. Irving, Francis Scott, Colonial Agent: Aristocratic Ideals and Empire in the 1840s (unpublished paper, 1986)—my thanks to Ass. Prof. Irving for allowing me to read this in manuscript.
[47] *SMH*, 18 November 1844.
[48] Wray to B. Boyd, 6 December 1842, PRO/J90/1422; see Jardine Matheson Papers; Brierly, Journal on Wanderer and at Sydney, 1843-44, 10 August 1843, 19 January 1844.
[49] Brierly, Journal on Wanderer and at Sydney, 1843-44, 1 November 1844; *SMH*, 18 November 1844, 21 January 1845.
[50] B. Boyd to J.W. Sutherland, 1 February 1845, in RBA, Minutes of General Meetings, 10 July 1845, PRO/J90/1331.

6 Boydtown

[1] B. Boyd to Russell, 11 December [1840], copy enclosed in Russell to Gipps, no. 187, 2 January 1841; *Boyd* v. *Royal Exchange Assurance*, Guildhall, July 1846 (H.P. Wellings, *Benjamin Boyd in Australia*, (Sydney: Ford, n.d.), p. 35 gives other slightly different estimates of size); Minute Book, RBA, 25, 26 August, 9 September 1840, PRO/J90/1332.
[2] Minute Book, RBA, 28 September 1841, 2 January 1842, PRO/J90/1332.
[3] *Hobart Town Courier*, 14 October 1842; *SMH*, 25 April 1842.
[4] Boyd and Robinson to Thomson, 29 December 1842, with Minute, 2 January [1843], Col. Sec. Dept, Letters received, 1843, 4/2616

AONSW; Gipps to Stanley, nos. 54 and 69, 14 March and 7 April 1845, PRO/CO201/357.
5 30 September 1842.
6 N. L. McKellar, *From Derby Round to Burketown: The A.U.S.N. Story* (Brisbane: University of Queensland Press, 1977) p. 15; P. P. King to Directors of the AAC, nos. 60 and 67, 22 March and 1 September 1842, AAC Papers.
7 Bunbury to La Trobe, 4 May 1843, Col. Sec. Dept, Letters received, 1843, 4/2614 AONSW.
8 *Boyd* v. *Royal Exchange Assurance*, op. cit., pp. 3-5.
9 Ibid., p. 6; *SMH*, 12, 14 June 1843; *Boyd* v. *Royal Exchange Assurance*, op. cit., p. 129.
10 Robert Lodge to Towns, 31 July 1846, Robert Towns and Co. Papers, Catalogued, vol. 5; certificate by John Koff (marine engineer), 16 August 1850, Robert Towns and Co. Papers, vol. 10; R. Towns to Robert Lodge, 11 February 1845, and R. Towns to R. Brooks, no. 25, 13 July 1844, in Robert Towns and Co. Papers, MSS 307—my thanks to Barrie Dyster and Frank Broeze for these references; *Australian*, 14 December 1847—the *Australian* at this date was under the control of Boyd.
12 *Atlas*, 24 May 1845; W. S. Boyd to G. H. Wray, no. 21, 24 August 1848, and W. S. Boyd to G. H. Wray, no. 29, 11 November 1848, PRO/J90/1419; J. P. Robinson to G. H. Wray, 2 January 1847 PRO/J90/1348; Ronald Parsons, *Ships of Australia and New Zealand Before 1850*, Part 1, A-J. (Adelaide: privately printed by R.Parsons, October 1983); W. S. Boyd to G. H. Wray, no. 32, 3 January 1849, PRO/J90/1419.
13 W. J. Dakin, *Whalemen Adventurers* (Sydney: Angus and Robertson, 1934) p. 99.
14 *Colonial Gazette*, 14 December 1842, extract in *New Zealand Gazette*, 30 April 1843.
15 Brierly, Journal ... of a Visit to Maneroo, 1842-3.
16 *SMH*, 11 March 1843.
17 Brierly, Journal on Wanderer and at Sydney, 1843-44.
18 Ibid.
19 *Southern Cross*, 15 June 1844—similar advertisements appeared in the Sydney and Hobart newspapers.
20 Brierly, 2 June, 7 August 1843, 28 October 1844, Journal on Wanderer and at Sydney, 1843-44.
21 *SMH*, 26, 29 March, 15 April, 23 May, 15 July 1844; Minute Book, RBA, 22 November 1848, PRO/J90/1331.
22 W.J. Dakin, op. cit., p. 104; Consignment Book, Boydtown and London, RBA, p. 66, PRO/J90/1390.

[23] J. M. R. Young, 'Australia's Pacific Frontier', *Historical Studies*, vol. 12, 1966, p. 381.
[24] Brierly, 2 June 1843, Journal on Wanderer and at Sydney, 1843-44.
[25] B. Boyd to Directors, 29 July 1846, Minutes of General Meetings, RBA, PRO/J90/1331; Benjamin Boyd, *A Letter to Sir William Denison*, p. 16.
[26] W. K. Hancock, *Discovering Monaro: A Study of Man's Impact on his Environment* (Cambridge: Cambridge University Press, 1972), pp. 51-3.
[27] B. Boyd, Evidence to the Select Committee on Immigration, 27 September 1843, NSW LC *V&P*, 1844; B. Boyd to J. W. Sutherland, 1 February 1845, PRO/J90/1446/B147.
[28] Brierly, 27 December 1842, Journals of the Wanderer.
[29] NSW *Government Gazette*, 9 March 1843.
[30] B. Boyd to P. P. King, 23 July 1846, Letters and papers chiefly from the correspondence of Phillip Parker King collected by the late H. O. Lethbridge Esq., A.3599 ML.
[31] 'Oswald Brierly was a pleasant, comfort-loving man; at this juncture, troubled with tired eyes and, consequently, unable to paint. Boyd said, in front of Georgiana [McCrae], "We must get him away from ships." That was the first suggestion. The next she heard of it was, when Dr. Greeves talked about Brierly's appointment as manager to Boyd's fishery, at Twofold Bay' (editorial commentary, inserted at 29 June 1842, in Hugh McCrae, ed., *Georgiana's Journal. Melbourne 1841-1865*, 2nd. ed., Sydney and Brisbane: Brookes, 1966, p. 94); Brierly, Journal on Wanderer and at Sydney, 1843-44.
[32] In early 1848 an anonymous advertisement appeared in the *SMH*: 'Marine Painting.—The whole theory of Marine Painting in Water Colours taught on a new principle, in six lessons, at half a guinea each lesson. Apply (by letter post-paid to Q. R. S., Herald office)' (quoted in *Heads of the People*, 12 February 1848).
[33] W. S. Moutry to J. P. Robinson, 30 March 1848, PRO/J90/1353.
[34] *Bell's Life in Sydney*, 4 March 1848.
[35] W. S. Boyd to G. H. Wray, no. 20, 23 August 1848, PRO/J90/1419; Brierly, 22, 25 December 1843, Journal on Wanderer and at Sydney, 1843-44; W. S. Moutry to J. P. Robinson, 22 December 1847, PRO/J90/1353.
[36] *SMH*, 14 June 1843.
[37] Brierly, 9 August 1844, Journal of the Wanderer, August to October 1844.
[38] Brierly, 5 June, 23 August 1847, Diary at Twofold Bay.
[39] Cockburn and Co. was owned by cousins of William Cockburn, a director of the RBA. B. Boyd to J. W. Sutherland, 17 August 1842, PRO/J90/1332.

⁴⁰ See Caroline Ralston, *Grass Huts and Warehouses: Pacific Beach Communities of the Nineteenth Century* (Canberra: ANU Press, 1977) for a study of this type of community; Brierly, 8 August 1844, Journal on Wanderer and at Sydney, 1843-44; Brierly, 10 September 1844, Journal of the Wanderer, August-October 1844.
⁴¹ Brierly, 8 August 1844, Journal on Wanderer and at Sydney, 1843-44.
⁴² 23 September 1846.
⁴³ *SMH*, 25 September 1846; *Sydney Chronicle*, 23 December 1846, 20 January 1847.
⁴⁴ 'Philo-Australis', 28 October 1846.

7 Labour Problems

¹ W. S. Boyd to G. H. Wray, no. 17, 8 August 1848, PRO/J90/1419/B91; Letter to the editor of the *SMH*, 22 May 1844.
² B. Boyd to J. W. Sutherland, 29 June 1847, PRO/J90/1446/B147; B. Boyd, Evidence to the Select Committee on Immigration, 27 September 1843, in NSW LC *V&P*, 1844.
³ B. Boyd to J. W. Sutherland, 19 September 1845, PRO/J90/1446/B147.
⁴ R. Madgwick, *Immigration into Eastern Australia, 1788-1851* (London: Longmans, Green, 1937), p. 233.
⁵ Richardson, 'The Parish of Penninghame', pp. 182-3; B. Boyd, Evidence to the Select Committee on Immigration, op. cit.
⁶ Report of the Committee on Immigration, NSW LC *V&P*, 1844; G. J. Abbott, *The Pastoral Age: A Re-examination* (Melbourne: Macmillan, 1971), pp. 95-7.
⁷ Abbott, op. cit., p. 103; B. Boyd, Evidence to the Select Committee on Immigration, 27 September 1843, op. cit.
⁸ J. P. Robinson, Evidence to the Select Committee on the Petition from Distressed Mechanics and Labourers, 16 November 1843, NSW LC *V&P*, 1843.
⁹ e.g. P. P. King to Directors of the AAC, no. 104, 29 July 1844: 'This [gratuity of tea and sugar] was given to enable me to withhold it occasionally according to their negligence or improper conduct' (AAC Papers).
¹⁰ Charles Campbell, Evidence to the Select Committee on Immigration, 28 September 1843, op. cit.; P. P. King to Directors of the AAC, no. 46, 19 March 1841, and no. 84, 20 September 1843, op. cit.
¹¹ Brierly, Journal on Wanderer and at Sydney, 1843-44.
¹² Extracted in the *Launceston Advertiser*, 2 May 1844; Webster, *The Last Cruise of the Wanderer*, pp. 3, 23.
¹³ Mark Boyd, *Reminiscences*, pp. 337-8.

228   Notes (Chapter 7)

[14] B. Boyd to J.W. Sutherland, 3 January 1844 and 1 December 1843, PRO/J90/1446/B147; *Launceston Advertiser*, 2 May 1844.
[15] B. Boyd, Evidence to the Select Committee on Immigration, 27 September 1843, op. cit.
[16] Ibid.; Sidney, *The Three Colonies of Australia*, pp. 131-2.
[17] Report from the Select Committee on Immigration, 5 December 1843, NSW LC V&P, 1843, p. 8.
[18] John Manning Ward, *James Macarthur: Colonial Conservative* (Sydney: Sydney University Press, 1981), p. 111; A. C. V. Melbourne, *Early Constitutional Development in Australia* (Brisbane: University of Queensland Press, 1963), p. 358; B. Boyd to J.W. Sutherland, 1 December 1843, PRO/J90/1446/B147; Robert Towns to Robert Brooks, no. 206, 2 April 1846, Robert Towns and Co. Papers, MSS 307.
[19] Gladstone to FitzRoy, 30 April 1846 (Private and Confidential) printed in NSW LC V&P, 1846.
[20] Evidence of B. Boyd to the Select Committee on the Renewal of Transportation, 19 October 1846, NSW LC V&P, 1846.
[21] J.P. Robinson to Samuel Browning, 28 June 1847, PRO/J90/1348.
[22] B. Boyd, *Letter to Sir William Denison*, pp. 13, 18.
[23] Alan Powell, *Patrician Democrat: The Political Life of Charles Cowper, 1843-1870* (Melbourne: Melbourne University Press, 1977), pp. 30-3; J.P. Robinson to Charles Cowper, Per favour of the Editor, *Australian*, 10 December 1846. In all, Boyd imported 'a large number' of exiles at £15 per annum, but after paying £4 per head expenses to get them to his squatting runs, 'Not more than half a dozen of them stayed beyond a month they all bolted & could not be got back except at an enormous expense' (W.S. Boyd to G.H. Wray, no. 54, 28 April 1849, PRO/J90/1419).
[24] T.P. Pugh, *Brisbane Courier*, 22 August 1863, quoted in K. Saunders, 'The Black Scourge' in Raymond Evans et al, *Exclusion, Exploitation and Extermination: Race Relations in Colonial Queensland* (Sydney: Australia and New Zealand Book Co., 1975), p. 149.
[25] Robert Towns to Robert Brooks, no. 204, 31 March 1846, Robert Towns and Co. Papers, MSS 307.
[26] B. Boyd, Evidence to the Select Committee on Immigration, 27 September 1843, op. cit.
[27] J.P. Robinson to George Robinson, 22 January 1847, Letters from J.P. Robinson and W.S. Boyd (ML).
[28] Brierly, 9 April 1847, Diary at Twofold Bay.
[29] *SMH*, 2 October 1847.
[30] Brierly, 9, 10, 14 April 1847, Diary at Twofold Bay; W.S. Moutry to Daniels, 15 April 1847, PRO/J90/1353.

Notes (Chapter 7) 229

³¹ W.S. Moutry to George Robinson, 26 May 1847, PRO/J90/1353; Brierly, 3 June 1847, Diary at Twofold Bay.
³² W.S. Moutry to George Robinson, 20 June 1847, PRO/J90/1353.
³³ *Australian*, 5 October 1847.
³⁴ *SMH*, 18 October 1847.
³⁵ 30 October 1847.
³⁶ 5 October 1847.
³⁷ B. Boyd, *Letter to Sir William Denison*, p. 16.
³⁸ *SMH*, 2 October 1847; or between a superior and an inferior grade of humanity, *Sydney Chronicle*, 2 October 1847 (the reports of the debate vary).
³⁹ *SMH*, 2 October 1847.
⁴⁰ Evidence of Henry Walpole, George Lancaster, Edward Kirsopp, enclosures in Attorney-General to Col. Sec., 25 November 1847, enclosure in FitzRoy to Earl Grey, Executive, no. 258, 24 December 1847 (AONSW).
⁴¹ FitzRoy to Earl Grey, ibid.; Minute, E[lliot?], 22 May, on ibid.
⁴² For details, see *The Colonial Intelligencer; or, Aborigines Friend*, 1848, pp. 47-51, 88-91, 115-20.
⁴³ J. Lang Innes JP and H.H. Braine JP to Col. Sec., 23 June 1848, enclosure in Plunkett to Col. Sec., 1 August 1848, enclosure in FitzRoy to Earl Grey, Executive, no. 41, 1 March 1849 (AONSW); W.P. Morrell, *Britain in the Pacific Islands* (Oxford: Clarendon Press, 1960), p. 312 (Grey's recommendation was based on a series of incidents, not just this one); Draft (Colonial Office) to Addington (Foreign Office), 30 July 1847, PRO/CO201/412.
⁴⁴ Enclosure, Plunkett to Col. Sec, 25 November 1847, PRO/CO201/386; quoted in *Sydney Chronicle*, 7 October 1847; William MacKenzie to 'My dear Matheson', 8 July 1848, B6/3/370, Jardine, Matheson Papers. My thanks to Ass. Prof. T.H. Irving for this reference; 'Wm. MacKenzie—I have advanced him £50, more in order to get his Bill on Lady MacKenzie of Gairlock for the whole; £125' (W.S. Boyd to G.H. Wray, no. 23, PRO/J90/1419).
⁴⁵ *Australian*, 29 October 1847; *Sydney Chronicle*, 7 October 1847.
⁴⁶ *SMH*, 2 October 1847.
⁴⁷ *Sydney Chronicle*, 7 October 1847.
⁴⁸ *SMH*, 4 November 1847.
⁴⁹ B. Boyd to J.W. Sutherland, 9 November 1847, PRO/J90/1446/B147; *The Colonial Intelligencer; or, Aborigines' Friend*, 1849, p. 91.
⁵⁰ 28 September 1847, quoting, with reference to Boyd, from an earlier editorial of 4 May 1847.
⁵¹ B. Boyd to J.W. Sutherland, 9 November 1847, PRO/J90/1446/B147.

230   Notes (Chapters 7-8)

⁵² *Bell's Life in Sydney*, 8 April 1848.
⁵³ B. Boyd to J.W. Sutherland, 17 March 1848, PRO/J90/1446/B147.

8 The British Lobby

¹ B. Boyd to J.W. Sutherland, 14 February 1847, PRO/J90/1446/B147.
² G.H. Wray to Webb, 25 April 1845, PRO/J90/1422.
³ B. Boyd to J.W. Sutherland, 1 February 1845, PRO/J90/1446/B147; G.H. Wray to B. Boyd, 2 August 1845, PRO/J90/1422.
⁴ 10 July 1845, Minutes of General Meetings, RBA, PRO/J90/1331.
⁵ 'I observe that no account currt. has been rendered by Messrs. Boyd Bros. & Co. of the numerous Shipments made to them & which for a long time were not drawn against. So far as I can understand there ought to be a large Balance due by them which ought to be looked to' (W.S. Boyd to G.H. Wray, no. 28, 14 October 1848, PRO/J90/1419); Wryghte Report.
⁶ G. H. Wray to J.P. Robinson, 9 March 1846, PRO/J90/1422.
⁷ B. Boyd to J.W. Sutherland, 1 February 1845, PRO/J90/1446.
⁸ Mark Boyd said at the London Tavern meeting that the journey took 26 days and 8 hours (*Colonial Gazette*, 18 April 1846, quoted in *Hobart Town Courier*, 15 August 1846); *Atlas*, 13 December 1845.
⁹ 4 September 1845, J.P. Robinson, Address to the Queen on Steam Communication, NSW LC *V&P*, 1845.
¹⁰ *Colonial Gazette*, 18 April 1846; Boyd Cable, *A Hundred Year History of the P. & O.* (London: Nicholson and Watson, 1937), p. 118.
¹¹ During 1844 the Australian colonies had received 66 318 letters and 105 087 newspapers from London, and another 2182 letters and 1013 newspapers from Liverpool, and sent, in return, 68 652 letters and 95 134 newspapers. A further 2855 letters and 651 newspapers were received from India (Mark Boyd, *Notes on our Australian Colonies*, pp. 5-7).
¹² Lieut. Waghorn, *Letter to the Rt. Hon. the Earl Grey*, [10 February] 1847, reprinted in *Hobart Town Courier*, 14 August 1847; Lieut. Waghorn, *Second Letter to the Rt. Hon. the Earl Grey*, [20 February] 1847, reprinted in *Hobart Town Courier*, 18 August 1847; G.H. Wray to B. Boyd, 17 February 1847, PRO/J90/1422; *Hobart Town Courier*, 28 August 1847.
¹³ *SMH*, 18, 26 April 1846; Bogue, *Steam to Australia*.
¹⁴ *Hobart Town Courier*, 28 August 1847; *The Times*, 10 August 1847.
¹⁵ John Yates (India and Australian Royal Mail Steam Packet Company) to Charles Nicholson (Speaker of the NSW LC) 15 December 1847, enclosure in Report of the Select Committee on Steam Communi-

cation with England, India and China, 1848, NSW LC V&P, 1848; *Hobart Town Courier*, 24 October 1849; see also Boyd Cable, *A Hundred Year History of the P. & O.*, op. cit., p. 119, and John Bach, *A Maritime History of Australia*, (Sydney: Pan Books, 1982) p. 109.

16 Boyd Cable, *A Hundred Year History of the P. & O.*, op. cit., pp. 118-32.
17 *Hobart Town Courier*, 30 December 1848.)
18 e.g. Evidence of Frederick Parbury, 23 March 1848:

1397. If you were allowed to take Men from any Sea Port, the South Seas, or otherwise, and supposing you paid them the same as the Americans, [1/130th lay] would you be enabled then to compete with them?

We could get Men at Sydney at a much lower Rate than the Americans, and, I think, equally good Whalers. There are a Number of South Sea Islanders that are ready to go on this Voyage.

1398. And New Zealanders?

Yes; we can take them now they are British Seamen. When I owned Whalers we could only take them as Foreigners. That is some Years ago.

(First Report from the Select Committee of the House of Lords appointed to Inquire into the Policy and Operation of the Navigation Laws, 19 May 1848.)

19 Evidence of Samuel Browning, 18 March 1847. First Report of the Select Committee from the House of Commons on Navigation Laws, 26 March 1847.
20 *SMH*, 2, 27 March 1846.
21 Donaldson was treasurer of the fund which collected money for Archibald Boyd during 1846. Ronald Parsons, *Ships of Australia and New Zealand before 1850*, Part 2, K-Z (Adelaide: privately printed by R. Parsons, 1983); *SMH*, 14 May 1846.
22 *Port Phillip Herald*, 8 July 1847; *SMH*, 4 October 1845.
23 B. Boyd to Mark Boyd, 11 July 1846, reprinted in *SMH*, 28 June 1847; P. A. Pemberton, *Pure Merinos and Others: The 'Shipping Lists' of The Australian Agricultural Company* (Canberra: ANU Printing Services, 1986) p. 104; Evidence of Samuel Browning, 16 March 1847, First Report of the Select Committee on Navigation Laws, op. cit.; see also entry on Samuel Browning (1802-1888) in *New Zealand Dictionary of Biography* (Wellington: Dept of Internal Affairs, 1940), pp. 106-7; Mark Boyd, *Notes on our Australian Colonies*, p. 16.
25 It is clear from his correspondence with Robert Towns at this time that Brooks feared the threat of change in the present regulations. Evidence of Robert Brooks, 23 March 1848, First Report from the Select Committee of the House of Lords...[on] Navigation Laws, op. cit.

Notes (Chapter 8)

26 Robert Towns to Robert Brooks, no. 585, 14 February 1849, Robert Towns and Co. Papers, MSS 307.
27 B. Boyd to J. W. Sutherland, 1, 14 February 1845, PRO/J90/1446/B147.
28 9 December 1848.
29 Bogue, *Steam to Australia*, p. 47.
30 B. Boyd to J. W. Sutherland, 3 September 1846, PRO/J90/1446.
31 J. M. Ward, 'Sir Charles FitzRoy', in *ADB*, vol. 1 (Melbourne: Melbourne University Press, 1966), p. 389; *SMH*, 27 June, 25 July 1846.
32 B. Boyd to J. W. Sutherland, 9 November 1846, 29 June 1847, PRO/J90/1446/B147.
33 B. Boyd to J. W. Sutherland, 17 March 1848, PRO/J90/1446/B147.
34 *Bell's Life in Sydney*, 8 April 1848, gives a full list of names, including 'John O'Connell' [sic] and Samuel Sydney [sic].
35 *Morning Herald*, 14 July 1848, quoted in Mark Boyd, *Notes on our Australian Colonies*, p. 19.
36 The ration Mark Boyd promised was considerably more generous than that offered on Ben Boyd's stations (Mark Boyd, *Notes on our Australian Colonies*).
37 B. Boyd to J. W. Sutherland, 17 March 1848, PRO/J90/1446/B147.
38 G. H. Wray to B. Boyd, 16 March 1847, PRO/J90/1422.
39 Minutes of Annual General Meeting, RBA, 29 July 1846, PRO/J90/1331; G. H. Wray to J. P. Robinson, 31 July 1846, PRO/J90/1422.
40 Edward Lennox Boyd to G. H. Wray, 29 July 1846 and B. and M. Boyd to 'Sir' [Wray?], 30 August 1848, PRO/J90/1346/3; R. Allan to G. H. Wray, 2 January 1847, 10 January 1848, PRO/J90/1346/1; G. H. Wray to J. P. Robinson, 17 August 1846, PRO/J90/1422.
41 'One thing I cannot understand. What became of all the property sent home during 1843, 1844, 1845, to Boyd Bros. & Co. which was not drawn against?' (W. S. Boyd to Adam Duff, 14 February 1849, PRO/J90/1346/5).
42 Wryghte Report, pp. 8-9; Robinson's total debt is extrapolated from individual letters from Robinson to Wray during this period, PRO/J90/1348.
43 J. W. Sutherland, G. N. Webster, Adam Duff, Mark Boyd, John Connell to B. Boyd and J. P. Robinson, 14 October 1846, PRO/J90/1422.
44 G. H. Wray to B. Boyd, 17 October 1846, PRO/J90/1422.
45 J. P. Robinson to G. H. Wray, 11 September, 1 October, 9 November 1847, PRO/J90/1348.
46 B. Boyd to J. W. Sutherland, 25 July 1846, PRO/J90/1446/B147.
47 Minutes of General Meetings, RBA, 11 August 1847, PRO/J90/1331; G. H. Wray to B. Boyd, 17 August 1847, PRO/J90/1422.
48 G. H. Wray to B. Boyd, 25 October, 1 November 1847, PRO/J90/1422.

9 Retrenchment

1. This meeting was called for Bathurst, and is an example of many similar (*Atlas*, 1 February 1845).
2. Gipps to Stanley, no. 205, Executive, 23 November 1845 (AONSW).
3. See e.g. Barrie Dyster, 'Support for the Squatters, 1844' in *Journal of the Royal Australian Historical Society*, vol. 51, 1965; Alan Powell, *Patrician Democrat: The Political Life of Charles Cowper, 1843-1870* (Melbourne: Melbourne University Press, 1977) p. 31.
4. J. P. Robinson to Sam Browning, 28 June 1847, PRO/J90/1348/2.
5. B. Boyd to J. W. Sutherland, 19 September 1845, PRO/J90/1446/B147.
6. E.g. 'I question if any of the revolting Americans suffered more in their property before they took arms in defence of self government ... a change of measures alone will prevent this country assuming independence as soon as strong enough' (Hobler MSS, vol. VII, 15 May 1850, in C. M. H. Clark, *Select Documents in Australian History*, vol. 1, 1788-1850, Sydney: Angus and Robertson, 1950, p. 294); Sidney, *The Three Colonies of Australia*, p. 131.
7. The fossils, which included the skull and lower jaw of a *Diprotodon*, were later sent to England by Curwen Boyd, but were lost in a shipwreck. Sydney Museum took casts (A. Mosley Moyal, ed., *Scientists in Nineteenth Century Australia: A Documentary History*, Sydney: Cassell, 1976, p. 205); *Australian*, 5, 15 June 1847.
8. W. S. Boyd to Alex. Matheson, 5 February 1844, letter no. 2385, London, In-correspondence, 1836-1844, Jardine, Matheson Papers; 'William goes into Parliament ... on the first vacancy', Archibald Boyd to B. Boyd, 11 July 1844, reprinted in *SMH*, 23 December 1844. W. S. Boyd was a member of the Reform Club and many of his letters are addressed from there.
9. 'when I hear ... that even some of my Brother Directors have suggested other persons being sent out. To these I do not pay the slightest attention, feeling assured that I was too well acquainted with my colleagues to suppose that any such interference would be proposed, I should be delighted to have the advice and cooperation of any of themselves in the Colony, but with regard to the interference of a third party they must be well aware that I would not submit to such a thing for a moment' (B. Boyd to J. W. Sutherland, 7 October 1843, PRO/J90/1446).
10. W. S. Boyd to [Donald?] Matheson, 8 December 1847, no. 3155, Unbound Correspondence, In-letters, London, January 1847-June 1850, Jardine, Matheson Papers; W. S. Boyd to Donald Matheson, 28 April 1848, Private, Australia 1837-1888, Jardine, Matheson Papers; W. A. Miles to J. P. Townsend, 23 April 1850, J. P. Townsend Papers.

234   Notes (Chapter 9)

[11] W. S. Boyd to Directors of the RBA, no. 1, 26 April 1848, PRO/J90/1419/B91.
[12] The minor loans were to William Elyard, on 80 horses at Illawarra, Andrew Lang, on 1200 cattle at Liverpool Plains, and Arthur Devlin, on 3000 cattle at Murrumbidgee (B. Boyd to W. S. Boyd, 20 April 1848, enclosure in W. S. Boyd to Directors of the RBA, no. 1, 26 April 1848).
[13] In 1848 he predicted a revenue as follows:

500 000 lbs of clean Wool at 1/3	£31 250
15 000 sheep sold & boil'd down at Stations at 5/-	4 500
6000 Cattle ″ ″ at 30/-	9 000
7 whalers at 40 Barrels p month will give 336 Tuns Sperm oil at £70	23 520
Juno Steamer per annum	5 000
Boyd Town ″	1 000
Other sources of revenue (horses now ready for Market)	1 000
	£75 270
And allowing for all expenses of Stock Loss & Outfits of Whalers, Repairs of Shipping & Cost of Establishments	34 929
It will leave to be remitted home	40 341

For 1849:

650 000 lbs of clean wool at 1/3	40 625
30 000 sheep sold & boiled down at 6/-	9 000
8000 cattle ″ ″ 30/-	12 000
150 Horses for India @ £20	3 000
7 whalers at 40 Barrels p month will give 336 Tuns Sperm Oil at £70	23 520
Juno Steamer	5 000
Boyd Town	1 000
Other sources of revenue	1 000
	95 145
And allowing for all expenses of Stock Loss & Outfits of whalers, repair of Shipping & Cost of Establishments	41 170
it will leave to be remitted home	53 975

—and so on, for 1850 to 1852.
(B. Boyd to W. S. Boyd, 20 April 1848, enclosure in W. S. Boyd to Directors of the RBA, no. 1, 26 April 1848, PRO/J90/1419/B91.)
[14] W. S. Boyd to G. H. Wray, no. 9, 6 July 1848, PRO/J90/1419/B91.
[15] Or so W. S. Boyd believed in May. But G. C. Forbes registered the

Notes (Chapter 9) 235

Velocity and the William in his own name in February 1848. Did Ben Boyd conceal the nature of this deal from his cousin? (W.S. Boyd to Directors of the RBA, no. 2, 24 May 1848, and W.S. Boyd to G.H. Wray, no. 5, 2 June 1848, PRO/J90/1419/B91; Ronald Parsons, *Ships of Australia and New Zealand before 1850*, Part 2, K-Z, (Adelaide: privately printed by R. Parsons, 1983).
16 See e. g., Thomas Craufurd to G. H. Wray, 10 October 1849, Misc. letters, RBA, PRO/J90/1346/4.
17 W.S. Boyd to Directors of the RBA, no. 1, 26 April 1848, PRO/J90/1419/B91.
18 W.S. Boyd to Directors of the RBA, no. 2, 24 May, and no. 9, 6 July 1848, PRO/J90/1419/B91.
19 W. A. Miles to J.P. Townsend, 15 May 1849, J.P. Townsend Papers.
20 W.S. Boyd to G. H. Wray, no. 18, 15 August 1848, PRO/J90/1419/B91; R. Want (for W.S. Boyd) to Col. Sec., 26 September 1848, Col. Sec. Dept., 48/10455, AONSW.
21 *Cornubia* was registered in the name of J.P. Robinson, then in February 1849 she was registered at Sydney in the name of James Paddon, master mariner (Parsons, *Ships of Australia and New Zealand before 1850*, op. cit.)
22 W.S. Boyd to G.H. Wray, no. 20, 23 August, no. 28, 14 October, no. 31, 17 November 1848, PRO/J90/1419.
23 W.S. Boyd to G.H. Wray, no. 21, 24 August, and no. 28, 14 October 1848, PRO/J90/1419/B91.
24 W.S. Boyd to G. H. Wray, no. 53, 13 April 1849, PRO/J90/1419.
25 *SMH*, 1 October 1847; W.S. Boyd to G.H. Wray, no. 42, 6 February 1848, PRO/J90/1419/B91.
26 W.A. Miles to Townsend, 23 June 1850, J.P. Townsend Papers
27 Cowper's biographer, Dr Alan Powell, confirms this, but assumes that the issue related in some way to Boyd's South Sea islanders. I am grateful to Dr Powell for his help.
28 See Paul de Serville, *Port Phillip Gentlemen and Good Society in Melbourne before the Gold Rushes* (Melbourne: Oxford University Press, 1980), ch. V; *Atlas*, 19, 26 August 1848.
29 W.S. Boyd to the electors of Port Phillip, *Australian*, 20 July 1848; Edward Curr to Archibald Cunninghame, 8 July 1848, Cunninghame Papers, vol. 3, 1845-56.
30 *Atlas*, 29 July 1848.
31 But Robinson was still alive when he attempted to nominate (W.S. Boyd to G.H. Wray, no. 43, 14 February 1849, PRO/J90/1419).
32 C. Nicholson to A. Cunninghame, 4 March 1849, Cunninghame Papers, vol. 3, 1845-56; R.L. Knight, 'Archibald Boyd', in *ADB*, vol. 1 (Melbourne: Melbourne University Press, 1966).
33 C. Nicholson to A. Cunninghame, 4 March 1849, Cunninghame

Papers, vol. 3, 1845-56; W. S. Boyd to G. H. Wray, no. 29, 11 November 1848, and no. 43, 14 February 1849, PRO/J90/1419/B91.
34 W. S. Boyd to G. H. Wray, no. 31, 17 November 1848, and no. 42, 6 February 1849, PRO/J90/1419; Ellis and Makinson, Solicitors, to G. P. Keon, 14 February 1884, in Wellings Papers, Box 4.
35 9 December 1848.
36 The Immigration Board, H. H. Massie and John Branwell, Twofold Bay, for the Agent for Immigration, Sydney, F. Merewether, 24 March 1849, enclosure in FitzRoy to Grey, no. 84, Executive, 5 May 1849, Governor's Despatches to the Secretary of State for the Colonies, vol. 61.
37 Wells, *Gazetteer*, pp. 69-85; *Morning Chronicle* (London), 2 February 1850.
38 W. S. Boyd to G. H. Wray, no. 32, 3 January 1849, PRO/J90/1419/B91; W. S. Boyd to Adam Duff, 14 February 1849, enclosure in Adam Duff to G. H. Wray, 5 June 1849, PRO/J90/1346/5.
39 This money amounted to more than £7000. The Royal Bank counter-claimed the money due on calls on shares from W. S. Boyd (A. Boyd to J. W. Sutherland, 9 December 1848, and A. Boyd to G. H. Wray, 30 January, 5 December 1849. PRO/J90/1346/3).
40 Minutes of General Meetings, RBA, 13 February 1849, PRO/J90/1331.
41 Sam Browning to G. H. Wray, 11 May 1849, PRO/J90/1346/3; W. A. Miles to J. P. Townsend, 23 June 1850, J. P. Townsend Papers.
42 W. A. Miles to J. P. Townsend, 15 May 1849, J. P. Townsend Papers; *Hobart Town Courier*, 21 July 1849.
43 Wryghte Report (Appendix); Boyd (Jervis Bay) to Sam [Browning], 1 November 1849, copy in Wellings Papers, Box 4.

10 The Wanderer

1 *Bell's Life in Sydney*, 2 June 1849; *SMH*, 23 December 1848; see Charles Bateson, *Gold Fleet for California: Forty-Niners from Australia and New Zealand* (Sydney: Ure Smith, 1963), pp. 156-61.
2 W. S. Boyd to G. H. Wray, no. 65, 23 July 1849, PRO/J90/1419/B91; Bateson, op. cit., pp. 51-2.
3 W. A. Miles to J. P. Townsend, 23 June 1850, J. P. Townsend Papers; B. Boyd to Sam [Browning], 1 November 1849, Wellings Papers.
4 *The Times*, 14 March 1842.
5 Marion Diamond, Charles St Julian 1818-1874: The Biography of a Colonial Visionary (Ph.D. thesis, University of Queensland, 1981); Merze Tate, 'Hawaii's Early Interest in Polynesia', *Australian Journal of Politics and History*, vol. 7, 1961; R. C. Wyllie to C. FitzRoy, 11 April 1850, enclosure in Merivale to Addington, 13 May 1851, PRO/FO58/72 (AJCP 1529).

Notes (Chapter 10) 237

6 *Polynesian*, 25 March 1850, extracted in *Bell's Life in Sydney*, 18 May 1850.
7 Herbert Asbury, *The Barbary Coast: An Informal History of the San Francisco Underworld* (New York: Alfred A. Knopf, 1933), p. 49; *Alta California*, 30 March, 3 April 1850.
8 C. Nicholson to A. Cunninghame, 12 February 1851, Cunninghame Papers, vol. 3; Audley Coote [?], typescript, 15 May 1907.
9 Roger W. Lotchin, *San Francisco, 1846-1856: From Hamlet to City* (New York: Oxford University Press, 1974), pp. 192-3.
10 Webster, *The Last Cruise of the Wanderer*, p. 1; Coote, op. cit.
11 Annabella Boswell, who entertained the men from *Wanderer* at Port Macquarie, referred to Ottiwell only, as an American (Annabella Boswell to [?], 29 December [1851], in Captain J. H. Watson, Cutting book of Port Macquarie; Webster, Journals and Papers.
12 Webster, *The Last Cruise of the Wanderer*, p. 13.
13 Ibid., p. 19; R. C. Wyllie to Governor of Oahu, 14 July 1851, copy in FO Box 17, p. 63, Hawaiian Archives.
14 Webster, *The Last Cruise of the Wanderer*, pp. ii, 22.
15 B. Boyd to Lord J. Russell, 8 October 1840, enclosure in Russell to Gipps, no. 164, 24 October 1840, *HRA*, series I, vol. 21, p. 54; B. Boyd to Lords of Her Majesty's Privy Council for Trade and Plantations, 24 October 1840; Draft, Russell to Boyd, 19 October 1840, PRO/CO201/302.
16 Webster, *The Last Cruise of the Wanderer*, pp. 24-5.
17 Ibid., p. 39.
18 Ibid., pp. 43, 58.
19 The document is signed (presumably by proxy) by Taano (King), Faro (his son) and Geo. Crawford. Benjamin Boyd's signature does not appear (Affidavit of John Webster, 25 August 1859 and enclosure A, St Julian Papers).
20 Webster, *The Last Cruise of the Wanderer*, pp. 69, 78.
21 Ibid., p. 76.
22 Ibid., pp. 97-101.
23 Signed Mauki, Barapooro, Lisitado, Arbi, Bai, Urpuru, Waraki, Keriweyo, Hara—all by crosses; also by Barnes and Crawford. Boyd's signature does not appear (Affidavit of John Webster, 25 August 1859, enclosure B, St Julian Papers).
24 B. Boyd, Makira Bay, 6 October 1851, copy, enclosure in Proceedings of Her Majesty's Ship Herald, Captain Denham, 24 November 1854-9 January 1855 to ascertain the fate of Benjamin Boyd. Papers transferred from Parliament House, 1918, A. 1384 ML.
25 I have chosen to use the modern form, but the island was consistently referred to as Guadalcanar, both by Webster, and later in newspaper reports of the incident; Webster, *The Last Cruise of the Wanderer*, pp. 106-8.

238   *Notes (Chapter 10)*

[26] Edward Reeve to John Webster, 24 December 1855, in Webster Papers.
[27] Webster, *The Last Cruise of the Wanderer*, pp. 113-16.
[28] Ibid., pp. 119-24.
[29] The log of the *Wanderer* was one of the documents presented by Mark Boyd in 1863, but since then, sadly, has disappeared (Inventory of Documents produced by Mr. Mark Boyd, in Petition for Special Service as Heir to his Brother Benjamin Boyd, Scottish Record Office); *Illustrated London News*, 10 April 1852.
[30] Letter to the editor of the *SMH* from L. W. S. Wright, 11 January 1960; Captain Boyd's Death at Wanderer Bay, 1851 (as related by 77 years old Paolo Kole), Alan Lennox-Boyd Papers. This account is unreferenced and undated, but was probably collected by Lord Boyd during his visit to Guadalcanal in 1960.
[31] Webster does not say what the firewood was used for, but as he also says that water was short after the first week at sea, I can only assume that this was the reason for their extraordinarily heavy use of firewood.
[32] Webster, *The Last Cruise of the Wanderer*, pp. 127-8; there is a portrait of Emma Green in the Alan Lennox-Boyd Papers.
[33] *Galloway Gazette*, 13 May 1899.
[34] 28, 29 March 1843.
[35] James Cowan, 'Famous New Zealanders, no. 43. John Webster of Hokianga' in *New Zealand Railways Magazine*, 1 October 1936.
[36] B. Boyd to J. W. Sutherland, 18 November 1841, PRO/J90/1446/B147; Florence Cantry to W. P. Wellings, 30 June 1956, in Wellings Papers. Mrs Cantry says in the letter that she was the granddaughter of the sailing master (unnamed) of the *Wanderer* on her original voyage to Australia.
[37] Webster's detailed and circumstantial account was only published later in the 1850s, and its justificatory style is a response to these innuendoes. In 1907, at the age of ninety-two, when the other protagonists were dead, he repeated his story, and it varies little from the published account (John Webster to [?], 31 April 1907, Five letters re the *Wanderer* FM3/389 ML).
[38] *Southern Cross*, 16 December 1851; Letter to the editor from O. O. Dangar, *SMH*, 9 May 1907; G. Crawford to R. F. Campbell, 1 December 1851, Five letters re the *Wanderer*.
[39] Annabella Boswell to [?], 29 December [1851], in Captain J. H. Watson, Cutting book of Port Macquarie.
[40] The issue of Boyd's possible survival was raised in the Court of Chancery in 1856 when the Official Receiver of the Royal Bank of Australia successfully appealed against Mark Boyd's discharge from Bankruptcy (Court of Chancery, 15 December 1856, Before the Lord

Justice of Appeal, In Bankruptcy.—ex parte Wryghte, in re Mark Boyd, *Banker's Magazine*, vol. 17, 1857).

41 Moequard to Edward Lennox Boyd, 30 April 1852, copy in *SMH*, 11 August 1852.
42 *Illustrated Sydney News*, 21 October, 9 December 1854; O. O. Dangar in *SMH*, 9 May 1907.
43 *People's Advocate*, 21 October 1854.
44 'He and my Wife's Brother Rear Admiral Robinson having married Sisters made him feel more than a common interest in the melancholy mission on which the Admiralty despatched him' (Mark Boyd to C. Roach Smith, 14 September 1866, C.205 ML); *The Times*, 10 August 1847.
45 Proceedings of H.M.S. *Herald*, Captain Denham, 24 November 1854 to 9 January 1855 to ascertain the fate of Mr. Benjamin Boyd (in papers transferred from Parliament House, 1918, A.1384 ML); Mark Boyd to C. Roach Smith, 14 September 1866, C.205 ML.
46 Inventory of Documents produced by Mr. Mark Boyd, in Petition for Special Service as Heir to his Brother Benjamin Boyd (Scottish Record Office).
Court of Chancery: re The Royal Bank of Australia, 16 February 1850; re The Royal Bank of Australia, 9, 26 March 1850; ex parte Robinson, 8 July 1852; ex parte Meux's Executors, 9 July 1852; ex parte Walker, 22 April 1854; re the Joint Stock Companies Winding-up Acts 1848 and 1849; re the Royal Bank of Australia, ex parte The Executors of J. P. Robinson, 26 November, 3, 15, 20 December 1855, 23, 24, 25, 28 January, 25, 28 June, 24 November, 4 December 1856; in bankruptcy ex parte Wryghte, in re Mark Boyd, 15 December 1856; in bankruptcy ex parte Wryghte, the claim of the Misses Boyd, 23 April, 22, 23 May 1857.
Court of Bankruptcy: Royal Bank of Australia, in re Mark Boyd, 14 April 1855, 26 June, 5 November 1856.
47 But this is the same source which claimed that Boyd was High Steward at her Coronation, and Cowan may have confused Webster with Oswald Brierly, who became Marine Painter to the Queen (James Cowan, 'Famous New Zealanders no. 43. John Webster of Hokianga' in *New Zealand Railways Magazine*, 1 October 1936).
48 *Southern Cross*, 16 December 1851; C. M. H. Clark, *A History of Australia*, vol. 3 (Melbourne: Melbourne University Press, 1973), p. 456.
49 Charles Archer to his father, in Archer Letters, Mfm A.3876 ML, quoted in Patricia Clarke, *A Colonial Woman: The Life and Times of Mary Braidwood Mowle, 1827-1857* (Sydney: Allen and Unwin, 1986), p. 196.
50 This is a theme pursued in Gavan Daws, *A Dream of Islands: Voyages of Self-discovery in the South Seas* (Brisbane: Jacaranda Press, 1980).

Select Bibliography

Government Archives and Official Sources

Archives Office of New South Wales

Colonial Secretary's Department. Letters received. 1843 4/2614, 4/2616.

Colonial Secretary's Department, correspondence with Governor. 48/10455.

Governor's Despatches to the Secretary of State.

Governor's Despatches from the Secretary of State.

Proceedings of Her Majesty's Ship Herald, Captain Denham, 24 November 1854-9 January 1855 to ascertain the fate of Benjamin Boyd. Papers transferred from Parliament House, 1918. ML A.1384.

Published papers (New South Wales)

New South Wales, Legislative Council, *Votes and Proceedings*.

New South Wales, *Government Gazette*.

Historical Records of Australia.

New Zealand Archives

Colonial Secretary's Department. Internal Affairs. I. 47/2344.

Guildhall, City of London

Register of Stockbrokers' applications. Guildhall, City of London. 1825, 1827.

Guildhall, July 1846. *In the Queen's Bench. Boyd v. The Corporation of the Royal Exchange Assurance.* Tried before Lord Denman and a Special Jury. From the Shorthand Writer's Notes.

Scottish Record Office
Summons of Reduction and Declarator, William Paul against Edward Boyd &c Outer-House. 2 March 1837. X CS46 Box 779.
Inventory of Documents produced by Mr. Mark Boyd. In Petition for Special Service as Heir to his Brother Benjamin Boyd, 2133SS, enclosure in C29/17/12, no. 22, Proof. In Petition Mark Boyd Esq. for Special Service to the Deceased Benjamin Boyd Esq. of Mertonhall, 17 November 1863, Additional Proof, 4 December 1863.

Hawaiian Archives
Foreign Office and Executive Files.

Public Record Office
The main collection of material on which this book is based is contained under the general heading PRO/90. Following the failure of the Royal Bank of Australia, the Court of Chancery collected from London and Australia as many documents as possible relating to the case. These were then used as the basis for the investigation by W. C. Wryghte, the Official Receiver of the bank. The collection is large but patchy. Some of the material has been destroyed by insects or water damage, and not all can be microfilmed. Nonetheless it remains a splendid collection of documents relating to many aspects of company investment in New South Wales in the 1840s, including stock and station books, letter books covering correspondence between the Royal Bank agencies in the colonies and between London and Australia, minute books, and miscellaneous letters from shareholders to the Royal Bank. The following list contains those sections most useful for this biography—but many more books are yet to be written from J90.

J90/1331 Minutes of General Meetings, Royal Bank of Australia.
J90/1332 Minutes, Royal Bank of Australia.
J90/1346/1-5 In-letters to London branch, mainly dealing with financial affairs of the bank.
J90/1347 Assorted letters to London branch.
J90/1348/2 In-letters to London branch, containing letters of J. P. Robinson.
J90/1348/3 In-letters to London branch.
J90/1349 Assorted papers—J90/1349/3 contains the will of Joseph Phelps Robinson.

242 Select Bibliography

J90/1353 Letter books from Boydtown, mostly Moutry to Robinson.
J90/1390 Royal Bank of Australia, Consignment Book, Boydtown and London.
J90/1419/B91 Letter book of W. S. Boyd to London branch.
J90/1422 Out-letters from London branch, mostly G. H. Wray to Australia (including B. and W. S. Boyd).
J90/1446/B147 Correspondence of Boyd to Sutherland.

CO201/302 Australia, Original Correspondence, Board of Trade 1840.
CO201/321 Governor's Despatches from New South Wales 1842.
CO201/345 Governor's Despatches 1844.
CO201/349 Governor's Despatches 1844.
CO201/354 Individuals, etc. I-Z 1844.
CO201/357 Despatches 1845.
CO201/363 Miscellaneous and Individuals, A-J 1845.
CO201/386 Despatches 1847.
CO201/412 Despatches 1849.

CO323/226 Colonies, General. Original Correspondence, Offices and Individuals 1840.

FO58/72 General Correspondence, Pacific Islands (Consul General for the Pacific) AJCP 1529.

Published Papers (Great Britain)

First Report from the Select Committee on Navigation Laws... Ordered, by The House of Commons, to be Printed, 26 March 1847.

First Report from the Select Committee of the House of Lords appointed to Inquire into the Policy and Operation of the Navigation Laws... Ordered, by the House of Commons, to be Printed, 19 May 1848.
Facsimile edition of both Reports (Shannon: Irish University Press, 1969).

[Wryghte Report] *In the matter of the Joint-Stock Companies Winding-up Acts, 1848 and 1849, and of the Royal Bank of Australia. Report of the Official Manager on the affairs of the above Company*, by order of the Master, dated May, 1854. Copy in Goldsmiths Library, University of London.

Private Papers

Australian Agricultural Company. Despatches etc. from New South Wales. ANU, Archives of Business and Labour, 78/1/17.
Mark Boyd to C. Roach Smith, 14 September 1866. C.205, ML.
O. H. Brierly, Journals of the Wanderer. A527/8, ML.
———, Journal of the Wanderer, August to October 1844. A.534, ML.
———, Journal of the Wanderer—Journal of a visit to Maneroo, 1842-3. A.537, ML.
———, Journal on Wanderer and at Sydney, 1843-44. A.539, ML.
———, Diary at Twofold Bay, April-September. 1847. A.540, ML.
Robert Brooks and Company Papers. AJCP M582-583.
Audley Coote [?], typescript, apparently written by Captain Audley Coote, 15 May 1907. Inserted between pp. 124 and 125, Newspaper cuttings, vol. 7, ML.
Cunninghame Papers, vol. 3, 1845-56. A 3180, ML.
Jardine, Matheson Papers. Cambridge University Library.
Letters and papers chiefly from the correspondence of Phillip Parker King. Collected by the late H.O. Lethbridge Esq. A.3599, ML.
Peter Laurie, Diary (1832). Copy at the Guildhall, MS. 20, 334.
Alan Lennox-Boyd Papers. Ince Castle, Cornwall—used with the permission of Patricia, Lady Boyd.
Macarthur Papers, vol. 31, James Macarthur, J. C. Pott and the Australian, 1842-1850. A.2927, ML.
Sir Thomas Mitchell Papers. ML.
North British Insurance Company, Minute Books (Edinburgh). Mitchell Library, Glasgow.
Letters (4) received from Joseph Phelps Robinson, Sydney... and William Sprott Boyd. ML, DOC 1116.
Indenture of the Royal Bank of Australia, 3 August 1840. Copy in the Goldsmiths Library, University of London.
St Julian Papers. ML.
J. P. Townsend Papers, MSS 1461(3). ML.
Robert Towns and Co. Papers, Catalogued, vol. 5, vol. 10. ML.
———, Uncatalogued MSS. 307, Letterbooks of correspondence to Robert Brooks and Co. ML.
Five letters re the *Wanderer*. FM3/389, ML.

Captain J. H. Watson, Cutting book of Port Macquarie (1923). ML.
John Webster, Journals and Papers, 1849-1886. Alexander Turnbull Library, Wellington, New Zealand.
Wellings Papers. NLA.

Newspapers and Journals

Alta California (San Francisco)
Arden's Sydney Magazine
Athenaeum (London)
Atlas (Sydney)
Australian (Sydney)
Bankers Magazine (London)
Bell's Life in London
Bell's Life in Sydney
Chambers Magazine (London)
Colonial Gazette (London)
Colonial Intelligencer; or, Aborigines Friend (London)
Croydon and Sutton Advertiser and East and Mid-Surrey Reporter
Dumfries and Galloway Courier
Dumfries Weekly Journal
Economist (London)
Galloway Gazette
Gentleman's Magazine (London)
Heads of the People (Sydney)
Hobart Town Courier
Illustrated London News
Illustrated Sydney News
Launceston Advertiser
London Post Office Directory
Morning Chronicle (London)
Morning Herald (London)
New Zealand Gazette (Auckland)
People's Advocate (Sydney)
Port Phillip Herald (Melbourne)
Punch (London)
Scotsman (Edinburgh)
Southern Cross (Auckland)
Sydney Chronicle (formerly *Australasian Chronicle* and *Morning Chronicle*)

Select Bibliography 245

Sydney Morning Herald (formerly *Sydney Herald*)
The Times (London)
Weekly Register (Sydney)
Wigton Free Press

Contemporary Published Works

Anon (June 1836). 'Parish of Cadder, Presbytery of Glasgow, Synod of Glasgow and Ayr' in *A New Statistical Account of Scotland by the Ministers of the Respective Parishes, under the Superintendence of a Committee of the Society for the Benefit of the Sons and Daughters of the Clergy*, vol. VI, Lanark (Edinburgh and London: William Blackwood and Sons, 1845).

Bogue, A. Esq. *Steam to Australia. A Letter addressed to the Right Honourable Earl Grey* (Sydney: W. and F. Ford, 1847).

Boyd, Benjamin Esq. *A Letter to His Excellency Sir William Denison, &c., &c., &c., Lieutenant-Governor of Van Diemen's Land, on the Expediency of Transferring the Unemployed Labor of that Colony to New South Wales* (Sydney: F. Wolfe, 1847).

Mr. Benjamin Boyd's Evidence before the Select Committee of the Legislative Council of New South Wales; with the Report of the Select Committee on the Renewal of Transportation (Cheapside: W. H. Bruce, 1847).

Boyd, Mark. *Notes on our Australian Colonies; in connexion with the Colonization Society* (London: T. Richards, 1864).

―― *Reminiscences of Fifty Years* (London: Longmans, Green and Co., 1871).

―― *Social Gleanings* (London: Longmans, Green and Co., 1875).

Campbell, John Logan. *Poenamo. Sketches of the Early Days of New Zealand* (London: William and Northgate, 1881).

'Garryowen' [Edmund Finn]. *The Chronicles of Early Melbourne, 1835 to 1852, historical, anecdotal and personal* (Melbourne: Fergusson and Mitchell, 1888).

Laurie, Sir Peter. *Killing no Murder; or, the effects of separate confinement on the bodily and mental condition of Prisoners in the Government Prisons and other gaols in Great Britain and America* (London: John Murray, 1846).

Laurie, P. G. *Sir Peter Laurie, a Family Memoir* (Brentwood: privately printed, William and Whitworth, 1901).
North British and Mercantile Insurance Company. *Centenary. 1809-1909.* (Edinburgh: privately printed, 1909). Guildhall Library. Pam. 5747.
Richardson, Rev. Samuel. 'The Parish of Penninghame' in *The New Statistical Account of Scotland...*, vol. IV, Dumfries—Kirkcudbright—Wigton (Edinburgh and London: William Blackwood and Sons, 1845).
Robinson, John R. and Hunter H. *The Life of Robert Coates better known as 'Romeo' and 'Diamond' Coates the celebrated 'Amateur of Fashion'* (London: Sampson Low, Marston, 1891).
Rusden, G. W. *History of New Zealand*, vol. 1 (Melbourne: Melville and Slade, 2nd ed., 1895).
Sidney, Samuel. *The Three Colonies of Australia: New South Wales, Victoria, South Australia; Their Pastures, Copper Mines, & Gold Fields* (London: Ingram, Cooke, 2nd ed., 1853).
Templer, John C. (ed.). *The Private Letters of Sir James Brooke, K.C.B., Rajah of Sarawak, narrating the events of his life, from 1838 to the present time* (London: Richard Bentley, 1853).
Waghorn, Lieut. R.N., F.R.A.S., etc. *Letter to the Rt. Hon. the Earl Grey, Secretary of State for the Colonies, on the Extension of Steam Navigation from Singapore to Port Jackson, Australia* (London: Smith, Elder, and Co., [10 February] 1847).
────── *Second Letter to the Rt. Hon. the Earl Grey, Secretary of State for the Colonies, on the Extension of Steam Navigation from Singapore to Port Jackson, Australia.* (London: Smith, Elder, and Co. [20 February] 1847).
Webster, John. *The Last Cruise of the Wanderer* (Sydney: Cunninghame, n.d.[185?]).
Wells, William Henry. *A Geographical Dictionary or Gazetteer of the Australian Colonies, 1848* (facsimile ed., Sydney: Council of the Library of New South Wales, 1970).
Westgarth, William. *Australia Felix; or, A Historical and Descriptive Account of the Settlement of Port Phillip, New South Wales...* (Edinburgh: Oliver and Boyd, 1848).
────── *Personal Reminiscences of Early Melbourne and Victoria* (Melbourne and Sydney: George Robertson, 1888).

Index

Aaron, Captain Frank, 190
Aboriginal labour, 98, 119-20
Aborigines' Protection Society, 135
Allan, Robert, 20
Aneityum, New Hebribes (Vanuatu), 128, 134-5
Atlas, 82-3, 166-8, 179-80
Australian, 83, 225
Australian Agricultural Company, 73, 95, 118, 152, 227
Australian Wool Company, 23-4, 38-9, 55, 143, 162, 175

Bank of Australasia, 17, 44
Bank of Australia, 36, 45
Bank of New South Wales, 17
banking, 12, 17, 24, 35-8
Barnes, Gillwell, 190, 194, 200, 202, 207
Beaudesert (Moreton Bay district), 58, 176
Bibbenluke (Maneroo district), 58, 103
Bland, Dr William, 86
Bligh district, 56
Boco Rock (Maneroo district), 58, 103
Bogue, Adam, 61, 147, 155, 180
boiling-down of livestock (for tallow production), 60, 103
Bombala, 103
Boswell, Annabella, 207, 237
Bourke, Sir Richard (Governor of New South Wales), 53

Boyd, Archibald (cousin, of Broadmeadows), 7, 14, 58, 77-9, 82, 83, 87, 90, 136, 158, 166-7, 172, 180-1, 185, 223, 231
Boyd, Archibald (cousin, of Hillhousefield and Leith), 7, 158, 171, 184-5
Boyd, Benjamin
  chronological: early life, 5-8, 12-14, 204-5; attends the Coronation, 13, 206; financial investments, 11-12; colonial investment, 14-16, 35, 75, 90, 93, 102-3, 142-3; establishment of Royal Bank of Australia, 17-20, 90, 211; share purchases, 20, 143; and the Australian Wool Company, 23-4, 38-9, 175; and yachting, 25-7, 63-5, 169, 185-6, 188, 190; voyage to Australia, 18, 27-9, 31-3, 166; loan to New Zealand government, 40-7, 65; land purchases, 34, 38-9, 55-61, 99, 104, 195, 198-9; squatting runs, 50-1, 55-60, 71-2, 89, 103, 128, 172-7, 175, 177-8; and Boydtown, 98-100, 102-10, 121, 162, 175, 177, 182; Chairman of Pastoral Association, 72-4, 82, 147, 166; co-ordinating British lobby, 77-9, 85, 87-90, 124-5, 139-40, 144-5, 147, 149, 151-2, 156-7; Member of the Legislative Council, 84-7, 90, 147; witness at Select Committee (on Crown Lands) 76-7, (on

247

248 Index

Immigration) 115-18, (on re-introduction of convicts) 123-4, 161; advocates re-introduction of convicts, 122-5, 132, 137, 228; and labour relations, 105-13, 115-18, 120-2, 126-7, 136-40, 157, 166, 168-9; and Pacific island labour, 112, 120-1, 126-40, 150, 155, 191-2, 209-10; duel with Cowper, 126, 179-80; relations with board of the Royal Bank of Australia, 141-4, 162-5, 170-1, 179, 210, 233; retrenchment and bankruptcy, 169-70, 174-9, 181-2, 185-6; goaled for debt, 181; illness, 171-2, 174; voyage to California, 188-9; voyage to the Pacific, 190-5; vision of a 'South Seas republic', 25, 32, 188, 192-3, 195; in the Solomon Islands, 195-203; death, 200-4, 208-9; suspicions surrounding death, 206-8; legends, 204-6, 209
general: attitude to race, 9, 120-1, 126-8, 137-8; character, 13-14, 32-5, 91-2, 95-7, 155-6, 162, 166, 168, 183, 185-6, 189; indirect political influence, 47-8, 108, 151, 166-7, 169; interest in China, 90-1, 121, 155; loyalty to kin, 7-8, 61-2; political attitudes, 64-5, 84-5, 154-6, 168; procrastination and poor management practices, 28-9, 32-3, 65-7, 90-2, 95, 105-6, 112-13, 128, 137, 141-3, 163, 172-3, 184; relationship with newspapers, 82-4, 108-9, 179, 183, 227; shipping and whaling interests, 93-8, 100-3, 106, 119-21, 148-55, 162, 172-5, 177, 184-5; social life, 61-5, 83, 169
Boyd, Edward (father), 5-10, 13, 78, 145
Boyd, Edward ('Dick', black servant), 9, 126
Boyd, Edward Lennox (brother), 81, 139, 158, 161-2, 164, 207
Boyd, Elizabeth (née Dreddington, Mrs Archibald Boyd of Broadmeadows), 185, 223

Boyd, Emma Anne (Mrs Mark Boyd, formerly Mrs Robert Coates, née Robinson), 217, 238
Boyd, James (brother), 28, 32, 61
Boyd, James (uncle), 5
Boyd, Janet (mother, née Yule), 6, 207
Boyd, John, MP (cousin, of Ulster), 158
Boyd, John (uncle), 5
Boyd, John Curwen Christian (brother), 15, 28, 61, 107, 169, 233
Boyd, Maitland (cousin), 81
Boyd, Margaret (née Campbell, Mrs J. C. C. Boyd), 15, 28
Boyd, Mark (brother), 5-6, 8-13, 26, 33, 56, 120, 155, 161, 206, 208, 230, 232: bankruptcy, 207, 209; director of Royal Bank of Australia, 21-2; financial activities, 10-12, 164; lobbying activities, 78, 80-2, 90, 91, 124, 140, 144-9, 152-3, 156-60, 170; partnerships with Benjamin Boyd, 23, 143, 147, 183
Boyd, Thomas Elder (no relation), 87
Boyd, William (grandfather), 5-6
Boyd, William (uncle), 5
Boyd, William Mitchell (cousin), 14-15, 58
Boyd, William Sprott (brother), 10, 15, 90
Boyd, William Sprott (cousin, of Hillhousefield), 7-8, 15, 79, 81, 91, 158, 165-6, 170-85, 187
Boyd, Wilson Maitland (cousin, of Broadmeadows), 7, 172, 215
Boyd Brothers (partnership), 23, 147, 162, 183, 230, 232
Boyd family, 15-16, 145: connections with Northern Ireland, 6; kin loyalty, 6-7, 80-2, 158, 164, 180
Boyd's Plains (New England), 58
Boydtown, 93, 98-110, 121, 128, 130, 150, 162, 173, 175, 177, 181-3; *see also* Twofold Bay
Bradley (first name unknown, master of the *Ariel*), 190, 194

Index 249

Brierly, Oswald Walters, 26, 32-4, 61, 91, 98-108, 119, 128-30, 137-8, 226
Brimadura (Wellington district), 60
British American Land Company, 21
Broadmeadows (Clarence River district), 58, 185
Broadmeadows (Selkirkshire), 7
Brooke, Sir James ('Rajah'), 14, 27, 40, 192
Brooks, Robert, 146, 148, 153-4, 231
Browning, Samuel, 30, 78, 81, 90, 124, 142, 147-8, 152-4, 156, 158, 167, 184-6, 190
Buller, Charles, 77
Bushby, Captain Tom, 31, 81

California, 186-90, 192-3; see also San Francisco
Cambalong (Maneroo district), 58, 103
Campbell, Charles, 118
Campbell, John Logan, 190, 219
Campbell, Margaret, see Margaret Boyd
Campbell, Robert Senior, 15
Campbell, Thomas Winder, 61-2, 107-8, 182, 188, 193, 195
Campbell and Co., of Calcutta, 15
Campbell family, 15
Canal Creek (Darling Downs district), 58, 176
Canterbury Association, 26
Capertee, 178
China, 8, 90-1, 120, 123, 134, 144-5, 153, 155, 170-1
Chisholm, Captain, 158
Church Hill, 31, 61, 86, 174, 179
Clarence River district, 58
Clark, C. M. H., 210
Clifton (Darling Downs district), 58
Clyde Company, 14
Coates, Robert 'Romeo', 217
Cockburn, Alexander, 11, 21-2
Cockburn, Robert, 21
Cockburn and Co., 107
Colac Station, 34, 39, 50-1, 57-8
Colonial Gazette, 78
Colonial Office, 24-5, 27, 37, 53-4, 56, 70, 74, 81-2, 88-90, 123, 135-6, 144

Commercial Bank of London, 12, 21
Condobolin (Wellington district), 60
Connell, John, 11, 21-2, 158
Connell, William, 44
convict labour, 114, 122-6, 132-4, 137
Coolee (Wellington district), 60
Cooper, George, 42-7
Cowper, Charles, 72, 76, 112, 113, 123-6, 132-4, 168-9, 179-80
Craignathan, 61
Craufurd (or Crawford), Thomas, 31, 50
Craufurd, William Petre, 17, 21-2
Crawford, George, 190, 197, 200, 202, 207
Curr, Edward, 180

Darling Downs district, 56, 58
Denholm, Captain, RN, 199, 208-9, 238
Deniliquin, 34, 58
Denison, Letter to Sir William, 125, 132, 140, 160
Donaldson, Stuart A., 61, 87, 151, 231
Drummond Island, 194
Duff, Adam, 21-2, 81, 148
Duke's Wharf, Sydney, 177
Dumfriesshire and Galloway Club, 8
Duncan, William Augustine, 62, 74, 84-5
Dunmore, 50

East India Company, 9-10, 15, 103
Eden, 98, 103-5, 177
Edingburgh and Glasgow Bank, 20
Edward River (Murrumbidgee district), 58, 130, 138
Eumerella, 50

Fawkner, John, 180
Fennell, Robert, 31, 51, 87
FitzRoy, Charles (Governor of New South Wales), 86, 123, 131, 134-5, 156, 169, 188, 208
FitzRoy, Robert (Governor of New Zealand), 46-7, 156

Flower, P. W., 148
Forbes, Captain George C., 174, 177
freemasonry, 6

Garnkirk, Glasgow, 7
Garra (Wellington district), 60
Gennong (Maneroo district), 58, 103
Gipps, Sir George, 27, 35, 37, 63-5, 86, 91, 108, 125, 167, 169: and land policy, 68-74, 77, 79, 83, 87-9, 144, 156; and New Zealand, 40-2, 44, 46; conflict with Boyd, 56, 64-5, 67, 83-5
Gladstone, William, 89, 123
Glasgow Association for the Protection of the Squatting and other General Interests of New South Wales, 80
Glass, Governor (Tristan da Cunha), 32
Gonoo (Wellington district), 60
Gore, John, and Co., 148
Green, Charles, 28
Green, Emma, 28, 61-2, 204
Grey, Earl, 140, 146-8, 161, 180-1
Grey, George (Governor of New Zealand), 135-6
Griffiths, G. R., 44
Griffiths, Gore, and Co., 44
Guadalcanal, Solomon Islands, 199-204, 206, 208-9
Gulgo (Wellington district), 60

Hamilton, Edward, 68, 73, 75, 222
Hamilton, James M., 51
Hawaii, 188-9, 191-3, 195, 205
Hawksley, Edward John, 108
Hobson, Captain William (Governor of New Zealand), 40, 43
'homestead regulations', 70-1, 73, 88
Hope, George, 89
House of Commons, Select Committee on the Navigation Laws (1847), 152-4
House of Lords, Select Committee on Steam Communication (1851), 148-9

Huggins, Thomas, 23
Hume, Joseph, MP, 152
Hunter River Steam Navigation Company, 95, 97

Imlay brothers (Peter, Alexander and George), 98, 106-7
immigration, 36, 45, 82, 90, 114-15, 122, 133, 139-40, 156-60, 182-3
India, 15-16, 91, 123, 128, 134, 144-5, 153
India and Australia Steam Packet Company, 147-9, 158, 208
Innes, Captain Archibald, 207
insurance industry, 9, 11, 96-7, 145
Isitado (or Lisitado), 196-9

Jardine, William, 8
Jardine, Matheson and Co., 8, 12, 15, 90, 136, 170-1
Java, 145-7, 153
Jemalong (or Gemalong, Lachlan district), 58

Kamehameha III (King of Hawaii), 188, 191, 205
Kapentaria, 200-1
Kennedy, Alexander, 44
King, Phillip Parker, 98, 118
Kingsmill Islands, 193-4, 196
Kirsopp, Captain Edward, 128, 131, 134-5, 138

Lachlan district, 56, 58
Laidley Plains (Moreton Bay district), 58, 176
Lancaster, Captain George, 134
land policy, 35-7, 51-7, 65, 68-73, 77, 81, 88-90, 143-4, 156, 166-8
Lang, Andrew, 50
Lang, John Dunmore, 8, 71, 86
Larpent, Sir George, 146-8
La Trobe, Charles, 95
Laurie, David M., 31, 65
Laurie, Sir Peter, 11-12, 21, 160-1, 166
Legislative Council, 37, 62-3, 68-9, 75, 79-80, 84-7, 90, 108, 122-3, 144-5,

147, 167: Select Committee on Immigration (1843), 115-19, 121-2; Select Committee on Crown Land Grievances (1844), 56, 75-7, 83, 125; Select Committee on the Renewal of Transportation (1846), 122-5, 161; Select Committee on Steam Communication (1848), 147; measures against Pacific island labour, 131-2; 1848 election, 179-81
Lifu, Loyalty Islands, New Caledonia, 128-30, 134-5
Liverpool, 12, 14, 22-3, 28
Logan, Charles D., 72, 83, 123, 148, 158
London Reversionary Interest Society, 12, 22
London Stock Exchange, 10-12
Lowe, Robert, 62, 71-2, 82, 113, 131-4, 137, 168-9, 176, 179, 223
Lyons, Samuel, 94, 177

Macarthur, Edward, 122
Macarthur, Hannibal, 72, 75, 86
Macarthur, James, 68, 74, 83, 112, 122-3
Macarthur, William, 74
McCrae, Georgiana, 33
MacKenzie, William, 134, 136-7
Mackillop, G., 80
MacKinnon, W. A., 78-9
Maitland, Frederick (Boyd's cousin), 81
Maitland, Joanna (Boyd's grandmother), 5
Mafra (or Maffra, Maneroo district), 58, 103, 128, 130, 133
Makira, Solomon Islands, 196-9
Maneroo district (also Monaro), 56, 58, 103-4, 121, 128, 133, 138, 221
Masters and Servants Act, 108, 115-16, 118, 131, 137-9
Matheson, James, 8, 12, 15
Mathews, Felton, 44
Matong (Maneroo district), 58, 103
Melbourne Club, 33

Memildra (Wellington district), 60
Merton Hall, 5, 11, 91
Meux, Thomas, 12, 21
Minore (Wellington district), 60
Mitchell, John, 21-2, 60
Mitchell, Sir Thomas, 21, 51, 60, 84, 158
Moequard (*Chef du Cabinet*, France), 207
Molesworth, Sir William, 158
Monaro, *see* Maneroo district
Montefiore, Jacob, 148, 158
Moreton Bay district, 58
Morris Augustus, 34
Moutry, William S., 105-6, 129-30, 136, 181-2, 185
Murray, Hon. James Erskine, 39-40, 47, 65
Murrumbidgee district, 56, 58
Myalla Downs (Maneroo district), 103

Nagle, Captain, 128
Napoleon III, Emperor of the French, 13, 207, 209
Navigation Acts, 120, 144, 149-55
Neutral Bay, 61
New Bank Buildings, London (No. 1) 155, (No. 4) 11, 23, 80
New England district, 15, 56, 58, 176
New Zealand, 14, 21, 25-6, 40-7, 65, 94, 98, 103, 146, 187-8, 190
New Zealand Banking Company, 41-4
Newton Boyd (Clarence River district), 58
Newton Stewart, Wigtonshire, 5-6, 57
Nicholson, Charles, 82, 189
North British Insurance Company, 11-12, 17, 21, 23, 26, 80, 164
Nyang (Murrumbidgee district), 58

'occupation regulations', 69-72, 77, 87-8
Ocean Island, 120, 193
O'Connell, Sir Maurice, 108
O'Connell, Captain Maurice, 108, 167
Ottiwell, Captain William, 190, 197-200, 202, 207, 237

Index

Pacific island labour ('kanakas'), 112, 119-21, 127-40, 150, 153, 155, 191-2, 210, 231
Pacific islands, 25, 102, 129, 135-6, 150, 153, 193
Pambula (Pampoola), 98
Pastoral Association, 72-7, 81-5, 123, 132, 147, 158, 166
Peel, Sir Robert, 152
Peninsular and Orient Steam Navigation Company, 146-7, 149
Penninghame, 57, 116, 204
Perth Banking Company, 20
Pim Joseph, 22
Plunkett, J. H. (Attorney-General), 131, 134-7
Polwarth, Lord, 78, 81
Poon Boon (Murrumbidgee district), 58
Port Macquarie, 204, 207
Port Phillip district, 14-15, 31-5, 50-1, 53, 56, 58, 61-3, 84-7, 167, 180-1

Raffles, Sir Stamford, 25
Ranken, George, 34
Rennie, Edward, 31, 38, 65
Riddell (Roxburghshire), 7-8
Robertson, William, 50
Robinson, Anthony, 22, 81
Robinson, Francis, 205
Robinson, George, 31, 128, 129
Robinson, Joseph Phelps, 12, 31, 61, 83, 84, 93, 105, 118, 184, 205: director of Royal Bank of Australia, 21-2, 142; departure for New South Wales, 28; business of Royal Bank of Australia, 65, 106, 143, 161-3, 172, 174; loan to New Zealand government, 43-6; land purchases, 56-7; and shipping, 93-5, 98, 145; Brierly's antagonism towards, 104-5; Member of the Legislative Council, 62-3, 75, 87, 106, 115, 123, 132-4, 145, 147, 167, 180-1; Treasurer, Pastoral Association, 72, 75-6, 82; co-ordinating British lobby, 78, 124, 157; and convict labour, 126; and Pacific island labour, 128, 130, 132-4, 137; death, 171, 175-6, 179
Ross, Clunies, 25
Rothschild, Lord, 13
Rotumah, 120, 135-6
Roxburghshire, 7-8, 11, 78
Royal Bank of Australia, 26, 28-9, 32, 35, 141, 171: annual general meetings, 18-19, 28-9, 47, 67, 91, 141-4, 161, 164; banknotes, 31, 37-8, 93, 206; books, 38, 65, 162; business in Australia, 37-9, 47-9, 90-1, 142, 162, 164, 171-3, 210; business in London, 28; capital, 19-20, 24, 142, 172; creditors, 39, 143, 161-2, 164-5, 173-4, 185; debentures, 20, 23-4, 161, 165, 185; debtors, 39-40, 55-6, 76, 163, 172, 181-2; directors, 21-2, 65-7, 91, 140-4, 161-5, 170, 179, 184 (*see also* individual names of directors); employees, 30-1, 38, 51, 93, 111, 162-3, 181-2; establishment, 17-21, 141; financial crisis, 161-5, 171-5, 184-5, 207; litigation, 96-7, 175, 181-2, 184, 207, 209; New Zealand loan, 40-9; political influence, 47-9, 72, 78, 80-1, 90, 140, 144, 149, 157, 167; shares, 18-20, 142-3, 170, 185; shareholders, 63, 66-7, 91, 141-3, 161, 175; shipping activities, 63, 93, 96, 145, 148-9, 184; stock and station, 55, 57, 91-2, 162-3, 172-3, 184; tokens, 105, 173
Royal Exchange Assurance, 96-7
Royal Hotel meeting (9 April 1844), 72, 74-7
Royal Thames Yacht Club, 25
Royal Yacht Squadron, 14, 25-7, 35, 39, 188-9, 192, 205
Russell, Lord John, 25, 60, 192

St George Steam Packet Company, 22-3, 97, 145
St Julian, Charles, 109
San Christoval, Solomon Islands, 195-9, 203, 208

Index 253

San Francisco, 187-90
Scott, Hon. Francis, 8, 77-9, 81, 88-90, 144, 146-8, 156, 158-60, 170
Scott, Sir Walter, 7-8
Sea Horse Inn, 102
Selkirkshire, 7
Selwyn, George (Bishop of New Zealand), 43
Sewell, Henry, 26, 34
Sewell, Isaac, 11, 26
Shannon Vale (New England district), 58, 176
Shepard, Alexander (Treasurer, New Zealand), 43-4
ships: *Arche d'Alliance*, 138; *Ariadne*, 196, 199; *Ariel*, 190, 194, 199, 206; *Bermondsey*, 182-3; *Bourbon*, 150, 154; *British Sovereign*, 209; *Cornubia*, 28, 30-1, 93-4, 98, 156; *Duchess of Kent*, 101; *Edward*, 101, 177; *Fame*, 101, 177, 185; *General Hewitt*, 63, 92; HMS *Herald*, 199, 208-9; *Juno* (paddlesteamer) 23, 28, 30, 93-5, 97-8, 103, 120, 170-1, 177, 187; *Juno* (bargue), 101, 177; *Lady Margaret*, 184; *Lucy Ann*, 101, 177; *Margaret*, 101, 151-2, 154, 177; *Oberon*, 207-8; *Portenia*, 101, 130-1, 134-5, 137, 174, 177; *Prince of Wales*, 101; *Rebecca*, 101, 177; *Royalist*, 14, 27; *Sea Horse*, 28, 30-1, 65, 93-7, 103, 106, 177; *Shamrock*, 95, 130; *Terror*, 30, 101, 175, 177; *Velocity*, 30, 35, 101, 121, 128-31, 134-7, 174; *Wanderer*, 25-8, 31-2, 34, 61, 91, 107, 120, 169, 177, 182, 185-201, 203-6; *William*, 101, 174
Shortland, Willoughby (Colonial Secretary and Acting Governor, New Zealand), 42-5
Sidney, Samuel, 158
Singapore, 25, 128, 144-7, 153
Smith, A. B., 23
Smith, William, 23
Society for the Promotion of Colonization, 139, 158, 170

Sprott (or Sprot), Alexander (Boyd's cousin), 7, 15, 123
Sprott, Mark (Boyd's uncle, of Garnkirk), 7-9, 14, 80
Sprott, Mary (Boyd's aunt, née Yule), 7
Sprott, Thomas (Boyd's cousin), 7
squatting, 51-60, 68-75, 79-80, 88-90, 114, 143, 156, 166-8
Stanley, Lord (Secretary of State for the Colonies), 46, 67, 74, 77-8, 81-2
steamships and steam communication, 30-1, 66, 82, 93-8, 140, 144-9, 156
Stephen, James, 27, 70
Stewarts Island (or Sikyana), 194-5
Strathmerton (Port Phillip district), 58, 129
Struthers, James, 29
Sutherland, John William, 18, 21-2, 38, 45, 66, 81, 107, 114, 120, 139-41, 143, 147, 155-8, 163-4, 170
Swainston, William (Attorney-General, New Zealand), 43
Sydney Chronicle, 108-9
Sydney Morning Herald, 84
systematic colonization, 53, 77, 158

Tana, New Hebrides (Vanuatu), 128, 134-5
Thomson, Edward Deas (Colonial Secretary), 131, 139
Timmararare, 193-4
Timnee (Wellington district), 60
Towns, Robert, 97, 123, 127, 133, 154, 190, 208
Tristan da Cunha, 32, 192
Turner, George Cooper, 108, 205
Twofold Bay, 39, 60, 62, 96, 98, 102, 119-22, 124, 128-30, 138, 155, 182-3, 210; *see also* Boydtown

Union Bank of Australia, 17
Union Bank of London, 12, 17, 23, 160, 164, 174, 184
United Kingdom Insurance Company, 161, 164
Urquhart, W. A., 11

254 Index

Van Diemen's Land Company, 21
Vice-Admiralty Court, 151, 155

Waghorn, Lieut., 145-8
Waitangi, Treaty of, 40-1
Wakefield, 14, 53, 75, 77
Walker, William, 86, 195
Walker family, 210
Wallawalla (Lachlan district), 58
Walpole, Henry, 134
Wanderer Inn, 58
Ward, J. M., 156
Warraberry (Wellington district), 60
Waterloo Place, London, 5-6
Webb, George, 34
Webb, Richard, 31, 65
Webster, Alexander, 21
Webster, George, 11, 21-2
Webster, John, 21, 190-2, 193-202, 204, 207
Weekly Register, 82-4
Wellington district, 56, 60
Wentworth, Major D'Arcy, 86
Wentworth, William Charles, 25, 54, 72, 82, 86, 102, 123-4, 133-5, 176
Westgarth, William, 34, 36, 39, 50-1, 58, 158
Whitmore (New England district), 58
Wilmont, Sir Eardley (Governor of Van Diemen's Land), 40
Windeyer, Richard, 72, 82
Wog Wog (Maneroo district), 58, 103
Woolshed (Murrumbidgee district), 58, 138
Wray, George Henry, 23, 46-7, 65-6, 79-81, 91-2, 142-3, 158, 161, 164
Wryghte, William Charles, 18, 23, 38
Wyllie, Robert C. (Hawaiian Minister of Foreign Relations), 188, 192

Yarborough, Earl of, 26-7
Yarrowitch (New England district), 58, 176
Yates, John, 158
Yule, Benjamin (Boyd's grandmother), 6
Yule, Janet (Boyd's mother), *see* Janet Boyd